The Revelation of Jesus Christ

The Revelation of Jesus Christ

Ray Frank Robbins

Wipf & Stock
PUBLISHERS
Eugene, Oregon

Wipf and Stock Publishers
199 W 8th Ave, Suite 3
Eugene, OR 97401

The Revelation of Jesus Christ
A Commentary on the Book of Revelation
By Robbins, Ray F.
Copyright©1975 by Robbins, Ray Frank
ISBN: 1-59752-007-1
Publication date 1/13/2005
Previously published by Broadman Press, 1975

To
Bob, Dixie, Ray, Sue,
Cecil, and John

Preface

A serious study of Revelation was begun while I was a college student more than thirty years ago. Through the years, my interpretations of this prophecy have changed. The conclusions reached in this book are the outcome of many years of study and teaching. The writing of this interpretation has been encouraged by the interest of and repeated requests from my students. Meanwhile, the immense literature in books, encyclopedias, dictionaries, and learned journals continues to increase. There has always been the temptation to delay the writing while many vital questions were still the subject of debate. It finally became apparent that one could spend his entire life in reading and evaluating the many contributions to this area of study and not write a word of his own interpretation.

This is not an attempt to write a formal commentary. It does not endeavor to explain the meaning of each word or each verse. Its aim is to bring out the meaning and message of the Revelation. Though it is based on scholarly study and deals with technical points whenever necessary, its aim throughout has been to bring out the meaning the prophet intended to convey to his original readers. It has been written, as far as possible, for "the Greekless." It does not deal, except subordinately, with questions of textual criticism or philology. Extended critical discussions have been avoided. Efforts have been made to assert nothing more strongly than the evidence warrants. However, it is difficult to be brief and yet not too positive.

The questions continually before the interpreter have been: Why was this said? What does it mean? What was it intended to teach? John wrote with a purpose. That purpose is sought. He wrote out of faith and for faith. It has been my aim to give the plain, straightforward, practical exposition of the prophecy. I have sought to omit what is needless. The results of labor, without the processes by which the interpretations were reached, are usually given. I have not attempted to refute other interpretations which, as I am well aware, exist in many and varied forms. Because realistic interpretation rather than argument has been aimed at, profuse bibliographical references have been avoided. However, as students will recognize, I am indebted to many scholars, including those with whom I disagree. I have sought to express my specific obligation and indebtedness to the various interpreters whose works I have freely used. The outline has also been used as the table of contents.

Regularly I have quoted the text of Revelation and other New Testament references from the Revised Standard Version of the Bible. I have quoted Old Testament passages from the American Standard Version.

These acknowledgments would not be in any sense adequate without a grateful reference to the trustees, administration, and fellow faculty members of the New Orleans Baptist Theological Seminary. Much of the research for the writing of this book was done during a sabbatical leave granted me in 1961-62. This study leave was spent in the Bodleian Library of Oxford University, which contains one of the largest collections of apocalyptic writings in the world. This leave was enhanced by a Sealantic Fund, Inc., Scholarship awarded by the American Association of Theological Schools. I am grateful for the grant. The actual writing has been done during a second sabbatical leave which was granted me for 1970-71.

I am indebted to my secretaries, Dr. Peggy Argo, Mrs. Woodrow Busch, and Mrs. Steve Turner, for typing and retyping the manuscript.

It is my hope and prayer that this interpretation will not only enable its readers to know the Revelation better but also bring them a little closer to that Lord and Savior whom John sought to reveal.

Ray F. Robbins

The New Testament text in this publication is from the Revised Standard Version of the Bible, copyrighted 1946 and 1952, by the Division of Christian Education, National Council of the Churches of Christ in the U.S.A. and is used by permission.

Contents

Introduction to the Interpretation 17

I. Introduction (1:1-20) 28
   1. The Preface (1:1-3) 28
   2. The Address and Greeting (1:4-8) 32
      (1) The Salutation (1:4-5a) 32
      (2) The Doxology (1:5b-6) 35
      (3) Summary and Prelude (1:7-8) 36
   3. Introductory Vision: Christ Among the Churches (1:9-20) 38
      (1) The Prophet's Commission to Write What He Sees to the Seven Churches (1:9-11) 38
      (2) A Vision of the Son of Man (1:12-16) 43
      (3) The Prophet's Commission to Write (1:17-20) ... 47

II. The Letters to the Seven Churches (2:1 to 3:22) 50
   1. The "Letter" to the Church in Ephesus (2:1-7) 52
   2. The "Letter" to the Church in Smyrna (2:8-11) 58
   3. The "Letter" to the Church in Pergamum (2:12-17) .. 61
   4. The "Letter" to the Church in Thyatira (2:18-29) 66
   5. The "Letter" to the Church in Sardis (3:1-6) 70
   6. The "Letter" to the Church in Philadelphia (3:7-13) .. 73
   7. The "Letter" to the Church in Laodicea (3:14-22) 77

III. The Sevenfold Vision of Conflict (4:1 to 22:5) 82
   1. The Vision of Heaven and Heavenly Worship (4:1 to 5:14) 82
      (1) The Vision of God as Creator (4:1-11) 82
         a. An Open Door in Heaven (4:1) 83
         b. The Throne and Its Occupant (4:2-3) 84
         c. The Twenty-four Elders (4:4) 86
         d. The Throne and the Torches (4:5) 87

e. The Glass-like Sea Around the Throne (4:6a)	87
f. The Four Living Creatures Worship and Serve God (4:6b-7)	88
g. The Ceaseless Hymn of Praise (4:8-11)	89
(2) The Vision of God as Redeemer (5:1-14)	90
a. The Sealed Scroll (5:1-4)	92
b. The Lion-Lamb (5:5-7)	93
c. The Adoration of the Lamb (5:8)	96
d. The New Song (5:9-10)	97
e. The Redeemed Worship the Redeemer (5:11-14)	99
2. The Opening of the Seals (6:1 to 8:1)	100
(1) The First Seal Opened—A White Horse (6:1-2)	102
(2) The Second Seal Opened—A Red Horse (6:3-4)	103
(3) The Third Seal Opened—A Black Horse (6:5-6)	104
(4) The Fourth Seal Opened—An Ashen Horse (6:7-8)	105
(5) The Fifth Seal Opened—The Martyred Souls Under the Altar (6:9-11)	105
(6) The Sixth Seal Opened—Judgments (6:12-17)	106
(7) First Interlude: God's Care for the Faithful (7:1-17)	109
a. The Church Militant, Assured Safety in the Midst of Judgment (7:1-8)	110
b. The Church Triumphant, Assured Safety Above Judgment (7:9-17)	113
(8) The Seventh Seal Opened—Silence of One-half Hour in Heaven (8:1)	116
3. The Seven Trumpets (8:2 to 11:19)	117
(1) Preface to the Vision of the Trumpets (8:2-6)	118
(2) The First Trumpet: Hail and Fire Mingled, Sent in Blood (8:7)	119
(3) The Second Trumpet: A Great Burning Mountain Cast into the Sea (8:8-9)	120
(4) The Third Trumpet: A Blazing Star Falls on the Waters (8:10-11)	121
(5) The Fourth Trumpet: Darkening of Sun, Moon, Stars (8:12)	121
(6) The Eagle's Warning (8:13)	122
(7) The Fifth Trumpet: Swarms of Locusts (9:1-12)	122
a. Smoke from the Abyss (9:1-2)	122
b. The Plague of Locusts (9:3-6)	123

      c. A Description of the Locusts (9:7-10) 125
      d. The Ruler of the Locusts (9:11) 126
  (8) Announcement of Two More Woes (9:12) 126
  (9) The Sixth Trumpet: External Enemies (9:13-21) 126
      a. The Releasing of the Agents of Divine
         Judgments (9:13-15) 127
      b. A Description of the Invading Army (9:16-19) 127
      c. The Response of the Stubborn to These
         Judgments (9:20-21) 128
  (10) The Second Interlude (10:1 to 11:14) 130
      a. The Strong Angel (10:1-7) 130
      b. The Little Scroll (Book) (10:8-11) 132
      c. The Measuring of the Temple and the Two
         Witnesses (11:1-14) 133
  (11) The Seventh Trumpet: Announcement of the Reign of
      God (11:15-19) 142
      a. Loud Voices in Heaven (11:15) 142
      b. The Song of the Twenty-four Elders (11:16-18) 143
      c. God's Response—the Open Temple and the Ark
         (11:19) 144

4. The War Between the Woman (Church) and the Dragon
  (Satan) (12:1 to 14:20) 145
  (1) The Dragon Seeks to Destroy the Child (12:1-12) 146
      a. The Woman, the Child, and the Dragon (12:1-6) .. 146
      b. The Effect of the Incarnation (12:7-12) 149
  (2) The Dragon Persecutes the Woman Who Brought
      Forth the Child (12:13-16) 153
  (3) The Dragon Persecutes the Rest of the Woman's
      Offspring (12:17) 154
  (4) The Beast Out of the Sea (13:1-10) 155
  (5) The Beast Out of the Earth (13:11-18) 160
  (6) The Third Interlude; Comfort in the Certainty of
      Victory (14:1-20) 165
      a. The Lamb and His Company (14:1-5) 166
      b. The First Angel Announcing the Triumph of the
         Gospel (14:6-7) 168
      c. The Second Angel Announcing the Fall of Babylon
         (14:8) 169
      d. The Third Angel Announcing the Doom of Those
         Worshiping the Beast (14:9-12) 170

- e. The Certainty of Those Who Die in the Lord (14:13) 172
- f. The Harvesting of the Saints (14:14-16) 172
- g. The Vintage of the Church's Enemies (14:17-20) 174

5. The Seven Bowls (15:1 to 20:15) 175
   (1) Introductory Vision: The Song of the Redeemed and the Seven Angels (15:1-8) 176
      - a. The Seven Angels with Seven Plagues (15:1) 176
      - b. The Conquerors Praise the Justice of God's Judgments (15:2-4) 177
      - c. The Seven Are Given Seven Bowls Full of the Wrath of God (15:5-8) 180
   (2) The First Four Bowls in the Sphere of the Physical (16:1-9) 182
      - a. A Command from the Temple to the Seven Angels (16:1) 182
      - b. The First Bowl: Evil Sores upon Men (16:2) 183
      - c. The Second Bowl: The Sea Like the Blood of a Dead Man (16:3) 183
      - d. The Third Bowl: Rivers and Fountains Become Blood (16:4-7) 184
      - e. The Fourth Bowl: The Sun's Scorching Heat (16:8-9) 186
   (3) The Last Three Bowls in the Spiritual Realm (16:10-21) 187
      - a. The Fifth Bowl: The Beast's Kingdom Darkened (16:10-11) 187
      - b. The Sixth Bowl: Drying Up the Euphrates and the Gathering of Kings of the World (16:12-16) 188
      - c. The Seventh Bowl: Contents Poured into the Air (16:17-21) 191
   (4) The Overthrow of Satan and His Subordinates (17:1 to 20:15) 193
      - a. The Nature and History of the Great Harlot Babylon (17:1-18) 193
      - b. The Fall of Babylon Depicted in Old Testament Doom Songs (18:1-24) 201
      - c. The Judgment of Heaven upon Babylon (19:1-10) 210

  d. The Vision of the Conquering Christ
    (19:11 to 20:15) 215
    (a) Christ the Captain and His Armies
      (19:11-16) 215
    (b) The Defeat of the Beast and His
      Allies (19:17-21) 219
    (c) The Abridgment of Satan's Power
      (20:1-6) 221
    (d) Satan's Final Defeat and Punishment
      (20:7-10) 226
    (e) The Judgment of All Enemies of Christ
      and His Church (20:11-15) 228
 5. The Blessedness of the New Jerusalem (21:1 to 22:5) 230
   (1) Fellowship with God in the Holy City (21:1-8) 231
   (2) A Description of the Holy City (21:9-27) 235
   (3) Life and Light in the Holy City (22:1-5) 241

IV. Conclusion (22:6-21) 245

Selected Bibliography 251

Introduction to the Interpretation

Authorship

The Revelation introduces itself with the name John. This name occurs four times in the writing (1:1,4,9; 22:8). This might well settle the problem of authorship; however, this is one of the most debated questions of New Testament study. This debate has been in progress since the second century. Conflicting traditions are found in the earliest writing about "John." According to one tradition, John the apostle, the son of Zebedee (Matt. 10:2; Mark 3:17; Luke 6:14; Acts 1:13), as well as James, was killed by the Jews in A.D. 44 (Mark 10:39; Acts 12:2). According to another tradition, in his old age, he lived and preached in Ephesus. This tradition also claims that he wrote five New Testament books: the Fourth Gospel, 1 John, 2 John, 3 John, and Revelation. According to another tradition, there were two people in Ephesus named John: the elder and the apostle. These traditions cannot be conclusively proved or emphatically denied. Where there is so much room for differences of opinion, dogmatism is out of place. With the present information, we prefer to leave the authorship an open question. The reader is referred to commentaries on Revelation for discussion on this difficult problem. Presumably the writer was sufficiently well-known to those to whom he was writing that he did not need to identify himself. For the purpose of this interpretation, we shall refer to the author as John, as the writer himself did.

Date

Early, weighty, clear, and positive external evidence is very strong for a date for the writing of Revelation near the end of the reign of Domitian (A.D. 81-96). The internal evidence also accords with a date during the reign of Domitian. There are some interpreters who think that it was written during the reign of Nero (A.D. 54-68).

Place of Writing

In 1:9 the writer says that he "was on the island called Patmos, because of the word of God and the testimony of Jesus." Patmos is a small island about ten miles long and from one to six miles wide, located about thirty-seven miles from Miletus. This rocky island in the Aegean Sea was used by the Roman government as a penal colony. According to tradition, John the apostle was arrested during the persecution of Domitian in A.D. 95 and was condemned to work in the mines on Patmos. This same tradition says that he was released eighteen months later by the emperor Nerva (A.D. 96-98). A monastery is located near the traditional cave where the Revelation was given. These traditions probably have some truth in them, but 1:9 may be interpreted to mean that John had gone to Patmos voluntarily as a missionary.

The Problem of Time

For the most part the interpreters of the Revelation agree on the meaning of the symbols and figures used in the book. The significance of these is not too difficult because there are so many extant apocalyptic writings with the same or similar symbolism. Also, many of these extant writings interpret these symbols. In the Revelation, many of these symbols used are interpreted (1:20; 4:5; 5:8; 7:13; 14; 12:9; 17:9,12,15,18). The real difference in interpretation has to do with time. When did the events narrated occur or when were they to occur? Over this issue many battles have been fought.

There is the so-called *preterist* interpretation which refers everything in the book to the past. The interpreters who hold this theory believe that the writer was reciting what was occurring in his own day. Some say that it was written to delineate the persecution during the reign of Nero, and others say that it depicts the persecution during the reign of Domitian. The interpreters who hold the preterist view maintain that the events and circumstances of the Revelation have been fulfilled.

There are also the *historical* methods of interpretations. There are several variations in these methods. In general, however, the scholars who hold to these interpretations believe that the fulfillment of the phenomena of the Revelation is going on throughout history, past, present, and future. Some interpreters see the series of seven as parallel, others see them as continuous. Some interpreters see the fulfillment as successive, others as sporadic. Some see the visions partly fulfilled, partly in the course of fulfillment, and partly unfulfilled.

The third general method of interpretation is the *futurist*. There are also many variations in this method of interpretation. In general, the interpreters who hold this view agree that the writer had in mind events that are still in the future. They agree that he deals primarily with events at the time of the second coming. Some of these scholars believe that the first three chapters of the Revelation refer to the historical situation of the seven churches and the remainder of the book refers to Christ's second advent and events immediately preceding it. Some of these interpreters hold that even the letters to the seven churches refer to the time of the end.

A fourth method of interpretation is the so-called *symbolic* theory. The scholars who hold this theory deny that the book has any reference to time as such. They claim that it is totally symbolical or spiritual.

In his book, *Syllabus for New Testament Study* (pp. 255-57), A. T. Robertson lists seven theories for the interpretation of the Revelation. Other interpretations can be added to the ones he discussed. It is apparent that the major difference between all these interpretations is the problem of time. There is truth in each of these theories, but it is not difficult to find objections to each interpretation. This problem of time can be solved if the interpreter keeps in mind the nature of the writing. What he saw was not a review of the past nor a preview of the future, but a superview by faith of the living Christ as he lives in his church and overcomes all opposition from within and from without. "A medley of tenses, present, future, perfect, preterite, testify to John's imaginative journeys from the present into the visionary future and back again" (Riddle, p. 361). The truths he discloses are common to every age—past, present, and future. They are timeless.

Prophecy and Apocalypse

The author associates himself with the prophets (10:7; 11:18; 22:9) and refers to his writing as prophecy (1:3; 22:7, 10, 18, 19). Apparently he was eager to establish the fact that he was in the succession of the great prophetic order through whom God spoke to his people. One element in the prophetic inspiration was a trance, bringing a heightened insight into moral and spiritual truths (Isa. 6:1 f.; John 12:41; Acts 11:5 f.; 2 Cor. 12:1-4). The grace gift *(charismata)* of prophecy is the gift of interpreting the will of God under the influence of the Holy Spirit (Liddell and Scott, p. 1539).

In the Bible, the word "prophecy" is used to express a forth-telling of the intuitively felt will of God for a specific situation in the life of an individual or a nation. In the Old Testament, and in the New Testament, the prophets were God's spokesmen. The etymology of the root word for prophet is not known. Apparently it is related to words meaning "to announce" or "to call." The Hebrew word for prophet means literally "one who speaks for another." The Greek word for prophet means "one who speaks forth." The prophets were men called of God to be his mouthpiece. They interpreted the divine will to individuals and to the covenant community. Their task was to assist the people of God in discerning the divine will in their daily living. These spokesmen had an invincible conviction that the messages which they delivered were not their own, but had come directly from God. God intensified and heightened their capacities as the Spirit of God spoke through them. Each prophet is "one who, moved by the Spirit of God and hence his organ or spokesman, solemnly declares to men what he has received by inspiration" (Thayer, p. 553).

The prophets interpreted contemporary history as the working out of a divine purpose. They saw the sovereign God as acting in the events of history to give it meaning and bring it to its goal. Usually these events of history were of a crisis nature, and the prophets interpreted them in the light of divine revelation. They saw that the ultimate victory in the events of history belonged to God. Their message proclaimed the mighty acts of God.

The prophetic message always included two aspects: judgment and salvation. Both of these were to take place by the action of God in history. The prophets' certainty that God would achieve his purpose was based on their knowledge of God as a living and dynamic God, an actual power at work in his creation. Their faith was an impassioned conviction that there is a living God at work in history and that he is Lord of history. They believe that God was always and at every event actively present. They viewed individuals and nations as instruments in God's hands to execute his will.

The prophets were primarily concerned with current events, yet they realized that the future is inherent in the present. The future arises out of the present. They spoke from the present viewpoint, and they spoke to their own generation. Even when the element of prediction was present in their message, it was not primarily for the sake of unfolding the future but for the purpose of bringing God's message to the people in their own day. They *were* contemporary, and they *are* contemporary. They addressed the age in which they spoke, and addressed also every age. Their messages were primarily God's word to his covenant community in their *Sitz-im-Leben* (life situation). This fact, however, does not destroy the principle of prophetic contemporaneity. They proclaimed picturesquely and forcefully truths of living and eternal validity for every age. They addressed themselves directly to the people, and that first and foremost through their oral utterances, and then by means of written discourse as well.

John, being a prophet, spoke to his own people in his own time. His writing has a firm historical anchorage. He started with the situation of the church in the first century. However, the message of his prophecy was not exhausted by its immediate purpose. His intention was to set forth principles on which God acts and to give a prophetic interpretation of the history which lies between the first and second advent of Jesus Christ. As a prophet, he was setting the contemporary against the background of the eternal.

The first word in the book is *Apokalupsis*. This word indicates that the document belongs to a group of writings usually called apocalyptic literature. This body of literature is a specific variety of prophetic composition. It was an outgrowth of and a direct continuation of prophetic literature. From the time of the Maccabees, it largely took the place of prophecy. This type of writing flourished between 200 B.C. and A.D. 100. It was used both by Jews and early Christians, and there are many extant apocalyptic writings (see James and Hennecke).

Apocalyptic had the same basis of revelation and inspiration as prophecy. Both apocalyptic and prophecy possessed an eschatology and were highly ethical. However, apocalyptic differed from prophecy in several essential ways. Apocalypses were usually pseudonymous. They were occasioned by the contradiction that existed between the ideal and the actual, between the promises which God gave to his people and the persecution and suffering which they were enduring. They arose in a time of trouble, distress, and trial. Most of them were occasioned by depressed circumstances. Therefore, they were primarily concerned to mediate a divine message of hope and encouragement and to awaken and quicken faith in the suffering people of God. They were also concerned to warn the ungodly. They held a close connection between righteousness and prosperity and between wickedness and calamity.

The apocalyptic writers had little faith in the present to produce the future. For them the future would not arise out of the present but would break into the present. The future would come to pass by direct catastrophic divine intervention or intrusion upon the world scene irrespective of human conduct. "Speaking generally, the prophets foretold the future that should arise out of the present, while the apocalyptists foretold the future that should break into the present" (Rowley, p. 35). The apocalyptic writers interpreted history as moving towards a great cataclysm. These writers stressed not so much what people have to do but what they have to expect. They saw the great world powers as the adversaries of God but who were under God's judgment and would be destroyed. They stressed the virtue of loyalty and stimulated faith by portraying in a vivid manner the certain overthrow of evil and the victory of righteousness. They sought to enlighten their readers with regard to the mysteries of nature, the supernatural and heavenly background of the operation of the natural world.

The apocalyptic writers used and adopted syncretistic ideas and highly symbolical language, visions, and imagery to convey their messages. Their enigmatical visions were often elaborated and rendered somewhat mysterious by their use of symbolical language. They were attempting to say what is really impossible to say, to define, or even to conceive. They were usually legalistic and emphasized the validity of the Law. They combined instruction and exhortation. They expressed loyalty to the Temple and its worship. They stressed the eschatology of the individual and held a firm belief in the future life. They believed in a new heaven and a new earth.

Revelation is an apocalypse. The method and approach mark the form of expression, and not the content of the message. The truth revealed came from the Holy Spirit. The form of the expression was derived from the writer's own age; the only conceivable source from which the means of expression could come (Dana, p. 123).

The Revelation is a prophecy *and* an apocalypse. "John regards his message as both a revelation (v. 1) and a prophecy (v. 3)" (Case, p. 188). He seeks to combine the prophetic view and the apocalyptic view. He saw that God had broken into history from without in the incarnation and was now working out his divine purpose in history through Jesus Christ in his church. He envisioned the sovereign God of the universe upon his throne carrying on his victorious program through Jesus Christ in his church.

Occasion

The Revelation has been called a tract for hard times, brought into existence to meet a particular and urgent situation in the church. The problem faced by the churches addressed seems to have been two-fold.

The members were being persecuted by the Roman officials because they refused to worship the emperor. During the reign of Domitian (81-96), emperor worship was compulsory. The Christians refused to burn incense to the statue of the emperor. Such refusal was interpreted as high treason punishable by death.

Also, the churches were being invaded by an insidious propaganda. The very integrity of the church's faith and morals was threatened by these subtle and apparently irresistible doctrines. In the second century, the teachings of this propaganda became known as gnosticism. C. H. Dodd says that gnosticism is "a label for a large and somewhat amorphous group of religious systems described by Irenaeus and Hippolytus in their works against Heresy . . . and similar systems known from other sources" (*The Interpretation of the Fourth Gospel,* p. 97).

The lines of divisions between these systems were not clearly defined. Gnosticism seems to have had affinities with elements of Judaism, Christianity, mystery religions, Greek philosophy, and Oriental Hellenism. No doubt, the teachings of Gnosticism in the second century go back to a milieu in which these elements were found.

It is difficult to reduce the teachings of the different systems to consistency, but in all of them there were some common elements. There seems to have been a fairly uniform scheme lying behind them all.

These systems did not appear in history fully developed, but there was a process of growth and development.

The basic assumption of gnosticism was an all inclusive dualism. It held that there are two mutually antagonistic principles in the universe, good and evil. It also held that the world is ultimately composed of two basic entities, spirit and matter. The principle of good was found in spirit, and the principle of evil was found in matter. The "spirit" God was held to be the embodiment of perfect goodness and the created world the personification of absolute evil. This Gnostic dualism was very convincing, and many church members became "Gnostic Christians." These teachings became a real threat when they were accepted by members of the churches.

This dualism was used to interpret the Christian doctrines in a general way as follows:

God. Logic forced a tragic split within the deity. The "spirit" God could not create an evil world. The Gnostics brought into being a fallen god called the "demiurge," who had by emanations descended from the "spirit" God, who was the creator-God.

Christ. Gnosticism denied the incarnation of Jesus Christ. He could not have been the spiritual Son of God and have a real human body at the same time. This problem was solved in two ways. First, the Docetists (from the Greek word *dokeo* meaning "to seem") claimed that Jesus was God, he just seemed to have been a man. They declared that Jesus was a god masquerading as a man, Second, Cerinthus claimed that Jesus was an ordinary man, but the divine Christ (Spirit-Logos) came upon him at baptism and left him before the crucifixion. The mission of Christ was to bring the secret rites knowledge *(gnosis)* of the "spirit" God to man.

Man. Gnosticism held that man has two natures, physical and spiritual. The body is a mere envelope holding the spirit. In his spiritual nature, he has a "divine spark" that is immortal and inviolable. Man could attain the goal of his existence only if he secured his release from his lowly fleshly substance through knowledge. This liberation was expressed in two ways: First, through stringent asceticism; and second, through the demonstration of freedom by unrestrained libertinism.

Salvation. Gnosticism held that redemption for the initiate was his release from the material body and his taking on the divine likeness through knowledge *(gnosis)*. It was through secret rites, visions, and mystical communion that the Gnostics were able to transcend "evil" flesh in which they were imprisoned. Through these means they had immediate knowledge of God; in fact, they had union with the divine spirit. Those who received the knowledge despised the ones who had not received it.

It seems that Revelation was written to meet this two-fold challenge to the church: persecution from without and heresy from within. The corruption of false teachers sapped its strength internally, and the heavy hand of the Roman Empire was attempting to destroy it by persecution.

The Use of Numbers

The Greeks were accustomed to attach to *numbers* a special notion of precision. The West has inherited this approach. We discover no poetry in arithmetic. It was quite otherwise in the East. In India, China, Persia, throughout Asia, and among the Jews themselves, at the time Revelation was written, numbers were continually used to express moral and spiritual ideas symbolically. A certain number would suggest a definite concept. Numbers became the symbols of ideas. This fact will help to unravel the meaning of the numbers found so often in the Revelation. The application of the method is not always certain, and it can be used for fanciful interpretation. However, this method was used by other apocalyptic writers, and most of the numbers had gained ideas that were understood by most writers of this literature. This method will save from the errors into which those have fallen, who, taking the numbers literally, have counted up years as if they were preparing a chronological table of historical events that have occurred and will occur since the Revelation was written. Much ingenuity has been shown in such attempts, which have generally been prefaced by some arbitrary assumption, such as that a prophetic day represents a year. Some have ventured to predict events, and again and again these predictions have failed. It is safer, and more in accord with first-century apocalyptic usage, to abandon these numerical computations and to read the numbers symbolically as the other metaphors are read.

In the book of Revelation several numbers seem to have been used as symbolic descriptions of ideas. The number *two* means companionship, increased strength, added courage, and mutual support. The number *three* was used to express the thought of the divine. *Three and a half* was a symbol of imperfection, incompleteness, or the interruption of the divine order of things. The number *four* stood for the visible creation, nature, or all creaturehood. The number *six* signified inability to reach the best, or it signifies failure to pass from the stage of incompletion. *Seven* was the number of perfection or completion. Seven is used fifty-four times symbolically in the Revelation.

The number *ten* came to symbolize human completeness. *Twelve* was the number used to symbolize organized religion in the world. Some multiples of these numbers were also used symbolically. These numbers in Revelation must not be interpreted with the literal exactness of mathematical formulae (Beckwith, Summers, Miles, and Lange provide excellent treatment of the subject of numbers).

I. Introduction
(1:1-20)

1. The Preface (1:1-3)

¹ The revelation of Jesus Christ, which God gave him to show to his servants what must soon take place; and he made it known by sending his angel to his servant John, ² who bore witness to the word of God and to the testimony of Jesus Christ, even to all that he saw. ³ Blessed is he who reads aloud the words of the prophecy, and blessed are those who hear, and who keep what is written therein; for the time is near.

The message begins with a brief statement as to the nature of the writing and the way in which the revelation it contained is given. This is followed by pronouncing a blessing on whosoever may read the prophecy in the Christian assembly and on those who hear it read and heed its moral instruction.

v. 1 The Greek word *apokalupsis* means "a revealing," "an uncovering," "an unveiling," or a "disclosure." The prophecy was intended to illumine the purpose of God in Christ to and through his church. It is not a revelation of a system of thought but of a living person. Jesus Christ is both the content of the revelation and the giver of it. He is the revealer and the revealed. No radical distinction is made between the revelation which God gives *through* Christ and *Christ* who is revealed. It is intended to illumine the purpose of God in the person of Christ. It is "a revelation of the infinite God, mighty to save; an uncovering for the consolation and inspiration of God's people of the all-conquering powers of an omnipotent Saviour" (Calkins, p. 12).

God expected the message to be given to **his servants,** i.e., the church. John expected the message to be understood. He is not attempting to conceal a truth but to make it known. **What** [thing]

INTRODUCTION

must soon take place (4:1; 22:6). The impersonal Greek verb *dei* (it is necessary) is used many times in the Septuagint to express the will of God revealed in the Law and the will of God revealed in general. It is used in the New Testament, especially in Lucan writings, to express moral necessity (Thayer, p. 126). It is also used in the Fourth Gospel to express the same moral necessity (John 3:7, 14, 30; 4:4,20,24; 9:4; 10:16; 12:34; 20:9). It is a necessity arising out of the laws of the divine nature, the inherent scheme or nature of things, and from the determinate will and counsel of God (Vine, Vol. III, pp. 93-94). Kittel says, it "expresses the necessity of the eschatological event, and is thus an eschatological term in the New Testament. It is well adapted for this role, since the eschatological event is one which is hidden from man, which can be known only by special revelation, and which sets man before an inconceivable necessity of historical occurrence grounded in the divine will."

These prophecies must be fulfilled because they are the word of God, and God is committed to these plans. This word of God is to be understood as more than just a message from heaven (Robbins, p. 183 f.). God's word is the outbreathing of the divine thought, the divine will, and purpose. It is his active power going out from him to achieve his purpose in the world. His word is of perpetual fulfillment. It not only is to be fulfilled, it has been fulfilled, and it is being fulfilled. The principles which were enunciated by John were not exhausted in the immediate fulfillment. The principles of divine government are applicable in all ages. John is in the true prophetic order.

The Greek prepositional phrase *en tachi* (with quickness, speed, suddenly, shortly, swiftness, hastiness; cf. Luke 18:8; Acts 12:7; 22:18; Rom. 16:20; Rev. 22:6) expresses John's faith in the living Christ. It was his conviction that the very nature of the redemptive kingdom of Christ requires that it be victorious. John certainly believed that the truth of his prophecy would be fulfilled in the near future. His faith was not mistaken. His faith was not emphasizing *time* but *certainty*. John was certain that in the coming struggle between good and evil, good would surely be victorious. This truth which must shortly be fulfilled, however, will not be exhausted by this particular fulfillment. John saw (and correctly) the great redemptive process, and he did not attempt to discern the incident of time relations (Dana, p. 99). To him, history was rooted in actual events, and he anticipated a real future. However, to him God provided the reason, the purpose, intention, and will for the future. At the same time, his God was an eternal presence. As a prophet, he saw God going before his people leading them to a goal, but he also saw Christ as present with his people in their witness and struggles of life (Matt. 28:20). God is the God of history and eschatology, and he is eternally present.

The words, **made it known,** are a translation of the Greek word *semainō* which is the verb form of the noun "sign" that is used so often in the Fourth Gospel (2:11,23; 3:2; 4:54; 6:2,14,26,30; 7:31; 9:16; 10:41; 11:47; 12:37; 20:30). This verb means to make known with "a sign," "to indicate," "to signify" (Thayer, p. 573). It was often used as a technical term for the response of an oracle. John here is simply telling how the truth is to be given, i.e., by signs, symbols, and figures. This fact should be kept in mind in interpreting Revelation. The word "angel" means messenger, i.e., Christ's messenger. Most of the apocalyptic messages were sent through angels. In Jewish thought, during the period between the Testaments, God was considered to be unapproachable in his majesty and, therefore, intermediary messengers were necessary. This verse says that the message came from the Father, through the Son, through Christ's messenger, to John, for the church. This verse also shows that John belonged to the true prophetic order because he was the agent through whom the word of God was transmitted to men.

v. 2 In this verse, John says he faithfully reproduced what had been communicated to him. He gives his personal witness to the word of God, that is, God's active power going out to achieve his purpose in the world. This probably refers to this book. John was testifying that suffering for righteousness' sake, in his own experience, has been turned by the grace of God into a blessing (1 Pet. 3:14). He *bore witness* in such a way as faithfully to reproduce the gospel in his own life. He had also learned by experience that suffering for righteousness brought him into fellowship with Christ (1 Pet. 4:12-14). John also bore witness to the testimony of Jesus Christ. Jesus Christ is the supreme example of victory through suffering (1 Pet. 2:21). Does John, in the statement *to all that he saw,* refer to the *visions* contained in this book or to the *truth* which he is proclaiming by the symbols? In other words, what did John see? Did he see the symbols, or did he see the profound prophetic truth that victory comes through suffering and use apocalyptic imagery to convey this truth to the church? In harmony with the vast majority of apocalyptic writers, the latter seems to be what John saw. The truth which he saw he presented in a composition which was characteristic of this literary type. He used the symbols and the figures to express the inexpressible. However, the value of the truth presented does not depend on any one theory concerning the nature of the vision, and the truth is not diminished because it is expressed by symbols and figures. He was conscious of giving personal witness to the word of God.

v. 3 The word *blessed* (*makarios*) is the same word used by Jesus in introducing each of the statements in Matthew 5:1-12. It is from a word which means "congratulation." This is the first of seven such "congratulations" (beatitudes) in Revelation (1:3; 14:13; 16:15; 19:9; 20:6; 22:7,14). Congratulations are pronounced upon the one *who reads aloud the words of the prophecy* in the assembly (cf. 2 Cor. 3:14 f.), upon those who *hear* with understanding the reading, and upon those *who keep what is written therein.* This promised blessedness is intended for those who reap the fruits of victory in the great conflict between God and the forces of evil. This statement also reflects the manner in which the message is to be communicated to the churches. The post filled by the reader in the Christian churches of primitive times was far more important when copies of the Scriptures were so very rare. (Smith, p. 29). The word "prophecy" is used here in its more literal sense of *forthtelling* the message of God. Basically, the word "prophecy" points to its divine origin. There is a sense of urgency in the prophecy, "for the time is near." This statement, **the time is near,** or "the season is near," has the same significance as the statement, "must soon take place," in 1:1. It means that the time is near for the things revealed in this book to be realized. The truths made known will be to each reader and hearer of immediate importance and great consequences.

2. The Address and Greeting (1:4-8)

The writer of the book again gives his name: John. He begins his message to seven churches (the church i.e., the one church in its sevenfold, universal experience) in the Roman province of Asia. There were no doubt other churches in this province (cf. Acts 20:5 ff.; Col. 1:2; 4:13). But the number seven is used to symbolize completeness, these seven represented the whole church of Asia, and indeed the whole church throughout the world. These seven churches signify the one church in her sevenfold universal experience. The revelation of "grace . . . and peace" is for the church. The salutation is from the Triune Source of all blessing; from the Eternal, from the sevenfold Spirit, and from Jesus Christ.

(1) The Salutation (1:4-5a)

⁴ John to the seven churches that are in Asia: Grace to you and peace from him who is and who was and who is to come, and from the seven spirits who are before his throne, ⁵ and from Jesus Christ the faithful witness, the first-born of the dead, and the ruler of kings on earth.

v. 4 The writer addresses seven churches in Asia. *Asia* was a Roman senatorial province located in the western part of Asia Minor which included all or part of Mysia, Lydia, Caria, Phrygia, the coastal areas, and the islands of the Aegean Sea. It consisted of a territory of approximately one hundred miles square. During the first century of the Christian era the capital of Asia was Ephesus.

From the second century, it has been pointed out that the number seven here is symbolical.

The earliest extant list of New Testament books is found in the Muratorian Canon. This is a fragment of an anonymous Latin manuscript which contained a part of a list of the Christian writings that were accepted as canonical by someone, probably at Rome, near the end of the second century. This fragment was discovered and published by L. A. Muratori in 1740. In this fragment, the writer says: "John in the Apocalypse, though he wrote to the seven churches, yet speaks to all [i.e., to all the churches]."

John Chrysostom (347-407), bishop of Constantinople, preacher, and theologian said: "The seven churches are all churches by reason of the seven Spirits."

Augustine (354-430), a bishop and theologian of northern Africa says: "By the seven is signified the perfection of the universal church, and by writing to the seven he shows the fulness of the one."

Bede ("the Venerable Bede," 673-735), an English monk and ecclesiastical historian, says: "Through these seven churches he writes to every church; for by the number seven is denoted universality." When John writes to seven churches, he is thus representatively writing to the whole church. The number seven denotes universality. It refers to the people of God, the church, the body of Christ, etc. (Matt. 16:18; Acts 9:31; Rom. 12:4,5; Gal. 1:3; 1 Cor. 12:4-6,11; 15:9; Eph. 1:22-23; 2:14-16: Col. 1:18,24; 2:16-19; 3:15). The word *ecclesia,* translated "church," occurs twenty times in Revelation. "Grace" and "peace" combine Greek and Hebrew elements. These are the customary words of salutation in the New Testament (cf. Rom. 1:7; 1 Cor. 1:3; 2 Cor. 1:2; Gal. 1:3; Eph. 1:2; Phil. 1:2; Col. 1:2; 1 Thess. 1:1; 2 Thess. 1:2; 1 Tim. 1:2; 2 Tim. 1:2; Titus 1:4; Philem. 3; 1 Pet. 1:2; 2 Pet. 1:2; 2 John 3).

The expression, *him who is and who was and who is to come*, refers to God's attribute of timelessness. God is perfect, unconditional, independent Existence. The Greek may be literally rendered: The "Being" and the "Was" and the "Coming." It is not grammatical, but it is an arresting way of stressing the changelessness and the eternity of God (Morris, pp. 47-48). He is "the Self-Existent." He is from everlasting. He embraces all duration, past, present, and future. Calkins says, "it means God is *here.*" This clause is an evident allusion and a new explanation of the venerable Old Testament name *JHVH* (Ex. 3:14), which means, "one eternally existing."

These three attributes are inseparably connected as belonging to God, from whom grace and peace are announced. The revelation is for the entire church, a message of "grace and peace." The writer is identifying God with the flow of creature-life with its familiar three tenses. However, since God is uncreated, he is not himself affected by the succession of consecutive changes we call time. The idea expressed by the clause is that of real, eternal, unconditioned, uncaused, self-existence. It says that God possesses endless being in the ultimate meaning of that term. He is the self-existent Self back of which no creature can think. He lives in the everlasting now. He has no past and no future. The whole book abounds with passages that set forth God as the living God (1:8,18; 2:10; 3:5; 10:5-6; 11:17; 15:7; 16:5; 17:8; 20:12; 21:1,6; 22:2,14,19).

The title *seven spirits who are before his throne* represents the Holy Spirit in the fullness of his activity and power in his manifold operations (cf. 4:5; 5:6; Isa. 11:2; Zech. 4:10). He is capable of perfect representation of God. The seven symbolizes perfection and universality. In Revelation, John speaks of the Spirit in the singular (2:7,11,17,29; 3:6,13,22; 14:13; 19:10; 22:17) and also as seven (1:4; 3:1; 4:5; 5:6). God in his Spirit is working through every part of creation. The position of the *seven spirits* before the throne means that the Holy Spirit is ever ready to accomplish God's mission.

v. 5a Jesus Christ is *the faithful witness.* The word "witness"

INTRODUCTION 35

is a translation of the Greek word *martus*, from which the English word "martyr" is derived. This was Jesus' function, "to bear witness to the truth" (John 3:32; 5:36; 18:37; 1 Tim. 6:13). Jesus was a faithful witness to God's way of victory over evil. This witness is the substance of the visions that John saw. These visions are graphic representations of God's prophetic message and redemptive purpose. Jesus Christ is the *first-born of the dead.* This simply states that Jesus was the first to permanently rise from the state of death (Rom. 8:29; Col. 1:15,18; Heb. 1:6). He rose from the grave, and became "the first fruits of those who have fallen asleep" (1 Cor. 15:20). He had indeed raised others—the widow's son, the daughter of Jairus, and Lazarus—but he himself alone in his own power rose as a conqueror of death and made others triumph with him. The statement, *the ruler of kings on earth,* is used to denote the exalted character and supremacy of Jesus. The rulers are seen as constituting a community over which Jesus rules (Matt. 11:27; 28:18; John 17:2; Eph. 1:20-22; Phil. 2:9-11; Col. 1:15-18). He is now the true ruler of all earthly rulers. The full realization of this title is yet to come, for, as the writer of Hebrews says, "We do not yet see everything in subjection to him" (Heb. 2:8b). The three titles of Jesus in this verse sum up Jesus Christ's relation to his church. This salutation links the Triune God with John's message.

(2) The Doxology (1:5b-6)

To him who loves us and has freed us from our sins by his blood ⁶ and made us a kingdom, priests to his God and Father, to him be glory and dominion for ever and ever. Amen.

This is the first of five doxologies to Jesus Christ in the Revelation (4:9; 4:11; 5:13; 7:12). The ascription of praise is twofold; glory and dominion. There is an increase later to a sevenfold ascription.

v. 5b The statement, *him who loves us,* is a translation of a present tense of the participle in the Greek. His love abides in God's ever-present now. In Greek, there is only one letter's difference in the spelling of "loosed" and "washed." The word "loosed" is much better attested in the manuscripts. The phrase means, "loosed us at the cost of his own blood." The power of sin is broken in the lives of those who receive the God of such love as manifested in the death of Christ. This proclaims a release or liberation; the removal of moral bondage. In the New Testament, God's love is a matter of free grace and is expressed most clearly and adequately in the forgiveness of sins (John 3:16). He gave himself unto death in order that the life which was in him may be set free for all men. The thought of Christ's redeeming work invokes the twofold doxology of praise, glory and dominion.

v. 6 This verse declares that the people of God are a kingdom of priests, the true spiritual Israel (Ex. 19:6; 1 Pet. 2:9). They have already been loosed from their sins by his blood and have already been made a kingdom—made to reign with Christ (Stagg, *New Testament Theology,* p. 318). This kingdom consists of people who have been loosed from their sins through Christ and now live to do his service (Morris, p. 46). The regal dignity belongs to the whole body of which Christ is the head. All Christians are *priests* because, being united with Christ, they share his actions and his victory. Each one has competency under God. Each one has direct access to God, and each one behaves as a priest to other people. Each one is also enabled "to offer spiritual sacrifices acceptable to God through Jesus Christ" (1 Pet. 2:5), and to present his body "a living sacrifice, holy and acceptable to God" (Rom. 12:1). Because Christians have received so bountifully, they occupy a position of privilege, opportunity, and service to their fellowmen. Thus, John declares the kingship and priesthood of the people of God (church), a sovereignty over the world by offering themselves unto God even unto death. This doxology refers to Jesus Christ.

(3) Summary and Prelude (1:7-8)

⁷ Behold, he is coming with the clouds, and every eye will see him, every one who pierced him; and all tribes of earth will wail on account of him. Even so. Amen.

INTRODUCTION 37

⁸ "I am the Alpha and the Omega," says the Lord God, who is and who was and who is to come, the Almighty.

v. 7 In this verse the prophet announces the *coming* of Christ. Not only in this verse but throughout the Revelation when Jesus' *coming* is referred to John uses a present tense, not a past tense, or a future tense. This is *true* prophetism. His *coming* includes his incarnation (past), his Spirit to build up the church (present), and his second coming to consummate the age or earthly history (future). These three aspects of his *coming* are an unbroken unity, the working out of a divine plan and purpose. His *coming* must not be interpreted to mean that he is now absent from his church. The early disciples were promised by Jesus that his presence would never be absent from them (Matt. 28:20). There are always two results of his *coming:* salvation and judgment. For some, his *coming* means manifestation, vindication, and glorification; for others his *coming* means manifestation, condemnation, and shame. This *coming* of Christ is the great central theme of the Revelation. It was fulfilled in the first advent of Christ; it is being fulfilled in the movement by which the purpose of God is being completed in history; and it will be fulfilled in a final crisis with a personal, visible reappearance of Jesus Christ. The phrase, *with the clouds,* is an appropriate symbol of majesty and glory. The apocalyptic writers often used clouds as clothing for deity and for vehicles of travel for deity (cf. Isa. 19:1; Dan. 7:13; Matt. 24:30; 26:64; Mark 13:26; 14:62; Luke 21:27; Rev. 14:14).

John's design in using this phrase seems to have been to impress the mind with a sense of the majesty and glory of Jesus Christ. He continues by saying that Jesus Christ will be visible in his glory to all that dwell upon the earth—in salvation or judgment. His murderers are singled out for special mention, while all the tribes of the earth wail the mourning of sorrowing repentance (Zech. 12:10-12; John 19:37). The design of this verse seems to be to show that the *coming* of Jesus Christ is an event of great interest to all mankind. Salvation or judgment will be upon every person because of Jesus Christ.

v. 8 Who is *the Lord God* that speaks the words of this verse? Is it God, the Father? Is it Jesus Christ (see 1:17 and Isa. 44:6)? It seems best to interpret these words as being from Jesus Christ, and if they are his words, they are a strong declaration of his deity (2 Cor. 6:18). The essential attributes of God are ascribed to the Son (see 22:13). In Jewish writings, it was customary to use the first and last letters of the Hebrew alphabet to denote the totality of anything. Alpha is the first, Omega the last letter of the Greek alphabet. The two include the whole series of letters, and, thus, are used as a symbol of the incomprehensibleness of Christ (or God). These words proclaim the totality of his divine being. The language here properly denotes eternity. It is a figure of speech for a spiritual fact really passing description or explanation. It is the equivalent of saying that he has always existed and that he will always exist. It means that Jesus Christ (or God) appears at the beginning and end of time simultaneously (Gen. 21:33; Ps. 90:2). It means that he is the Almighty One of eternity past and eternity future. The word *Almighty* expresses the all-embracing sovereignty which Christ exercises.

3. Introductory Vision: Christ Among the Churches (1:9-20)

This division introduces not merely the epistles to the churches, but the other visions in the book. Several of the Old Testament prophets began their ministry with an overwhelming vision of the glory and power of God (Isa. 6; Jer. 1; Ezek. 1; Dan. 10). At the beginning of his prophecy, John describes in detail how he was commissioned to give his message. He saw a vision of the triumphant Christ in his glory and power.

(1) The Prophet's Commission to Write What He Sees to the Seven Churches (1:9-11)

⁹ I John, your brother, who share with you in Jesus the tribulation and the kingdom and the patient endurance, was on the island called Patmos on account of the word of God and the testimony of Jesus. ¹⁰ I was in

the Spirit on the Lord's day, and I heard behind me a loud voice like a trumpet " saying, "Write what you see in a book and send it to the seven churches, to Ephesus and to Smyrna and to Pergamum and to Thyatira and to Sardis and to Philadelphia and to Laodicea."

v. 9 John took it for granted that the recipients of his prophecy knew his identity. One simple sentence of identification would have prevented volumes of speculation about him during the last eighteen centuries. Whoever he was, he was in Jesus a *brother* and fellow partaker in the tribulation. It is in keeping with the position of one who suffers with them, to speak of himself as a *brother.* His is a message of a sufferer to the suffering (Matt. 5:10-11). It has been pointed out for centuries that believers in times of tribulation especially love this book. Note the order of the words: *tribulation, kingdom,* and *patient endurance.* The word "tribulation" is a translation of the Greek word *thlipsis* which literally means "a pressing, pressing together, pressure." It came to mean in New Testament usage "oppression, affliction, tribulation, distress, straits" (Thayer). This word is used some fifty-two times in the New Testament, and each one emphasizes some kind of distress or affliction (cf. John 16:33). It is evident from its use here that the Christians, including John, were suffering on account of their religion. Some form of persecution was in progress, and the churches were suffering because of it.

The word that is translated *patient endurance* means steadfastness and endurance in trying circumstances. In the New Testament, it is used many times to express the characteristic of a Christian who is unswerved from his deliberate purpose and his loyalty to Christ by even the greatest trials and sufferings (Thayer). John had been banished. He was a fellow-sharer of tribulation with the other Christians, and he shares that patient endurance which draws its life and energy of endurance from Jesus Christ. He wrote to show the churches how the tribulation could lead to the kingdom (2:2-3,19; 3:10; 13:10; 14:12). Suffering can be used to develop endurance, mature faith, and prepare for more intense spiritual warfare (Jas. 1:2 f.). The same truth is found in other places of the New Testament (Luke 21:19; Rom. 5:3; Acts 14:22). This tribulation characterizes the whole End time (cf. 7:14). The purpose of the writing of Revelation was to bless the church in the tribulation. Tribulation arises inevitably from the fact that the church is not of the world and yet is in the world. John wanted the Christians to know that the kingdom of God can be realized only through tribulation and perseverance. Jesus is King. He had declared to Pilate that he was a king, though not of this world (John 18:36). Pilate's statement placed over Jesus' head on the cross, "This is the King of the Jews," declared his testimony to the agelong hope of Israel. By his spiritual presence, his disciples are constituted into a fellowship of mutual love of suffering and service. The fact that they reign through and in Christ is a truth repeated in the New Testament (5:9 f.; 20:4; 22:5; cf. Matt. 5:3,10; Luke 12:32; 22:28-30; Rom. 5:17; 2 Tim. 2:11 f.; 1 Pet. 2:9). It is a present and eternal reign of all the redeemed in Christ. The beginning, struggle, progress, and triumph of this *kingdom* of Jesus Christ is the theme of the Revelation. *Patmos* (now called Patino or Patmas) is a small rocky island in the Aegean Sea. It is about ten miles long and it is from one to six miles wide. Its small size and rugged character made it a suitable place for a prison. The Roman naturalist Pliny said, "They [the prisoners] were thrown together into any ship that could be found, and such as escaped the dangers of the waves and storms and reached the place assigned for their habitation, found there nothing but bare rocks and an inhospitable rugged shore where they had to pass a life of hardship and misery."

There is some evidence that prisoners on Patmos had to work in the quarries. A natural grotto in a rock is the traditional cave where John saw his vision. John states that he is on this island **on account of [*because of*] the word of God and the testimony of Jesus.** This statement could mean that he was there for the purpose of receiving the word; however, the context favors the interpretation that John was there because he had been faithful in his witness concerning Christ.

v. 10 In this verse John tells why he was capable of receiving a revelation. He was prepared to apprehend it. He says that he came to be *in the Spirit* (cf. 4:2; 17:3; 21:10). This means more than being in the spirit in a moral sense. It means being in an elevated state of mind, a kind of ecstasy in which a man is lifted out of himself (cf. Ezek. 1:1; Acts 10:10; 22:7; Rom. 8:9; 2 Cor. 12:1-10). It was the Holy Spirit who gave this power of spiritual insight, but it was through John's natural abilities that the power was bestowed. He was open to the Holy Spirit and ready to hear and see. In this unusual state of spiritual ecstasy, through faith, he was able to look beyond the present suffering and tragedy to God revealed in Jesus Christ who is stronger than the forces of evil at work in the world. Earthly limitations were removed and the heavenly temple itself was opened to his inward eye, as it had been opened to Isaiah (Isa. 6:1). He saw the two powers (Jesus Christ in his church and the world) set in array against each other. The world seemed by far the stronger of the two.

In John's day the world was well represented in the person of Domitian. He styled himself habitually: "The Lord and God." Any resistance to his claims was punished with death. The Christians who only called Jesus Lord could not escape. Exile and death were their lot, and they whose faith was so sorely tried must have asked themselves what would be the outcome of the conflict. The vision given to John was the answer to this inquiry. The prophecy points first to the overthrow of the church's immediate enemies. There is without doubt distinct references to Rome and the Emperor. However, the conflict of the church with the world was not confined to the first century, nor did it end when the Roman Empire fell. This prophecy extends further. It points to the battle then raging as the first of a mighty and continuous warfare which was to follow to the end of time. God's purpose then in the Revelation was to make known the general principles upon which he orders the advancement of his church. He, for a time, allows the world seemingly to prevail, yet he guides all to the substantial victory of the church.

The term *Lord's day* occurs nowhere else in the New Testament but it probably means, the first day of the week, or Sunday (Matt. 28:1; Mark 16:2; Luke 24:1; John 20:1; Acts 20:7; 1 Cor. 16:2). This day was dedicated especially to the Lord because this was the day on which Jesus arose from the dead. This was one way the early Christians memorialized his resurrection each week. John heard *a loud voice like a trumpet* (Ezek. 3:12). This means that the voice was clear, distinct, intelligible, and compelling. Because of its clearness, the trumpet is often referred to in the Old Testament as the instrument to summon people together (Ex. 19:13,16,19; Num. 10:10; Judg. 7:18 ff; Isa. 18:3; 2 Sam. 15:10). The trumpet was used to emphasize authority; for solemnity, alarm, or gladness (Num. 10:1-10; Lev. 25:9; Zech. 9:14). John being *in the Spirit* was so delivered from the dominion of the senses that he could hear spiritual voices and see spiritual forms.

v. 11 In this verse John states, the first of twelve times, that he writes the book by divine command (1:11,19; 2:1,8,12,18; 3:1,7,14; 14:13; 19:9; 21:5). He was in the "goodly fellowship" of a long succession of prophets in Hebrew history. He was to communicate God's message to his fellow Christians. He was God's herald, authoritative agent, and messenger to the churches. The *loud voice like a trumpet* commands him to *write* into a book *what you see* and *send it to the seven churches* (cf. Hab. 2:2; Isa. 8:1; 30:8; Jer. 36:2). The phrase, *what you see,* corresponds with "all that he saw" (1:2). What John saw was the truth which he presents with the entire book. It was a vision of victory of Jesus Christ through his church. This truth is to be sent *to the seven churches: Ephesus, Smyrna, Pergamum, Thyatira, Sardis, Philadelphia,* and *Laodicea;* i.e., the church. These churches are listed here and are addressed in chapters two and three in the order in which a messenger from Ephesus would follow in visiting each of them. They were probably chosen because of their locations and their importance. These seven individual churches represent the total church. The message is to be communicated to the church. The churches should also *see* that Christ would ultimately triumph over all his enemies. This victory of Christ would take place in and through his churches.

(2) *A Vision of the Son of Man (1:12-16)*

¹² Then I turned to see the voice that was speaking to me, and on turning I saw seven golden lampstands, ¹³ and in the midst of the lampstands one like a son of man, clothed with a long robe and with a golden girdle round his breast; ¹⁴ his head and his hair were white as white wool, white as snow; his eyes were like a flame of fire; ¹⁵ his feet were like burnished bronze, refined as in a furnace, and his voice was like the sound of many waters; ¹⁶ in his right hand he held seven stars, from his mouth issued a sharp two-edged sword, and his face was like the sun shining in full strength.

v. 12 The prophet's turning to *see* was an indication of his receptivity to the revelation about to be given. Words can be seen with the inner eyes (cf. Isa. 2:1, etc.). John was able to distinguish this voice from his own personal consciousness. The importance of the truth spoken is emphasized by his "seeing" the voice (Gen. 3:8,10; 4:10; Ex. 19:19; Num. 7:89; Deut. 4:33; 5:22; Mark 1:3; John 1:23). He *saw seven golden lampstands* (churches, see 1:20) in the middle of which was one like a son of man (Dan. 7:13). (This was Jesus' favorite title for himself.) This vision, like most of the others, is unrepresentable in art. The truth that it represents is everything; the external form is incidental. John was writing in symbols, and it is the truth of the symbolism that is important, not the possibility of reconstructing the scene.

The directions for making the lampstand of the tabernacle are recorded in Exodus 25:31 ff. It was a golden stand with a central stem, with three branches on either side of the shaft. Each branch held a lamp which was fed with oil through the central stem and the branches. The lampstand in the tabernacle represented the testimony of God's truth borne by God's Chosen People. John possibly used the lampstand in the tabernacle for the source of this symbol, but he made several changes in the representation. The lampstand in this vision symbolizes the churches' function of witnessing which the Son of man is inspecting as he walks among them (Tenney, p. 55).

Jesus compared his disciples to a lamp set upon a stand to give light to all in the house (Matt. 5:15; see 11:4). He is present with all branches of his church, however distant one from the other, providing the needed light. The symbolism of the lampstands (and the stars) indicates that it is a night scene. The darkness which is symbolized is not an absolute mode of being, existing in its own right, but a metaphor describing what life becomes when God is rejected. The only light shining in the dark world is in the churches. The church's capacity for dispelling the darkness of the world depends upon the presence of the Light of the world in the churches (John 1:4; 8:12; 9:5; 12:35; Matt. 5:14-16). It is characteristic of John that for him light and darkness are not static terms but describe God in motion to his world and the negative response of the world to this movement. It follows that the shining of light is a process of salvation or judgment, depending on whether men will turn to or from God.

v. 13 Being turned, John "saw" a dramatic and inspiring vision of Christ in the middle of the churches. He perceived that a church is a human fellowship arising spontaneously from a divine fellowship. The background of the vision is to be found in Daniel 7:9-14; 10:5-6. The church is in the midst of conflict, but the exalted Christ the Son of man, is in the midst of the church. He has not departed from them, leaving them to the mercy of their enemies. He is still right in their midst. His presence, power, and guidance assure the church of victory. His function in the churches is suggested by his clothing. His garments represent the mark of a person of distinction, the offices of king and priest. The "robe reaching to the feet" symbolizes his priesthood (Lev. 16:4) and kingship. The **golden girdle** was a mark of royal majesty and authority. Each detail mus be understood to have a symbolic meaning and to represent some characteristic of the living Lord.

vv. 14-16 In these verses, John gives, in symbolic representation, the character of the Christ (Son of man) in the middle of the churches. Only as Christ is seen for what he really is can anything else be seen in true perspective. For these persecuted Christians, it was important that his glory and majesty be brought out (Morris, p. 52). The whiteness (pure brightness) of his head and hair suggest the fact of his purity and the fact of his eternity (Dan. 7:9). Throughout the Revelation, "pure brightness" is used to refer to heavenly persons and things (2:17; 6:2; 7:9; 20:11). It symbolizes ripe knowledge, mature judgment, and solid wisdom. The symbolism, *eyes . . . like a flame of fire,* means that he has power to search the hearts of men. His eyes are penetrative. He has power to penetrate into the thoughts of men. He is omniscient. He has infinite insight and infallible knowledge (Dan. 10:6). He knows man completely (Ps. 139; John 2:24-25). He walked among us, felt our pains. His knowledge of our afflictions and adversities is more than theoretic: it is personal, warm, and compassionate.

The *feet . . . like burnished bronze* probably symbolizes strength, might, firmness, durability, stability, and splendor (Ezek. 1:7; Dan. 10:6). It symbolizes the ability to progress and advance. It also symbolizes his tread of inspection among the churches. The Son of man has the power, as he moves in the churches, to lead them to victory (Isa. 60:13). His *voice . . . like the sound of many waters* seems to signify the majesty and authority of his voice over peoples and nations (Ezek. 1:24; 43:2; Rev. 14:2; 19:6; Pss. 29:4; 65:7; 93:4; Dan. 10:6). The voice of Christ is strong and majestic amid the Babel-sounds of the world.

The *right hand* was used by apocalyptic writers to symbolize strength, power, energy, and authority. In the Old Testament, God's right hand is the instrument of salvation, guidance, and protection of his people. In the *right hand* of the Son of man, John saw *seven stars* (cf. Jer. 22:24). He interprets the meaning of the *stars* in

1:20. The number *seven* was used to signify all, complete, the whole, entire, a totality. The prophet saw that all "messengers" of all the churches were held in the powerful protective hand of Christ.

There have been many interpretations of the "angels" (literally, "messengers") of the churches. However, most commentators, ancient and modern, have held the "angels" to mean the "ministers" of the churches. These "messengers" have been set by God over his flock, for whose welfare they must give an account. In chapters 2 and 3, these "messengers" are identified with their churches. It was to these "messengers" that Christ spoke (2:1,8,12,18; 3:1,7,14).

The *sharp two-edged sword* which issued from his mouth represents his speech, the word of God. It is God's word in general, regarded as a single and complete revelation of his will. It is his weapon of conquest and victory. It is that word which is sharper than any two-edged sword. It suggests the penetrativeness of divine truth (see 2:12,16; 19:13,15,21; Luke 2:35; Eph. 6:17; Heb. 4:12; Pss. 14:3; 57:4; 59:7; 64:3; 149:6; Prov. 12:18; Isa. 11:4; 49:2). This symbol is a figurative representation, not photographic art, of the double character of God's word: salvation and judgment. The message of God is either salvation or judgment, depending upon the response made by the hearer.

John concluded the representation of the Son of man by saying, **His face was like the sun shining in full strength.** This expresses the utmost brilliancy that man can conceive; it symbolizes a revelation of the essential deity of Christ (1 Tim. 6:16). His majesty and glory are compared with the overpowering splendor of the sun. In verses 12-16 the writer has used various figures to impress the readers with certain truths. It would not accord with his purpose to attempt to transfer to canvass the symbols he employed. These various figures must not be combined in an effort to represent a figure of the Son of man. It is the spiritual truth which gives meaning to these descriptions. The purpose of this portrait was to exhibit by a series of symbols the authority and majesty of Christ.

INTRODUCTION   47

In this mental and spiritual vision, John "saw" the victorious, glorified Christ dwelling in and ruling over the churches. He "saw" in these seven churches, in their sevenfold diversity and unity, the whole church in the End time. It is the actual church (the people of God) on the earth. It is in this church that Christ is to be found in the world. This church, with the risen, living Christ in her midst, is in conflict. Her warfare is inevitable. Nothing could more quickly and certainly give hope to the persecuted and discouraged Christians than a vision of the triumphant Christ present in their midst. His presence and his power are their assurance of victory. He holds them in his strong hand.

(3) The Prophet's Commission to Write (1:17-20)

[17] When I saw him, I fell at his feet as though dead. But he laid his right hand upon me, saying, "Fear not, I am the first and the last, [18] and the living one; I died, and behold I am alive for evermore, and I have the keys of Death and Hades. [19] Now write what you see, what is and what is to take place hereafter. [20] As for the mystery of the seven stars which you saw in my right hand, and the seven golden lampstands, the seven stars are the angels of the seven churches and the seven lampstands are the seven churches.

vv. 17-18 The prophet heightens the portrayal of the previous vision by stating that at the sight of the heavenly Christ, he fell at his feet as if he were dead. Every vision of God inspires awe and reverence. The supernatural manifestations on other occasions as recorded in the Bible had similar effects (Gen. 17:3; Ex. 33:20; Josh. 5:14; Judg. 6:22-23; 13:20; Job 42:5-6; Isa. 6:5; Ezek. 1:28; 3:23; 43:3; 44:4; Dan. 8:7,17,27; 10:8-9,15-17; Matt. 17:6; Luke 1:12; 5:8; Acts 9:4; 26:14). For every man it is a dreadful thing to encounter the living God (Ex. 33:18,20). John is overcome with a consciousness of his unworthiness in the presence of the heavenly Christ, but he is reassured. The *right hand* (see 1:16 above) of the Son of man is laid upon him and he is told not to be afraid. This gesture is designed to give reassurance. Every disclosure of the Divine Being brings a sense of unworthiness and also a sense of acceptance. The epithet, *I am the first and the last,* is similar to the one ascribed to God in 1:8. The Son of man is the eternal One, the self-existent One. The End time has entered history in the person of Christ to redeem it (Stagg, *New Testament Theology,* p. 328). He is God, though he is man. He also is the living One that became dead and the dead One who is *alive for evermore.* He not only has life in himself but he is the source of life in others (John 1:4; 14:6). Stagg says, "Not only did he die for us; he died in order to enable us to die the death that issues into life" (Stagg, *New Testament Theology,* p. 123). He not only has control over the passage of life from this world but over Hades, the vast unseen realm of death itself. The *keys* are the emblems of his authority and right. He has *the keys of Death and Hades,* because he has destroyed death by his own death and resurrection. He now is the conqueror of that resistless foe and that mysterious realm which man dreads (Heb. 2:14 f.). If he has authority over life and death, then he is victorious over all foes. If he has supremacy over the spirit world, then he has all supremacy. The churches have nothing to fear because the victorious living Christ is in control of the entire situation (Summers, p. 101).

v. 19 It was only because John had seen the divine Person with such divine power that he was commissioned to write. He had seen the divine Christ, the Priest and King, who is self-existent, who has all knowledge, who has all power, who judges all men, who speaks the word of God, who is God and man, standing in the midst of the churches. It was because of this vision of Christ in the churches and his faith that God would be victorious that John was commissioned to write. The vision which he "had seen," he was to share with the churches. The commission was to write *what is and what is to take place hereafter.* It is well to notice the words, *now write;* it gives the practical thought to the whole of the previous vision. This commission to write is a repetition of the command given in 1:11. There the commission included the whole vision which the prophet saw: past, present, and future. The commission here was to write **what is and what is to take place hereafter.** The first clause, **what you see,** comprehends the other two clauses, **what is** and **what is to take place hereafter.** What John saw in the vision were eternal principles and truths which operate anytime and all the time. His vision embraced great spiritual realities that are timeless. He was told to write what he had received from Christ concerning both the present and the future. There are serious objections to the popular interpretation that this is an outline of the book. His message, all of his message, was contemporary and relevant, and it is always contemporary and relevant.

v. 20 In this verse, John defines his prophecy and gives the interpretation to the symbolism he used. **Mystery,** in the New Testament, means something which has been made known by God but which could not otherwise have been known by man. His usage of **stars** and **lampstands** have hidden meanings which must be explained before they can be known. The stars, he says, symbolize the messengers (angels) of the churches. It seems best to interpret his explanation of the mystery by understanding the messengers (angels) to refer to the leader or leaders of each church (see 1:16). The lampstands represent the churches themselves. His prophecy is to relate to the church.

II. The Letters to the Seven Churches
(2:1 to 3:22)

In the preceding majestic vision, the prophet "saw" the glorified Christ in the church (cf. Isa. 6:1-13). He saw that Christ is in her midst; seeing, knowing, judging, and rewarding. He saw that Christ is the center of her unity and life, the source of her authority and power. He saw that Christ's guidance, power, and discipline guarantee the church's victory. In the vision of the seven churches, John saw the church as it is. He knew the churches. There was much in common that confronted each of them; and yet, each church had its own peculiar problem. He knew that the churches were loveless, unfaithful, weak, immoral, indifferent, and compromising. He also knew that the churches were loving, faithful, strong, moral, compassionate, and steadfast.

John was a visionary; however, this fact did not keep him from being a realist. He knew that the churches must become the church if they were to fulfill their mission in the world. The only way the churches could become the church was to receive (John 1:12) Christ more into their life. Only he could enable them to maintain pure doctrine and practice. In order to encourage them to become the church, he wrote seven literary creations designed for this purpose. He writes "letters" to seven churches located in cities of the Roman province of Asia. Each "letter" has a special message suited to the actual condition of each church. These "letters" are both historical and prophetical. They belong together and supplement each other. They refer very directly and clearly to their own ecclesiastical contemporary situation; however, they are also intended in their combination for the church or churches at any time throughout the ages.

These "letters" are not merely separate exhortations addressed only to each particular church, but all the "letters" were meant for all the seven churches, i.e., the whole people of God. The warnings are intended for all. The rewards mentioned are not really distinct recompenses, but rather different phases of one great whole. All the rewards will be enjoyed in their entirety by those who have been victorious in the trials and temptations of life. The descriptions of the seven churches combined furnish the vision of the church at any time. During the warfare which John discusses, any church at any time may find its own message and draw forth according to its need, warning, encouragement, and consolation.

The seven "letters" are written according to a common sevenfold plan. First comes a superscription to the church being addressed through a special messenger. Next comes a reference to some of the attributes of Christ, drawn for the most part from the description in the preceding vision of Christ in the church. The only exception to this is the designation of Christ in the "letter" to the Laodiceans (3:14). Then an account of the spiritual condition of the particular church is given. After this comes a message of praise and/or blame. Next comes exhortation in view of the spiritual condition. Then a promise is made to the morally victorious. Finally, there is a call to attention to the voice of the Spirit (Peake, *The Revelation of John,* p. 224).

In the "letters" to the churches in Ephesus, Pergamos, and Thyatira, commendation and blame are mingled. In the "letters" to the churches in Smyrna and Philadelphia, there is no blame for anything in doctrine, discipline, or manner of life. In the "letters" to the churches in Sardis and Laodicea, there is no commendation.

The definitive work on the cities and churches of Revelation was done by Sir William M. Ramsay in his book, *The Letters to the Seven Churches.* The work was first published in 1904. It was reprinted by Baker Book House, Grand Rapids, Michigan, in 1963. Many other helpful books are available on this interesting study;

however, most of them are dependent upon the work done by Ramsay.

1. The "Letter" to the Church in Ephesus (2:1-7)

¹ "To the angel of the church in Ephesus write: 'The words of him who holds the seven stars in his right hand, who walks among the seven golden lampstands.

² " 'I know your works, your toil and your patient endurance, and how you cannot bear evil men but have tested those who call themselves apostles but are not, and found them to be false; ³ I know you are enduring patiently and bearing up for my name's sake, and you have not grown weary. ⁴ But I have this against you, that you have abandoned the love you had at first. ⁵ Remember then from what you have fallen, repent and do the works you did at first. If not, I will come to you and remove your lampstand from its place, unless you repent. ⁶ Yet this you have, you hate the works of the Nicolaitans, which I also hate. ⁷ He who has an ear, let him hear what the Spirit says to the churches. To him who conquers I will grant to eat of the tree of life, which is in the paradise of God.'

Ephesus, in the first century, was the capital and foremost city of the Roman province of Asia. It was a free city. It was noted for its wealth, culture, corruptness, commerce, politics, and religion. It was "the metropolis of Asia," and the most thickly populated city in the province. It was the most important strategic center for world communication between the East and West. Three great roads from the East converged on Ephesus. It became a leading city in the Christian Way from the founding of a church there by Paul (Acts 19:1 to 20:1,18-35). Paul spent three years of his ministry there (Acts 20:31), which was the longest time he spent in any city. Tradition associates the apostle John, the elder John, Mary (the mother of Jesus), Timothy, Onesimus, and many other leaders of early Christianity with Ephesus.

v. 1 *Angel.* In the Old Testament the Hebrew word *Malākh* (Gen. 16:11, etc.) and in the New Testament the Greek word *angelos* (Matt. 1:20, etc.) mean messenger, envoy, or angel. It is not always easy in each case to discern whether the writer is referring to a heavenly messenger or to an earthly messenger. Usually, however, the context makes the reference understandable. In the seven "letters," it is the *angel* of the church in the city that is addressed. The *angel* is so identified with the church that the qualities and actions of the church are referred to as his own. He is praised for the good qualities of the church and blamed for its failures. The *angel* seems to be the bishop or pastor of the church, but he may be the celestial counterpart of the earthly organism. The one *who holds* [i.e., has full control over] *the seven stars in his right hand* is an epithet of Christ taken from the vision of the glorified Christ in 1:16. This special attribute indicates his absolute power and sovereign protection over the churches as he moves among them. He maintains their spiritual life. He holds the messengers of the churches in his right hand, the hand of power. He has power to protect, to guard, to support, to reward, to chastise, and to control the messengers of the church. The one *who walks among the seven golden lampstands* is an epithet in a slightly different form of the one given in 1:13. In this appellation, Christ declares his relation to the church and not just to the messengers. Christ is present in his church: the center of her unity and authority, the source of her power and life. The church is his body—his medium of expression in the world (Eph. 1:22-23; 3:3-13; 4:1-16; Col. 1:18-27; 2:16-19; 3:15, etc.). Paul had learned this profound truth in his vision on the road to Damascus (Acts 9:4 f.; 22:7 f.; 26:14 f.). Jesus had prayed for this oneness with his people (John 17:20-23). Christ dwells energetically, not just passively, in his people, the church.

v. 2 *I know.* This introductory verb (*oida*, not *ginōskō*) is used in all seven "letters" (2:2,9,13,19; 3:1,8,15). The design of this verb is obvious. It stresses the fact that Christ is intimately acquainted with the conditions of each church. There is nothing in the church, good or bad, which is not perfectly known by the indwelling Christ. Several characteristics are mentioned to show that Christ knows the church in Ephesus. *I know your works, your toil and your patient endurance* (cf. 1 Thess. 1:3). Perhaps the meaning can be seen by translating it, "I know your works; i.e., your toil and your patient endurance." The primary meaning of the word *works* (*erga*) is business, employment, or that with which anyone is occupied (Thayer, pp. 247-48). It is used in the Johannine writings to refer to the whole conduct of man, good and bad (John 3:19-20; 5:36; 7:3,7; 8:39,41; 1 John 3:8,12; 2 John 10; Rev. 2:5-6,9; 3:8; etc.). The word *toil* (*kopos*) means a beating, but its derived meaning is excessive labor united with trouble. The words *patient endurance* (*hupomonēn*, see 1:9 above) comes from two Greek words which mean "to abide under." This suggests that steadfastness which bears up under burdens of service or suffering. Christ knew the work being done, and he knew the circumstances in which the patient toil was accomplished. "You cannot endure evil men . . . false." These *evil men* were probably gnosticizing Christians. They claimed for themselves "the deep things of Satan" (2:24). They were partisans of the prophetess "Jezebel" and were known as "Nicolaitans" (2:14-16,20-24; cf. Bultmann, Vol. 1, p. 170). Christ also knew that the church was adverse to the encroachment of these false pretenders and evil workers. The church had no sympathy with their practices or their teachings.

v. 3 Christ also knew the trouble which the Ephesians had experienced on account of the evil and false teachers. Even in this trouble, they kept on *enduring patiently.* Christ knew these remarkable characteristics of both works and doctrine in the church in Ephesus. "Tired in loyalty, not of it. The Ephesian church can bear anything except the presence of impostors in her membership" (Moffatt).

v. 4 *I have this against you . . . you have abandoned the love you had at first.* Christ also knew that in their efforts to serve and to preserve orthodoxy, they had left their self-giving love (*agapē*) for Christ and for fellow Christians (1 John 4:20). He knew that they had left the Christian love which they had once demonstrated. Christ also knew that their hatred of heresy had left no room for love for those who differed in their beliefs. They had transformed virtues into a vice. Their Christian action and their watchful spirit had been used in a human way and not in continual obedience to God. In their struggle to maintain the standard of belief and practice, they had become self-opinionated and self-righteous, and had developed a censorious and hypercritical spirit. They had left the primary Christian virtue (1 Cor. 13; 1 John 4:8). Their lack of love had distorted their perspective. In the battle against evil, they had lost the one quality without which all others are worthless—love, the preeminent Christian virtue.

v. 5 To correct the spiritual declension into which the church had fallen, Christ speaks to the church with three imperatives: remember, repent, and do. This leaving of the love which they once displayed should be a matter for deep concern. Christ commands effort on their own part at self-recovery, **remember** (*mnēmoneue*); i.e., "continue to remember." There must be a continual calling to remembrance the fact that zeal for good works and truth may obliterate the most important truth, i.e., God is love (1 John 4:8). To forget to love is to fail to live. It is forgetfulness of this fact that leads to coldheartedness. **Repent** (*metanoēson*). This is a command for an instant change of mind, attitude, and conduct. They were to change their minds toward Christ and their fellow Christians. They must see, really see, what they have done in its true character and its full dimension. They must see what they have done, and that means seeing that they have done it to God, whose righteousness is love.

Do the works you did at first (*poieō*). This means that they are to begin immediately to do the works of love which they first did as followers of Christ. Their struggle against false doctrine and their efforts in Christian service must follow nothing but the guidance of God. This verse concludes with a sharp warning that if they did not heed the commands, they could expect sudden judgment and removal of the lampstand. The church is essentially a light-bearing community; if it ceases to give light, it ceases to be the church. With all of its orthodoxy, strength, and vigor, this church was in danger of ceasing to be a church. It could be a church only under the lordship of Christ, and under his lordship it must be a fellowship (*koinōnia*). To destroy the dimension of love toward men is to destroy the dimension of love toward God (1 John 1:3; 2:9-11; 4:7-21). If a church leaves these vertical and horizontal dimensions of love, it ceases to be a church. *I will come to you* (literally, "I am coming to you"). Christ's coming must not be thought of as his second coming (*parousia*), nor to imply that he is absent from his church (John 14:18; Matt. 28:20). He is in his church (Matt. 18:20). A congregation is a church to the extent that the faith and works of its members are motivated by the love of Christ. The church which has ceased to love has lost its reason for existence—has ceased to exist as a church. This is Christ's coming in special judgment. To remove the lampstand indicates that the church is in danger of disappearing; it warns of the lasting results of lovelessness. A loveless church does not and cannot represent Christ in the world. The only way to save the church from stagnation and spiritual death is to repent of the sin of failing in love.

v. 6 *Nicolaitans.* The evidence for identifying this sect is not sufficient to be dogmatic. They are mentioned by name in the New Testament only here and in 2:15. The early church fathers describe their tenets as profligate and immoral, pretending to combine the teachings of Christ with the impurities of paganism. Tertullian (*ca.* 150—after 220), Clement of Alexandria (*ca.* 150—*ca.* 215), and Eusebius of Caesarea (*ca.* 264—*ca.* 349) say that they were unrestrained in their licentious ways. Irenaeus (*ca.* 130—*ca.* 202) and Hippolytus (d., *ca.* 236) identify the founder of the sect with Nicolas, one of the seven appointed to serve tables (Acts 6:5). It has been thought by some that Nicolas is no historical name but simply a designation of Balaam. According to this view, the teachings of the Nicolaitans are identical with the teachings of Balaam (2:14). It seems that the Nicolaitans were corrupt in doctrine and in practice; they practiced immorality on the ground of spiritual liberty. The church in Ephesus, as well as Christ, deeply disapproved of the teaching and practice of the Nicolaitans. However, the Ephesian Christians hated what Christ hated without loving those whom he loved.

v. 7 The "letter" to the church in Ephesus concludes with an exhortation and a promise, but the introductory formula widens the application to include all churches and all Christians. The use of the plural *churches* in each exhortation (2:7,11,17,29; 3:6,13,22) is significant, indicating that no letter is addressed to a single church, but is directed to all seven, and through the seven, to all churches everywhere at all times (Rist). The Christ (2:1) exhorts attention to the voice of the Spirit. "The Spirit of Christ in the prophet is the interpreter of Christ's voice" (Swete). Each Christian in each church must hear for himself (Ezek. 3:27; Matt. 11:15; 13:9,43; Mark 4:9,23; Luke 8:8; 14:35). Each one who has the capacity to understand the message is exhorted to respond and obey (Blaney). Continuous victory is possible for all Christians who fall into the temptation to pervert the virtue of opposition to falsehood into the vice of lovelessness. They share in Christ's victory; he opposed sin in every form, yet he loved the sinner enough to die for him. The "overcomer" depicts the Christian as a faithful warrior for Christ, "the victorious member of the church, as such, apart from all consideration of the circumstances" (Swete).

The promise of *the tree of life* is a reference to the Garden of Eden. It is a general description of what is available to every Christian. The word *life* means fellowship with God through Christ, here and hereafter. The word *paradise* was first used by the Persians to refer to royal pleasure parks. The Jews learned the word during their captivity in Babylonia. When the Hebrew Old Testament was translated into Greek, this word was used to refer to the Garden of Eden. In the New Testament, the word is used three times (Luke 23:43; 2 Cor. 12:4; Rev. 2:7) as an equivalent of heaven, the abode of the redeemed. In the exercise of the love of Christ, paradise is restored and the way to the tree of life is opened. Out of a loving church the healing river of living waters flow and beside it the tree of life stands, as it once stood by the river which flowed through Eden (Gen. 2:9 f.). This promise was designed to rekindle and restore their "first love." For him who overcomes his lovelessness there will be the satisfying fruit of the tree of life in his earthly life and in his future life. The *tree of life* (Gen. 3:22) symbolizes man's participation in eternal life with all the blessings and privileges which that life can bring (21:10; 22:2,14,19).

2. The "Letter" to the Church in Smyrna (2:8-11)

⁸ "And to the angel of the church in Smyrna write: 'The words of the first and the last, who died and came to life.
⁹ " 'I know your tribulation and your poverty (but you are rich) and the slander of those who say that they are Jews and are not, but are a synagogue of Satan. ¹⁰ Do not fear what you are about to suffer. Behold, the devil is about to throw some of you into prison, that you may be tested, and for ten days you will have tribulation. Be faithful unto death, and I will give you the crown of life. ¹¹ He who has an ear, let him hear what the Spirit says to the churches. He who conquers shall not be hurt by the second death.'

Smyrna is located about forty miles almost due north of the site of Ephesus. It remains today as a flourishing and prosperous seaport city, named Izmir. In Roman times, the city rivalled Ephesus as a trading center. Smyrna was also a beautiful city with spacious streets and magnificent temples, including temples to Apollo, Asklepios, Aphrodite, Zeus, and Homer. Strabo calls it "the most beautiful of all" the cities of Asia (*Geography* XIV, 1. 37): The inhabitants claimed that it was the birthplace of Homer and also the first to worship Caesar. Cicero speaks of Smyrna's faithfulness to all treaties and alliances. Through the centuries it has remained a strong Christian witness and is today one of the great centers of piety and learning of the Orthodox church. The Muslims call it the "Infidel City" because of its Christian witness. Ramsay calls it the "City of Life." Some scholars think that this is the oldest continuous Christian witness in the church. This is the city where Polycarp was martyred in 168.

v. 8 The words of the address are taken from the titles of Christ in the introductory vision (see the discussion on 1:17-18). These two titles are especially suited to those who are about to suffer for their faith. The title, **the first and the last,** reminds them that while their sufferings, hardships, and possible death are for a short time he whom they worship and serve is eternal. He is the beginning and end of all things. Before these changeful scenes began, he is; after these changeful scenes have passed, he remains. He has always existed and will always exist. He has lived through all the past and will live through all the future; and, therefore, he can accomplish his purpose and fulfill every promise. He is also identified in this verse as the conqueror of death. He knows what they are going through, he personally has been through it. He conquered death and proved himself superior to it. He **died** (i.e., "became dead") and **came to life** and will continue to live forever. Death was to him the gate to life eternal. These two titles strongly emphasize deity and declare his ability to execute all he says.

v. 9 *I know.* The word "works" has been added to some manuscripts by later hands (see 2:2). **Tribulation** (*thlipsis*) is a general term which describes all the sufferings of the church (see 1:9). This distress was probably produced by the persecutions—which the Christians were experiencing. **Poverty** (*ptocheia*) describes the condition of one who is destitute. It is not the word "poor" (*penes*), which described the condition of a person who worked for a living. The poverty which these Christians were experiencing was probably caused by the oppression which they were undergoing. They probably had become poor because of their faith. **But you are rich** (*plousios*). The word *plousios* means "abounding" and "abundantly supplied." Though the Christians in Smyrna were paupers in material things, they had an abundance of true and durable riches.

Slander (*blasphēmia*) means railing, reviling, slander, detraction, and speech injurious to another's good name. The Jews, by national descent, in Smyrna who did not accept Christ as their Messiah opposed all Christians who did. These Jews were demonstrating the national apostasy and were now slandering the Christians (cf.

Rom. 2:28; Gal. 6:15 f.). By their opposition and unbelief, they had turned their synagogue into *a synagogue of Satan* (John 8:39). Satan was using them for his own purpose as an instrument of evil. The dramatic account of the martyrdom of Polycarp in Smyrna says that the Jews urged his execution.

v. 10 *Do not fear.* The church is addressed through its messenger. Christ not only knew the persecution, destitution, and reviling of the past, he also knew that they were about to suffer more severely than ever. He specifies the manner in which their sufferings would occur, and he commands them not to be afraid. Worse things are to come than poverty and blasphemy. Some of them were to be cast *into prison,* and prison was not a place for punishment. It was a place for those who were awaiting death or trial. Their future persecutions were to be more intense. Some of them would suffer imprisonment and torture unto death. They were to be accused and treated as criminals. The purpose of these future persecutions was that they might be tempted from their allegiance to Christ. This oppression (*thlipsis,* see v. 9) will last *ten days.* The number ten is a round number which represents a measured and very brief period of time (Gen. 24:55; Num. 11:19). The fact that the testing will be for a short period of time is often used in apocalyptic teachings as the ground of encouragement and consolation. The *ten days* was probably intended to remind them that the severe persecution would be but a little while when compared with the life with which they would be crowned. The time of the persecution is short; the duration of the joy is forever.

Be faithful until death. This command means, "Keep on being faithful, even though it cost you your life" (see Heb. 12:3). It does not say how long they are to be faithful, but how faithful they are to be. Keep on being faithful even if faithfulness brings death. *I will give you the crown of life.* The crown (*stephonos,* not *diadems*) was the crown of a king, athlete, and a triumphant warrior (1 Cor. 9:25; 2 Tim. 4:8). The crown that was given was the life itself. The *existence* which was given up in faithfulness was transformed into a *life*. The one who is faithful unto dying, looking as if he has lost all, finds life. The one who is faithful may die, but he dies to live. The badge of the Christian life is a cross.

v. 11 *He who has an ear, let him hear.* The Spirit is saying to each member of the church, "Be faithful." *He who conquers shall not be hurt by the second death.* The expression, *second death*, is a rabbinic phrase which occurs in the Bible only in Revelation (20:6,14; 21:8). However, it is used often in the intertestamental writings to refer to final perdition. It is a state of living torments and final separation from God. The prophet describes it as "the lake that burns with fire and brimstone," (21:8). The word "death" occurs in the Bible many times. The "first death" or "death" means natural, physical death, that which separates one from physical life and the hope of physical life. The "second death" separates one from God, the source of all life. The temporary pain of the first "death" is contrasted with the enduring pain of the *second death*. The *second death* also separates one from hope of eternal life. One must make his choice. If he fears the hurt of the first "death" so much that he is unfaithful, then he must suffer the unspeakable hurt of the second. The one who is faithful not only receives a reward of eternal life, but he also escapes a dreadful death. The exhortation by the Spirit and the promise by the conqueror of death were given to sustain the struggling Christians in their trials and to help them to be faithful. The one who has more faith in God than he has a love for his life lives with God.

3. The "Letter" to the Church in Pergamum (2:12-17)

[12] "And to the angel of the church in Pergamum write: 'The words of him who has the sharp two-edged sword.

[13] "'I know where you dwell, where Satan's throne is; you hold fast my name and you did not deny my faith even in the days of Antipas my witness, my faithful one, who was killed among you, where Satan dwells. [14] But I have a few things against you: you have some there who hold the teaching of Balaam, who taught Balak to put a stumbling block before the sons of Israel, that they might eat food sacrificed to idols and practice immorality. [15] So you also have some who hold the teaching

of the Nicolaitans. ¹⁶ Repent then. If not, I will come to you soon and war against them with the sword of my mouth. ¹⁷ He who has an ear, let him hear what the Spirit says to the churches. To him who conquers I will give some of the hidden manna, and I will give him a white stone, with a new name written on the stone which no one knows except him who receives it.'

Pergamum was about fifty-five miles northeast of Smyrna. It was the most northern of the seven churches mentioned in the Revelation. It was located in the valley of the river Caicus and for a long time was the capital city of the Roman province of Asia. This city was left to the Roman government in a will.

Historically this was the greatest city of Asia. Ramsay calls it, "the royal city, the city of authority." Pliny calls it the most illustrious city in Asia. There were many points of greatness about Pergamum. It was famous, first of all, for a literary center. The library here contained 200,000 volumes. It was second in volume only to Alexandria in Egypt. One of the writing materials of the early centuries of Christianity got its names from Pergamum. It was called parchment from Latin *pergamena charta* (paper of Pergamum). Parchment was made from animal skins.

In Greek mythology, Pergamum was the birthplace of Zeus. It was a city of religion. This was the first place in all the empire to give divine honors to the Emperor. In 29 B.C. an altar was dedicated to "divine Augustus." It was from this city that emperor worship spread into other parts of the province and then into other provinces of the empire.

It was the home of an insidious and ornate paganism. Behind the city stood a hill on which there were temples to Zeus, Athena, Dionysus, and Aesculapius. The altar of Zeus, on a platform cut out of the rock-hill, dominated the city. The ruins still testify that it was a "city of temples."

Pergamum was also the last outpost of Greek civilization. Many of the Greek writers spoke of this city as being the last point of civilization. When one went beyond Pergamum, he entered heathendom.

v. 12 The words of the address are taken from the description of Christ in the introductory vision (see 1:16). Christ is represented as having a sword with two edges (cf. Isa. 49:2; Heb. 4:12). The two edges were designed to cut both ways. This sword emphasizes the penetration of truth. Christ distinguishes between truth and error. Truth is the only weapon which Christ will use in his struggle with evil. It is a weapon of blessing or judgment. It is greater than the sword of a pagan government.

v. 13 *I know where you dwell, where Satan's throne is.* The Christ with the two-edged sword knows the peculiar wickedness of the environment of the church. This statement may refer to the fact that Pergamum was a pagan religious center but probably refers to the fact that it was a center of emperor worship. Satan himself had his *throne* there, i.e., the main seat of power of the imperial cult in the province. He, in mimicry of God's throne, had set up his throne (4:2). The church was ministering in the most difficult situation imaginable and was undergoing persecution while doing so.

You hold fast my name. This statement in the original language emphasizes the fact that the whole name is being continually held. This loyal, steadfast church had been true to Christ personally. The members had not been ashamed or denied that they were disciples of Christ. The name of Christ stands for his life revealed in the events of history, in a word for his very self. To *hold fast* his *name* means to hold fast to his "personality" or "character." The church had come into a real and living relationship with Christ.

Did not deny my faith. This may be an objective genitive in the Greek which would mean, "their faith in Christ," or it may be a subjective genitive which would mean, "the faith which was Christ's." It may include both of these ideas. These Christians had clung to their faith in Christ in spite of all opposition, and the faith they had was the same high faith in God that Christ held (Heb. 12:2; Matt. 27:43). The phrase in the Greek is in a tense which indicates that it is a reference to some specific incident. There had been some outburst of persecution, some crisis in which they had remained faithful. There were some members who refused to deny Christ to save their own lives.

Antipas. This is the only reliable reference to this early martyr. Traditions grew up concerning him, but they are not reliable. The Greek word for witness is *martus*. So many of the early faithful witnesses were killed because of their faith, the word came to mean martyr (Acts 1:8; 22:20; 1 Tim. 6:13; Rev. 1:5; 17:6). At least one Christian at Pergamum had died for his faith.

The repetition of the phrase ***where Satan dwells*** is probably given to emphasize the general character of the city.

v. 14 This verse points out the fact that there were certain members in the church who had learned a way to escape martyrdom. They had insight and knowledge. They were in favor of sharing the social life of their pagan neighbors. They were broad-minded and tolerant. Like Balaam (Num. 22:1 to 25:9; 31:15 f.), they debased spiritual gifts to evil purposes and practiced impurity as expressive of the purest form of divine worship. Like some of the Corinthians (1 Cor. 8:1-13), these members were allowing their knowledge and Christian liberty to become a ***stumbling block*** to their weak brothers. Like ***Balaam,*** they were teaching the way of compromise, the way of conformity. They were prostituting their gifts to the seducing of their fellow Christians into idolatry and impurity (Rom. 6:15). Like Israel in the plains of Moab, some of these Christians were bringing a curse upon themselves by yielding to sin.

v. 15 For a discussion of ***Nicolaitans,*** see 2:6.

v. 16 ***Repent*** and ***I will come to you soon*** (see 2:5). The whole church is to repent of its tolerance of this evil. Christ makes war on those who hold to the teachings of Balaam and the Nicolaitans. His opposition is principally directed against the false teachers, but also against the church for tolerating them. The weapon for this resistance is truth (1:16). Christ's spoken words are like a sharp sword. They cut and penetrate deep into the soul (Isa. 49:2; Eph.

6:17; Heb. 4:12).

v. 17 Again the introductory formula widens the application to include all churches and all Christians (see 2:7). Any church or Christian can gain the victory in his conflict with compromise and sin. Christ promises two rewards to the victorious.

Hidden manna. In the intertestamental period a belief was held that the ark and other sacred treasures of the Temple had been buried by Jeremiah in a secret and safe place on "the mountain where Moses went up and beheld God's inheritance.... 'The place shall be unknown until God gathers the congregation of his people together and shows his mercy'" (2 Macc. 2:4-7). There was also a Jewish expectation that manna would descend from heaven during the messianic age. These beliefs about the manna probably suggested the image for "the true bread from heaven" (John 6:32). As the Hebrews were sustained by manna from heaven in the desert (Ex. 16:16-35), so the Christian who "overcomes" or who gains the victory over sin will be nourished by "the bread of God . . . which comes down from heaven, and gives life to the world" (John 6:33). Those Christians who refused to eat of the forbidden food of sin would be fed from heaven with *the hidden manna* (spiritual life) now restored by the victorious Christ.

White stone. The stone may refer to the Urim and Thummim (official lots of the priests) which was a medium through which the word of God was communicated to his people in the Old Testament (Ex. 28:30). Some see in it a reference to Christ. The *white stone* was associated with and was used as a symbol of hospitality, friendship, acquittal, public honor, admission ticket, a happy day, dole ticket, token of victory, token of nobility, and an amulet. It is possible that the prophet included many of these ideas in his symbolism. The sense of the symbolism seems to be that Christ would give to the one who overcomes a token of his favor which would have some renewed and heavenly name inscribed upon it, which would be intelligible to him only (3:12; Isa. 62:2). The name stands for the totality of a person's life. It expresses the nature, the character, the being of the person who hears it. No one else can understand the evidence of Christ's favor but the Christian himself.

4. The "Letter" to the Church in Thyatira (2:18-29)

[18] "And to the angel of the church in Thyatira write: 'The words of the Son of God, who has eyes like a flame of fire, and whose feet are like burnished bronze.
[19] " 'I know your works, your love and faith and service and patient endurance, and that your latter works exceed the first. [20] But I have this against you, that you tolerate the woman Jezebel, who calls herself a prophetess and is teaching and beguiling my servants to practice immorality and to eat food sacrificed to idols. [21] I gave her time to repent, but she refuses to repent of her immorality. [22] Behold, I will throw her on a sickbed, and those who commit adultery with her I will throw into great tribulation, unless they repent of her doings; [23] and I will strike her children dead. And all the churches shall know that I am he who searches mind and heart, and I will give to each of you as your works deserve. [24] But to the rest of you in Thyatira, who do not hold this teaching, who have not learned what some call the deep things of Satan, to you I say, I do not lay upon you any other burden; [25] only hold fast what you have, until I come. [26] He who conquers and who keeps my works until the end, I will give him power over the nations, [27] and he shall rule them with a rod of iron, as when earthen pots are broken in pieces, even as I myself have received power from my Father; [28] and I will give him the morning star. [29] He who has an ear, let him hear what the Spirit says to the churches.'

Thyatira was located on the Lycus river near the Roman road between Pergamum and Sardis. It was about forty miles southeast of Pergamum. Its location made it a city of some commercial importance, a center of communication, and a garrison headquarters. It was refounded as a Macedonian colony by Seleucus Nicator after the death of Alexander the Great. It was strongly Macedonian. Lydia (Acts 16:14-15) was from Thyatira. It was not noted for its culture or beauty. It was the smallest of the seven cities. The elder Pliny's evaluation can be seen in his comment: "Thyatira and other unimportant communities . . ." It was a manufacturing center. It was especially famous for its wool trade and for its purple-dye works. These industries and many others were under the control of powerful trade guilds. Authorities disagree about its survival. Some think that it survives in the present town of Akhisar (White Castle).

The "letter" to Thyatira is the longest and most obscure of the "letters" to the churches in Revelation, and, like the one to Pergamum, it is severe in its tone.

v. 18 The words in the address *to the angel of the church in Thyatira* are taken from the titles of Christ in the introductory vision (see 1:14-16). The message is sent from *the Son of God* (Matt. 26:63 f.; John 11:4). This is noteworthy because the term "Son of man" is usually used in Revelation, and this is the only time the phrase *Son of God* is used. This descriptive phrase suits because the message in this "letter" is expressed in language of sovereignty and sternness. The two titles, *who has eyes like a flame of fire,* and *whose feet are like burnished bronze,* emphasize Christ's all-searching gaze and his power to trample down and destroy enmity and resistance.

v. 19 The Son of God has intimate personal knowledge of the church's love, faith, service, and patient endurance. He also knows that they are making progress in good works; the last are more than the first. They are enlarging their activities and increasing the energy put forth. The church was advancing in works of active service.

v. 20 The "messenger" of the church is rebuked for tolerating the presence of some powerful evil influence in the congregation. The wife of King Ahab was instrumental in leading ancient Israel into the practice of idolatry (1 Kings 16:31 f.; 2 Kings 9:22). John evidently uses the name *Jezebel* figuratively to carry us back to the wicked wife of Ahab. He seems to use the name *Jezebel* symbolically to signify a form of false doctrine personified. This symbolical Jezebel was to the church in Thyatira what Jezebel, Ahab's wife, was to him. The error represented by the name seems to have been antinomian gnosticism. Like Jezebel of old, these teachers were leading some of the members into the adoption of heathen ways and into compromise with a pagan faith. The spirit of Jezebel was showing itself in the church. This spirit made pretensions to divine inspiration (cf. John 2:19; 4:1-3). No protest was being made to this evil in the church by the "messenger."

Jezebel's teachings were the same as the teachings of the Nicolaitans, though *to practice immorality* precedes *to eat food sacrificed to idols.* This change signifies her particular emphasis. The metaphor of adultery is often used in the Old Testament to represent Israel's unfaithfulness to God (1 Chron. 5:25; Ezek. 25:37; Hos. 9:1; etc.). Although, according to the teachings of antinomian gnosticism the words can be taken quite literally.

v. 21 Jezebel had been given opportunity to repent but had refused. Nothing but disaster can come to those who do not respond to the repeated warnings of God. God's delay of judgment does not mean indifference but an unwillingness that any should perish (cf. 2 Pet. 3:9).

vv. 22-23 Jezebel's lovers and children are probably the devotees and disciples of her teachings. Forbearance having failed, God uses severity (Jer. 3:8; 5:7; Ezek. 16:22). The devices of evil practices become the devices of retribution. The bed of sin becomes the bed of sickness, anguish, and punishment. Those who have become partakers in Jezebel's passions have abandoned their own works for hers and are, therefore, commanded to repent of her works. The object of judgment is both disciplinary and corrective. All who share her evil practices share her death to all that makes life meaningful and worthwhile. The ones who practice Jezebel's sins meet with Jezebel's retribution (1 Kings 18:40; 2 Kings 10:6-7,24-25). Jezebel's sins pollute the mind, ruin the body, destroy the conscience, and paralyze the will of those who practice them. The Son of God knows completely the feelings and the inmost thoughts of each one (cf. Jer. 11:20).

vv. 24-25 Some of the members in Thyatira did not practice the sins of Jezebel. These faithful Christians are protected from the consequences of her sins. The Gnostics claimed that a special secret knowledge was needed for full salvation, and they claimed that they could supply that knowledge. They also claimed that they possessed an inner life which made conduct irrelevant. They taught that all human experience was to be explored. Those who did not know the deep things of God were scorned. The Son of God says that their teachings are not the deep things of God but the deep things of Satan.

The faithful members are commanded to *hold fast* (get a grip on) the love, faith, service, patience, and the growth in these virtues for which they had been commended in 2:19. These members must beware of relaxing their hold on the Christian principles by which they are at present guided.

vv. 26-27 These verses are a free quotation from Psalm 2:9. John saw the church, united with the victorious Christ, in complete triumph. The power of Christ is a moral and spiritual power. In this realm he is supreme. Christ gives or shares this moral and spiritual power *over the nations* with the faithful Christians. The promise here is of *power* ("the might of right") to share in the shepherd-like sovereignty of the anointed king. The *rod* is the same word used in the Septuagint in Psalm 23:4. It signifies the shepherd's rule over his flock. It is made of *iron* indicating the unbreakable rule thus symbolized. The word *rule* should be translated "to shepherd."

The world's resistance shall be overcome completely, and the world's opposition shall be *broken in pieces.* This victory will be won by Christ's own power, but this power will work through his faithful people. The reward for faithfulness is a share in the power of the "faithful-unto-death" Christ. To "conquer" is not simply to triumph at last but to overcome continuously. The faithful Christian life consists of lifelong fidelity.

vv. 28-29 The *morning star* was proverbial for brightness and beauty. It was also used to express perpetual expectation and hope. It is the sign of dawn, the herald and promise of a new day. Christ is called *the morning star* (22:16). Each faithful member in Thyatira is promised victory in his struggle as he is exposed to the ravages of a morally compromising heresy.

In the first three "letters" the promise to the "overcomer" is placed before the call to attention, and in the last four "letters" the call to attention is placed after the concluding words of promise.

5. The "Letter" to the Church in Sardis (3:1-6)

¹ "And to the angel of the church in Sardis write: 'The words of him who has the seven spirits of God and the seven stars.

" 'I know your works; you have the name of being alive, and you are dead. ² Awake, and strengthen what remains and is on the point of death, for I have not found your works perfect in the sight of my God. ³ Remember then what you received and heard; keep that, and repent. If you will not awake, I will come like a thief, and you will not know at what hour I will come upon you. ⁴ Yet you have still a few names in Sardis, people who have not soiled their garments; and they shall walk with me in white, for they are worthy. ⁵ He who conquers shall be clad thus in white garments, and I will not blot his name out of the book of life; I will confess his name before my Father and before his angels. ⁶ He who has an ear, let him hear what the Spirit says to the churches.'

Sardis was located thirty-three miles southeast of Thyatira at the foot of Mount Tmolus on an inaccessible hill. It was situated at the juncture of five roads and was on the highway between Thyatira and Philadelphia. It commanded the fruitful Hermus valley, and the commerce of that rich valley centered upon it. Its position made it one of the world's great trading centers. It was famous for its woolen fabrics, and the art of dyeing is said to have been devised here. The manufacture of a special kind of bronze was carried on in Sardis. Gold dust was found in the little stream which flowed through the city. It is the place where modern money was first coined.

Sardis was the capital of the ancient kingdom of Lydia. In 560 B.C., Croesus, whose name has become a proverb for extravagant wealth, was its king. It was captured by Cyrus in 548 B.C. and by Antiochus the Great in 216 B.C., although it was thought to be impregnable. The inhabitants of Sardis, some of whom were Jews, had a reputation for luxurious living. They were noted for luxury and licentiousness. In A.D. 17 it, along with eleven other cities, was destroyed by an earthquake. Tiberius helped to rebuild it. Its chief god was Cybele (or Cybebe).

The church in Sardis reflected the history of the city. It was sadly degenerated. No conflict is mentioned with foes within or without the church. The church had ceased to witness sufficiently to excite the opposition of the world. It seems to have been a perfect model of inoffensive Christianity. There was no occasion to oppose a church that had given up her testimony.

v. 1 The designation of the one who addresses the "messenger" of the church in Sardis does not occur in the introductory vision of Christ. The reference to the one *who has the seven spirits of God and the seven stars* (cf. 1:20; 4:5) emphasizes Christ as the source of life and light to his church. The number *seven* denotes completeness and perfection. He has the fullness of God's Spirit. The *seven spirits* are the sevenfold (complete) operation of the Holy Spirit (1:4). This attribute expresses his power by the Spirit to convict of sin and of a worthless profession. *The seven stars* are the "messengers" of the churches (1:16,20). Christ holds in his hand these *stars* for safety in danger and punishment in unfaithfulness. This title of Christ is appropriate in addressing a church which is all but dead to spiritual things. He not only has the spirit with which he enlivens the churches but he also has complete control over the "messengers" of the churches.

I know introduces a precise diagnosis of the attainments and failures of the congregation. The church stands before him exactly as it is, stripped of all its pretense. The One who could look beyond the deceiving form of appearance saw that on the whole the church was alive only in name (Eph. 2:1,5; 5:14; 1 Tim. 5:6; 2 Tim. 3:5; Titus 1:16). It was not lacking in reputation or in outward manifestations of life and activity, yet in the sight of him who has the seven spirits of God (omniscience), it was dead. This church was "the paradox of death under the name of life" (Swete).

v. 2 *Awake.* The original is more vivid, being equivalent to "become wakeful," "awake and watch," or "become a watcher." *Strengthen what remains* refers to the residue of faith and practice or spiritual vitality that still lingered among them. Even this small residue was just ready to become extinct. Whatever may have been the church's appearance before men, "before my God" no work of the church was *perfect,* "complete," or "fulfilled."

v. 3 The church is reminded of the spiritual condition from which its members had declined (2:5). They are also reminded of the permanent result of the act of receiving the spiritual residue in their lives and the act of hearing at some definite period in their past. They are commanded to *keep,* or "continue to keep," and *repent,* or "repent once for all." The basic sin of the church, as well as the other churches of the Revelation, was unrepentance, which excludes forgiveness and renewing grace (cf. 2:5,16,21; 3:18 f.).

If the church does not *awake,* Christ will come as a thief. This proverbial expression is used in the New Testament to stress the unexpectedness of Christ's "coming" (16:15; Matt. 24:43; Luke 12:39; 1 Thess. 5:2; 2 Pet. 3:10). Christ comes in many ways in salvation or judgment. His judgment is God's judgment (John 5:22) *Hour* is used in Revelation to denote a very short time or a point in time. It is used here to indicate a period whose shortness should be emphasized (Rissi, p. 28).

v. 4 There was a small remnant left in the church who had not shared in the spiritual decline of the majority. They had not been defiled by the moral atmosphere around them and had not besmirched their Christian profession. These undefiled ones shall enjoy glory in a continuous life of victory with Christ as their constant companion. *They are worthy* of this walk with Christ because they have done nothing to forfeit it.

v. 5 The blessings in store for the small remnant are continued in this verse. The ones who overcome the condition of spiritua

THE LETTERS TO THE SEVEN CHURCHES   73

death will be arrayed in *white garments* (symbolic of moral purity, character, vestments of the soul, cf. 4:4; 7:13-14; 19:8; 2 Cor. 5:4) and will not have their names removed from *the book of life.* The *name* is synonymous with "person." In Revelation the "book of life" is a figure which means the register of heavenly citizens. The metaphor goes back to the register of inhabitants of Jerusalem (Isa. 4:3; Ezek. 13:9). It was also used to refer to the register of God's people (13:8; 20:12,15; 21:27; Ex. 32:32; Ps. 69:28; Isa. 8:16; 29:11 f., 18; Dan. 12:1; Mal. 3:16 f.; Luke 10:20; Phil. 4:3; Heb. 12:23). It occurs frequently in apocalyptic literature. The heavenly standing of him *who conquers* is further stressed by the statement that Christ *will confess his name* before God. When Christ vouches for a man, he is accepted (Luke 12:8 f.).

v. 6 See 2:29 above.

6. The "Letter" to the Church in Philadelphia (3:7-13)

⁷ "And to the angel of the church in Philadelphia write: 'The words of the holy one, the true one, who has the key of David, who opens and no one shall shut, who shuts and no one opens.
⁸ "I know your works. Behold, I have set before you an open door, which no one is able to shut; I know that you have but little power, and yet you have kept my word and have not denied my name. ⁹ Behold, I will make those of the synagogue of Satan who say that they are Jews and are not, but lie—behold, I will make them come and bow down before your feet, and learn that I have loved you. ¹⁰ Because you have kept my word of patient endurance, I will keep you from the hour of trial which is coming on the whole world, to try those who dwell upon the earth. ¹¹ I am coming soon; hold fast what you have, so that no one may seize your crown. ¹² He who conquers, I will make him a pillar in the temple of my God; never shall he go out of it, and I will write on him the name of my God, and the name of the city of my God, the new Jerusalem which comes down from my God out of heaven, and my own new name.
¹³ He who has an ear, let him hear what the Spirit says to the churches.'

Philadelphia was twenty-eight miles southeast of Sardis on the road to Laodicea. It was named for Attalus Philadelphus, who founded it in 140 B.C. It was located on one of the most strategic sites in Asia Minor. For its own protection, it was less favorably situated than any other of the seven cities mentioned in Revelation. It was situated at a place where the borders of Mysia, Lydia, and Phrygia met. It was the gateway to the East. It was founded for the purpose of spreading Greek culture and language to the barbaric tribes. It was intended to be missionary.

Philadelphia was located on the flat summit of Mount Tmolus, a volcanic mountain range. Its citizens were in constant fear of earthquakes and volcanic eruptions. It was destroyed by an earthquake in A.D. 17. It was rich in hot springs to which the infirm came to bathe in medicinal waters.

It was famous for its vintages and its wines. Dionysus, the god of wine, was its principle deity, but it had so many gods it was sometimes called "Little Athens."

The church in Philadelphia was inwardly faithful, but outwardly weak and suffering. It was not rebuked or warned, simply commended and exhorted. The reward promised is the presence of Christ and greater opportunities for service.

v. 7 The "messenger" *of the church in Philadelphia* is addressed by one who is *holy* (6:10), *true* (1 John 2:20; 5:20), *has the key of David* (Isa. 22:22), and who *opens and no one shall shut, who shuts and no one opens* (Job 12:14; Isa. 22:22). Each of these appellations used indicates that which belongs to the essential nature of Christ. None of the titles comes from the introductory vision in 1:13-16. This verse indicates that the authority which Christ exercises as king is holy, true or genuine, absolute, and final. He alone gives or withholds admission to the city of David, the new Jerusalem (3:21; 19:11-16; 20:4; Eph. 1:22). He acts resolutely, and no one can interfere. This sovereignty he uses, even in delegating authority to his church (Dan. 7:13 ff.; Matt. 26:64; 28:18-20; 16:19). The church is representing him. He is always the head of the church. Whatever degrees of authority may have been committed to the church, the supreme power belongs to Christ alone (Matt. 28:18; Eph. 1:22).

v. 8 Christ's commendation is based upon intimate personal knowledge. He speaks here by way of encouragement. He knows all the facts about the condition of the church. The **open door** symbolizes a gift of missionary opportunity and spiritual usefulness to the church by Christ (John 10:7-9; Acts 14:27; 1 Cor. 16:9; 2 Cor. 2:12; Col. 4:3). It means that he gave them greater opportunities and privileges for service as a reward for faithful service, which also led to greater glory. This opportunity which he gave to them could not be taken from them. The strength of the church was little, but it was genuine. Its reality and genuineness are witnessed by its fidelity. The church's little strength was made strong in Christ (Zech. 4:6). The members had been obedient and had not renounced the name of Christ.

v. 9 The Christians in Philadelphia are told that they shall be victorious over their Jewish opponents (Rom. 9—11). The power of their testimony and the faithfulness of their lives would conquer and win their enemies (1 Cor. 14:24). By their rejection of the Messiah and their slanderous accusations of the Christians, the Jews had constituted themselves into a *synagogue of Satan.* They spoke falsely in calling themselves *Jews,* that is, God's favored people. They were lacking in all that was characteristic of the true Israel.

The name *Jews* was a name of honor which the synagogue could no longer bear (2:9). The true *Jews* are those who accept the Messiah (Rom. 2:28 ff.). The faithful Christians are promised that the malicious opposition which they encounter shall not prevail but shall be overcome and humbled. In contrast to a Jewish expectation that the Gentiles would eventually recognize Israel's primacy (Isa. 45:14; 49:6,22-23; 56:1-5; 60:14; Ezek. 36:23; 37:27-28), these Jews will be made to see that the church is the true Israel. Hope is held out of converting the Jews. It is to Christ in his church that all men, Jews included, must make their submission (Morris, p. 79).

v. 10 The faithful Christians had manifested in their trials which they had experienced the ***patient endurance*** (*hupomonē*, i.e., steadfastness and endurance in trying circumstances) which Christ requires. Christ promises them that because they had kept his command to endure he would bring them safe out of the future trials that would come upon the world. This does not mean exemption from trials but rather deliverance out of trials. ***The hour of trial*** seems to be the same as the all-inclusive "great tribulation" which is present during the whole End time. These trials affect all the inhabitants of the world (12:9; Luke 2:1). They put faithfulness to the test and disclose character. They often bring temptation (Jas. 1:2,13). They provide opportunities for the unfaithful and the unbelievers to repent. No exemption was promised from trials and suffering. However, God will not allow his people to be tried above that which they are able to bear, but will with the trial make a way of escape (1 Cor. 10:13). The Lord of End time is in the midst of his church to keep it.

v. 11 The declaration by Christ ***I am coming soon*** is a promise and is intended to be an incentive to faithfulness and encouragement to the church. He kept his promise. This is the "keynote of the book" (Beckwith). The "coming Jesus" has already decided all things for the believers because life and death have been overcome by him. He comes in every trial either for salvation or judgment. Christ commands the faithful Christian in Philadelphia to ***hold fast***, or "keep a firm grip on" whatever faithfulness they then possessed. Those who would take their crown (*stephanos*, i.e., a badge of victory) are not competitors for it; but such as would prevent their attainment of it by enticing them to unfaithfulness (Smith).

v. 12 The promised reward to him ***who conquers*** is that he would be a pillar in the temple of God. The "conquering" is a present continuous process. In apocalyptic writings, a ***pillar*** stood for something that was firmly fixed and stable. The temple (*naos*) must be taken metaphorically, as there is no temple in the heavenly city (21:22). It seems that John uses the temple here, as do Paul and Peter, to refer to the dwelling place of God, the church (1 Cor. 3:16-17; 6:19; 2 Cor. 6:16; 1 Tim. 3:15; 1 Pet. 2:5). This is an assurance of inseparable unity between God and his people. *Never shall he go out of it* means that the faithful will be a permanent part of the spiritual temple. Notice that there are three marks which are given to the faithful Christians to assure them that they are God's own, incapable of being removed or claimed by another (7:3; 14:1; 22:4; John 3:33). First, *the name of my God* means that they belong and would be known and recognized as belonging to God. Second, *the name of the city of my God* means that they are heavenly citizens and would be known and recognized as belonging to the holy city (Phil. 3:20). Third, *my own new name* means the name of Christ which is the revelation of himself that is necessarily concealed from those who dwell in this world (2:17). John declares that *the new Jerusalem . . . comes down.* In this statement, the spirituality and holiness of the church are set forth (Ezek. 48:35). Its creation and sustenance are wholly due to God. The new Jerusalem is continually coming down out of heaven from God (21:2,10; Gal. 4:26; Heb. 12:22). This is John's way of saying that it is God's work. *My God* receives emphasis from being repeated four times in this verse. This fourfold repetition makes absolute and real the inseparable unity between the victorious Christ and those who confess him in shame (3:8-9).

v. 13 See 3:6 above.

7. The "Letter" to the Church in Laodicea (3:14-22)

[14] "And to the angel of the church in Laodicea write: 'The words of the Amen, the faithful and true witness, the beginning of God's creation.
[15] "'I know your works: you are neither cold nor hot. Would that you were cold or hot! [16] So, because you are lukewarm, and neither cold nor hot, I will spew you out of my mouth. [17] For you say, I am rich, I have prospered, and I need nothing; not knowing that you are wretched, pitiable, poor, blind, and naked. [18] Therefore I counsel you to buy from me gold refined by fire, that you may be rich, and white garments to clothe you and to keep the shame of your nakedness from being seen, and salve to anoint your eyes, that you may see. [19] Those whom I love, I reprove and chasten; so be zealous and repent. [20] Behold, I stand at the door and knock; if any one hears my voice and opens the door, I will come in to him and eat with him, and he with me. [21] He who conquers,

I will grant him to sit with me on my throne, as I myself conquered and sat down with my Father on his throne. ²² He who has an ear, let him hear what the Spirit says to the churches.' "

Laodicea was forty-three miles southeast of Philadelphia, twelve miles from Colosse and about one hundred miles from Ephesus. It was founded by Antiochus and was named after his wife, Laodicea, in 250 B.C. It was situated at the intersection of three well-travelled roads and in the Roman times had grown rapidly. It was a wealthy banking and manufacturing center. It manufactured cloth and carpets from its native, glossy, black wool. It was the seat of a well-known medical school that compounded medicines for eyes and ears. It was famous for its warm springs which provided water for bathing but was utterly unfit for drinking. The Phrygian god, Men Karou, was its chief deity, although it was a center for emperor worship.

Paul wrote a letter to this church (Col. 4:16).

v. 14 The attributes of the speaker to the "messenger" of the church in Laodicea are *Amen, the faithful and true witness,* and *the beginning of God's creation.*

Amen. The Hebrew word "amen" (Isa. 65:16) is the acknowledgment of a word which is valid, and the validity of which is binding (Kittel). It is a word expressive of life and unchanging faithfulness. It is the word with which Jesus introduces his most solemn declarations, especially in the Fourth Gospel, which is liturgically doubled twenty-five times. It is here applied to Christ, "whose testimony never falls short of the truth" (Swete). It indicates that Christ's every word is certainly and assuredly true. His unchanging faithfulness, "amen," contrasts with Laodicea's unfaithfulness, "neither cold nor hot."

Faithful and true witness is in some measure appositional and is an amplification of the *amen.* It asserts the truthfulness, trustworthiness, and completeness of Christ's work as a witness in the strongest manner. As the faithful and true witness, he judges evil and exposes the true condition of the person.

The beginning of God's creation indicates that Christ is the originating principle, source or instrument of creation through whom God works (John 1:3; Col. 1:15,18; Heb. 1:2). These titles stress Christ's faithfulness and authority. His faithfulness stands in sharp contrast to the church's unfaithfulness and self-sufficiency. Also these titles stress his ability to tell the church how it is with them, though they know it not and keep saying the very opposite.

v. 15 The One described in the preceding verse knows well the moral elements and spiritual temperature of the church. This statement was designed to impress upon the church the fact that Christ was not only acquainted with what they did but also with their inner motives and purposes. He knew that the members were ***neither cold nor hot.*** These figurative words describe persons who are neither in earnest for God nor utterly indifferent to him. There was a profession but no warmhearted faithfulness. There was no real love, and yet there was an appearance of it, the pretense to it. ***Would that you were cold or hot!*** This wish about the present condition expressed in an exclamation does not mean that he wishes them to become cold or hot. The wish is that they may not remain as an abiding condition in their lukewarm state.

v. 16 The distaste and nausea produced by lukewarm water are used as an intensely strong figure to express the extreme disgust which Christ feels toward insincerity and hypocrisy. This startling language expresses in the strongest possible fashion a vigorous repudiation of the sanctimonious pretense of the Laodiceans (Tyndale, p. 83).

v. 17 ***For you say.*** The church was habitually making claims about their own riches, and they claimed that their wealth was entirely due to their own efforts. They were continually imagining riches which they did not possess. The riches and poverty referred to here are no doubt spiritual. However, a state of wealth and ease can easily produce such a mental condition, and the wealth of Laodicea may have produced the condition of the church. The contrast between their imagined state as they saw it and their real state as Christ saw it is expressed in bold and striking words. They said, *I am rich;* Christ said, *You are wretched, pitiable, poor, blind, and naked.* Self-sufficiency is the fatal danger of a lukewarm condition. Many think that this statement hits at Laodicea's banking business, medical school, and clothing manufacturers.

v. 18 The remedy for the threefold spiritual deficiency is Christ. He would have them procure from him *gold refined by fire,* that is, real genuine wealth. He can also provide *white garments* which will contrast with the black wool garments which the wealthy Laodiceans wore. These white garments will provide real honor (Gen. 41:42; Esther 6:6-11; Dan. 5:29). The eye salve which he provides in contrast to their famous collyrium will enable them to really see.

Apparently the church in Laodicea had escaped persecution; however, Christ is about to show his love by bringing upon it outward affliction. This shows the loving purpose of Christ in permitting the persecutions of the church which the Revelation describes.

v. 19 Discipline is the lot of all whom God loves (Prov. 3:12) He chastens because he is love (Heb. 12:6). The chastening comes from the Lord of the church, not hostile forces. Christ is still sovereign, and he is in his church. Rebuke and chastening may be signs of the tenacity of his love, even when they indicate displeasure. His judgments are but the expression of a deep affection that should lead to repentance.

Be zealous. That is, "Keep on being zealous." This has reference to the problem of lukewarmness. *Repent.* Repentance is the whole purpose for the severe disclosure which he has made of their faults This church was so self-satisfied that it was all but devoid of fellowship with Christ.

vv. 20-21 The figurative language here is so plain that it needs no interpretation. Holman Hunt's great picture interprets this passage better than words. This is a metaphorical description of fellowship in the church and in the messianic kingdom (Matt. 26:29

Mark 14:25; Luke 22:30). The highest promises are contained in the figure: First, close communion with Christ, under the common figure of a feast, at which Christ is both the provider and the guest. Second, victory and exaltation to the heavenly realm where Christ allows them to sit and reign with him. In the same way that Christ is seated with God on his throne (22:1,3), the faithful Christian is seated with Christ on his throne (cf. Matt. 19:28; Luke 22:30). Christ's victory and exaltation was by way of the cross (John 16:33; Phil. 2:5-11), and this sets the pattern for the church. They who conquer as he conquered sit with him on his throne (Eph. 1:3,20; 2:6; 3:10; 6:12). His seeming defeat was his victory, and the seeming defeat for the suffering Christian can be his victory.

v. 22 See notes on 2:7.

III. The Sevenfold Vision of Conflict
(4:1 to 22:5)

1. The Vision of Heaven and Heavenly Worship (4:1 to 5:14)

(1) The Vision of God as Creator (4:1-11)

The fourth chapter is a call to the church for the conflict—a call to believe in God. It provides a brief vision of the transcendent greatness, majesty, power, and kingly authority of God. To John, sovereignty and omnipotence go together. This chapter stresses the revelation of God as Creator, the ultimate source of all existence, and the sovereign over all the universe. He called all things into existence and commanded them to obey his will. Nearly all the images come from the Old Testament, especially from Ezekiel, Isaiah, and Daniel. The writer accepts the great affirmation of faith with which the Bible opens, "In the beginning God created the heavens and the earth" (Gen. 1:1).

This chapter is intended to impress the reader with God's incomprehensible plenitude of power, a potency that is absolute. John has the same faith as the psalmist who says, "Power belongeth unto God" (Ps. 62:11), and as Paul who declares that nature itself gives evidence of the eternal power of God (Rom. 1:20). The writer's faith sees God as having limitless power and as being the source of all the power. He is the source of all things and the master of every phenomenon. John's faith envisions a God who can do whatever he wills to do, for whom nothing is difficult or hard, because he possesses absolute power. He envisions a God who is in absolute control of events; nothing escapes him; nothing frustrates his plan; and nothing fails to serve its appointed purpose. This divine reign which exists and has always existed must paradoxically "come" on earth (Ps. 145:13; Matt. 6:10). God has not abandoned his throne (seat of authority) at the center of the universe. The word "throne" occurs fourteen times in the Greek text in this chapter. This vision is closely related to the letters to the churches. It shows what power is available for the church in the struggle. These Christians could feel safe only if they were sure of God's protecting care. This chapter makes us vividly conscious of the sovereignty of God which is the comfort of the believer in every trial.

a. An Open Door in Heaven (4:1)

¹ After this I looked, and lo, in heaven an open door! And the first voice, which I had heard speaking to me like a trumpet, said, "Come up hither, and I will show you what must take place after this."

v. 1 The natural sense of the introductory phrase of this verse is that there is given a new phase or variety of the vision. The prophet does not say he saw the door as it opened, but already being "in the spirit" he saw a door from earth to heaven which had been set open, through which he could in prophetic rapture observe what was within. This is the ***open door*** of revelation (Swete).

The former voice (1:10) calls for him to "come up here." This means that he was to receive greater insight into spiritual things. He is still "in the Spirit" (1:10). He had a receptive and responsive spiritual nature. He possessed a spiritual susceptibility and energy. He does not hear with the physical ear or see with the physical eye. John, as all Hebrews, conceived of the entire person as functioning through the eyes and ears. For him, a person hears and sees with the whole self. To "hear" or to "see" was a call to heed, to obey. He is able to hear and see the things of God because they are spiritually examined (1 Cor. 14:15). The impersonal verb *dei* ("it is necessary") means that it must happen because it is the declaration of divine truth. This "it is necessary" means that

God has predestined the course of things. His sovereign will stands above the events of history. He is in history; he helps to shape its ends (Blaney). He will not be frustrated or defeated.

The last phrase, "after these things" (*meta touta*), is placed by Westcott and Hort at the beginning of verse 2. (There are, of course, no verse divisions in the Greek Manuscripts). This is probably the correct interpretation for it follows the ordinary sense of the text. The expression is used by John not to change the chronology but to introduce a new phase of the vision (see 1:19; 7:1,9; 9:12; 15:5; 18:1; 19:1; 20:3). For John, the way into the presence of God lies open (Heb. 10:19-20). "The *heaven* which is the scene of John's vision . . . is part of the created universe . . . which is entered by the opening of the Spiritual eye rather than by any more literal form of transit" (Caird, *The Revelation of St. John the Divine*, p. 62). No journey to a heavenly world would bring John any closer to God (Ezek. 1:1; Mark 1:10; John 1:51). He needed only to be "in the spirit" to recognize and enjoy the eternal presence, which makes heaven wherever one is.

b. The Throne and Its Occupant (4:2-3)

² At once I was in the Spirit, and lo, a throne stood in heaven, with one seated on the throne! ³ And he who sat there appeared like jasper and carnelian, and round the throne was a rainbow that looked like an emerald.

v. 2 The prophetic vision now unfolds itself with new distinctness. John's spiritual rapture was now intensified, enabling him to see more clearly the truth of the sovereignty of God. In a vision of resplendent imagery, God was seen sitting on the throne. The God who dwells in heaven possesses absolute authority over the universe (1 Kings 22:19, Pss. 11:4; 47:8; Isa. 6:1 f.; Ezek. 1:26-28; Dan. 7:9 f.). He has not abdicated his right to be the judge of all his creatures. God himself is never described in the Scriptures (Ex. 20:4). The Old Testament theophanies were revelations of God in human disguise; they were not visions of God as he is

THE SEVENFOLD VISION OF CONFLICT 85

in his essential being. In Revelation *throne* stands for authority, and God's enthronement implies his supremacy. His rulership is over the world as a whole. It is one way to emphasize God's all-controlling authority (Rev. 5:13; 7:10; 19:4).

Much of the imagery with which his presence is described here is that employed by Ezekiel (1:26-28). In such figurative visions, the outward signs must be understood as only describing the deep spiritual realities which they represent for God is indeed invisible (John 1:18; Col. 1:15; 1 Tim. 1:17; Heb. 11:27). The signs are figures of speech for spiritual facts which are beyond description or explanation. This is an obscure and restrained mention of God in his might, majesty, and power. However, these symbols describe the truth in terms which our frail minds are able to comprehend, but they are only visual metaphors from the language of the earth. These symbols seem to express the truth that the almighty, omnipresent, sovereign Ruler of the universe is able to overrule the trials and tribulations of his church here on the earth to his ultimate glory.

v. 3 The one on the throne is not described (Ex. 20:4) with anthropomorphic terms, but his nature is suggested through various symbols (contrast Dan. 7:9). The three stones mentioned were the most costly and precious things the ancient man could conceive. The *jasper* of the Bible is a translucent stone of many colors, somewhat transparent, probably the modern diamond. It was characterized by purity and brilliancy. It is used to symbolize the holiness, righteousness, and glory of God coming into visibility. It was the last stone on the breastplate of the high priest (Ex. 28:17), and the first stone in the foundation and walls of the new Jerusalem (Rev. 21:18-19). The *carnelian* is always red, though it varies in shade. This stone was used to symbolize God's justice, judgment, and wrath. It was the first stone on the breastplate of the high priest (Ex. 28:17) and the sixth stone in the foundation of the new Jerusalem (Rev. 21:20). The rainbow around the throne, *like an emerald,* is an emblem of God's covenant which he established with Noah (Gen. 9:12-16), and a pledge of God's mercy and faithfulness in keeping his promise to restrain his wrath from sinful men. It is a symbol of living hope. God's sovereignty and God's mercy are never separated. The whole symbol is a way of conveying the idea of a Being, perfect in holiness, goodness, and majesty, supreme and all-merciful. The purpose of the vision is to fill us with awe at the radiant glory of the unfathomable mystery of God's omnipotent majesty.

c. The Twenty-four Elders (4:4)

⁴ Round the throne were twenty-four thrones, and seated on the thrones were twenty-four elders, clad in white garments, with golden crowns upon their heads.

v. 4 These *twenty-four elders* offer intelligent worship, explain certain things to John, and possibly sing that they have been redeemed to God by the Lamb's blood (Rev. 5:9). (The text here is uncertain.) The symbolism is from the Temple, and as the heads of the twenty-four courses of priests instituted by David (1 Chron 24:1-19), these elders could stand for the whole church of God in the past and in the future, called in 1 Peter 2:9 "a royal priesthood." The number 24, a double of 12 (organized religion), is designed to represent the glorified people of God of both the old and new covenants, the victorious church in her fullness. The elders therefore, seem to represent all the redeemed (Rev. 5:9). The *white garments* are the robes of priests and are emblems of purity (1:6 5:10). These robes represent the character of the triumphant church The *golden crowns* are symbolical of their victory over their enemies The *golden crowns upon their heads* and the fact that they sit on thrones indicate that the prophet intended to convey the idea that the elders are of a kingly order or have a regal character (3:21 5:10; 1 Pet. 2:9). The representatives of the church are here visualized as reigning with Christ (Matt. 19:27-29; Luke 22:30). God's people share in his reign. These symbols also indicate that the members of the church have received holiness of character and exaltation of condition promised to those who are faithful unto death (2:10).

d. The Throne and the Torches (4:5)

⁵ From the throne issue flashes of lightning, and voices and peals of thunder, and before the throne burn seven torches of fire, which are the seven spirits of God;

v. 5 The symbolism for the first part of this verse comes from Exodus 19 to 20 (cf. Job 37:4; Ps. 77:18; Ezek. 1:13). The *lightning, and voices and peals of thunder* were heard in connection with the great Theophany (i.e., appearance of God) at Sinai, when the Law was given. In the scene at Sinai, the clouds and lightnings were not so much tokens of coming judgment as the symbols of that righteous power which can show itself in judgment. The imagery is regularly connected with the presence and power of God. These symbols are used here as signs of divine power, majesty, and judgment (Ex. 19:16). God has not left his people to the mercy of their foes.

The second part of the verse, *torches of fire* (i.e., burning torches), is a mode of representation for the Holy Spirit. The *seven spirits* refer to the presence and energies of the Holy Spirit in his fullness (1:4; 3:1; Matt. 3:11-12). The description was possibly derived from Isaiah 11:2 and probably refers to one Spirit with a sevenfold manifestation. In Zechariah 4, the seven-branched lampstand of the Law is made to symbolize the Holy Spirit, without some mention of whom the symbol of the throne of God would be incomplete. The Holy Spirit is manifested to and through the church and is ever active in his judging and purifying power.

e. The Glass-like Sea Around the Throne (4:6a)

⁶ and before the throne there is as it were a sea of glass, like crystal.

v. 6a The symbolism of the appearance of a sea here seems to indicate deep tranquillity and separation. A great gulf separates the holy, peaceful God and frail, struggling humanity (Isa. 55:9).

Forever God stands apart. The "King of kings and Lord of lords . . . dwells in unapproachable light" (1 Tim. 6:15-16). God is invisible (1 Tim. 1:17), and no "one has ever seen God" (John 1:18). God is unlike anything we have known in our familiar world of time, space, and matter. He is as high above his highest creation as he is his lowest creation, for the gulf that separates the highest from the lowest is finite, while the gulf between God and the highest creation is infinite. John was separated by the sea from those he loved. Someday the sea will be no more (21:1). The redeemed will then stand in God's presence and will not be separated from each other.

f. The Four Living Creatures Worship and Serve God (4:6b-7)

And round the throne, on each side of the throne, are four living creatures, full of eyes in front and behind: ⁷ the first living creature like a lion, the second living creature like an ox, the third living creature with the face of a man, and the fourth living creature like a flying eagle.

v. 6b-7 There have been at least thirteen interpretations of the phrase *four living creatures.* In the Revelation, these creatures worship, do service, and instruct John. It seems best to interpret this exotic imagery in accordance with the symbolical use of numbers to mean the fullness of inanimate creation in its energy and variety. "The four forms represent whatever is noblest, strongest, wisest, and swiftest in nature" (Swete). Four was used as the number of the material world viewed as the creation of God. The whole chapter relates to the majesty of God, so it seems more natural to suppose that the figure is symbolic of all creation fulfilling its proper office; waiting upon God, fulfilling his will, and setting forth his glory. It seems to be a picture of all nature praising God (Pss. 19:1-2; 103:22; 145:10; 148). Everything which fulfills its function for which it was created praises God.

The language used to describe things and movements in this passage is not intended for us to make a mental picture. It is better not to make the attempt. Perhaps there is the suggestion of God's consciousness in and through nature. God's power is to be found operative through all the universe. The passage is thus a personification of the works of God as Creator, Preserver, and Mover. It shows forth the immanent power and wisdom of God, so active in all created nature, offering to God the homage of nature as its Maker, and Preserver, its Source and its End (Eaton, p. 58).

The figure comes from Ezekiel (1:6,10,22,26; 10:20,22). Most commentators point out that the three pairs of wings are for reverence, humility, and swift obedience (cf. Isa. 6:2). They also represent the speed with which the *living creatures* execute the divine command. With *eyes in front and behind* the living creatures are ever watchful to render adoration and praise to God, which they continually do "day and night" (4:8). They display the characteristics of creation in its fullest energy. They, in their eternal watchfulness, observe all that transpires in heaven and on earth. They worship God because by him they were created. Multiplicity of eyes symbolize omnivision, vitality, and vigilance (Ezek. 1:18; 10:12; Zech. 3:9). They observe and reflect on all sides of the divine majesty of creation, and they see the power and authority which God exercises over it and expresses through it.

g. The Ceaseless Hymn of Praise (4:8-11)

[8] And the four living creatures, each of them with six wings, are full of eyes all round and within, and day and night they never cease to sing,
"Holy, holy, holy, is the Lord God Almighty,
who was and is and is to come!"
[9] And whenever the living creatures give glory and honor and thanks to him who is seated on the throne, who lives for ever and ever, [10] the twenty-four elders fall down before him who is seated on the throne and worship him who lives for ever and ever; they cast their crowns before the throne, singing,
[11] "Worthy art thou, our Lord and God,
to receive glory and honor and power,
for thou didst create all things,
and by thy will they existed and were created."

God is the creator of all things; therefore, they are only rightly used when they are used in accordance with his will. At all times the world that God made is praising him. The use of the future tense of worship implies the eternal repetition of the act.

vv. 8-9 John heard, as it were, the voice of creation sounding through the universe. In the vision, God's unapproachable glory as creator is clothed in forms of thought and language which had been hallowed by the tradition of centuries. He is thrice holy, that is completely holy. He is the *Almighty.* The Greek word translated *Almighty* is literally "All-ruler." He rules over all, brings good out of evil, overrules the purposes and devices of men, and guides all the processes of history. He is worthy of the highest praise, because he is the creator of all that is. This ascription of praise by the creation is intended to attribute to God the qualities of holiness, omnipotence, and eternal existence. All of God's creation gives continual praise to him.

v. 10 The church now joins creation in a common hymn ascribing to God all glory, eternal holiness, and power (Isa. 6:1-4). John saw the elders *cast their crowns before the throne.* These were crowns of victory, and this act was a recognition on the part of the church that victory had been won in the power of God.

v. 11 In this prophetic vision, John sees all creation and the church join in a common hymn ascribing to God all thanksgiving, glory, and honor. His transcendent majesty and power are recognized by all creation and the church (Heb. 2:10). He is the Creator and Lord of the universe and the church. He is manifested most clearly in the spheres of creation and redemption. He rules and holds sovereign sway over all creation, and his purpose must be victorious. It was in this vision of the sovereignty of God that the Christians could find the source of their confidence of ultimate triumph. God has power to rescue the church from its internal and external peril.

(2) *The Vision of God as Redeemer (5:1-14)*

The truth declared in this vision is an addition to the truth revealed in the previous chapter. Chapters 4 and 5 should be read together. In chapter 4, "the theme is that of the omnipotent Creator, reigning majestic and remote in a heaven from which man is excluded. . . . In v [chap. 5], the focus of the seer's eyes changes, and with incomparable dramatic force he describes his vision of the Redeemer in whom lies every hope of man's salvation, every hope of a future kingdom of justice" (Kiddle, p. 67).

These two chapters demonstrate the inseparable unity between the Father and the Son by having creation and the church render equal homage to both (John 10:30; 12:45; 14:9-10). What is set forth in these two chapters gives us the ground of confidence in the triumph of the kingdom of God. The creator God on the throne, the twenty-four elders, the seven lamps of fire, the sea of glass, and the four living creatures all remain. These symbols have shown God enthroned supreme in the midst of all his creations. God is Creator, but what is to be done with the creation? How does the Creator relate himself to his creation? The world and the church need to know. He not only created, but he also seeks to save his creatures who have come to moral shipwreck.

God has from the beginning related himself to his creatures in their sins as their redeemer (Job 19:25; Pss. 19:14; 78:35; Prov. 23:11; Isa. 41:14; 43:14; 44:6,24; 47:4; 48:17; 49:7,26; 54:5,8; 59:20; 60:16; 63:16; Jer. 50:34). Supremely he revealed himself as redeemer in Jesus Christ. He was God's representative, revealer, or agent, who came into the world to show the truth about him, to act for him, to die as a sacrifice for sin, and to rise again and return to God as his glorified Son. Paul declared this truth when he said, "God was in Christ reconciling the world to himself" (2 Cor. 5:19). The writer of Hebrews also emphasized this truth when he said, "Being made perfect he [Son] became the source of eternal salvation to all who obey him" (Heb. 5:9), and again when he said, "He [Christ] entered once for all into the Holy Place . . . thus securing an eternal redemption (Heb. 9:12). Therefore, Jesus Christ is a trustworthy and indubitable self-revelation of God as redeemer in human language and in a human person. He was God's self-manifestation in a human life. The basis of hope for the Christian and the church lies in the conviction of a powerful God and a redeeming Savior.

a. The Sealed Scroll (5:1-4)

¹ And I saw in the right hand of him who was seated on the throne a scroll written within and on the back, sealed with seven seals; ² and I saw a strong angel proclaiming with a loud voice, "Who is worthy to open the scroll and break its seals?" ³ And no one in heaven or on earth or under the earth was able to open the scroll or to look into it, ⁴ and I wept much that no one was found worthy to open the scroll or to look into it.

v. 1 The phrase *And I saw* introduces a new incident in the vision. That which had been witnessed remained, but a further development was taking place.

The phrase *in* [on] *the right hand* (literally, "upon the right hand"; that is, laid upon the palm of the right hand of him who sat upon the throne, ready for someone to take, as in v. 7), indicates that the hand of power (right hand) was extended in the act of offering the scroll (*biblion*) to anyone who should be able to open and read it. It was not his will that the contents of the scroll should be kept from any. However, the content or meaning of a "sealed book" was unknown (Pss. 68; 138; Isa. 29:11). This scroll, such as the one Ezekiel saw, was written upon both sides. Papyrus scrolls were usually inscribed on one side only. This one was so crowded with writing that not only was the inside of it full but the writing was continued upon the back also. The fact that it was written on both sides suggests the completeness and fullness of the contents. There was no space for addition to that which was written. The scroll was completely full of declarations of the divine will. It symbolizes God's complete will and purpose for humanity and the principles of God's government in his creation. It contains especially the purposes of God insofar as they are achieved by the Lamb of salvation (Rom. 16:25-26), the interpretation of life which Christ alone can give. It is the book of the world's destiny or the purpose of creation (Isa. 29:11-12; Ezek. 2:9-10; Dan. 12:4).

Christ is God's answer to the questions raised by human history. Without Christ, God's plan for the world could never be translated into history (Calkins). A will in Roman law bore seven seals of the seven witnesses to the will (Charles). The number seven indicates that it was completely sealed. God alone knew what was written in the book. "The seal gave to a writing in ancient times the writer's imprimatur and assured its genuineness, and at the same time served as a warning to any who would open the document without authority" (McDowell, p. 79; cf. Rom. 4:11; 1 Cor. 9:2).

v. 2 A *strong angel* with a loud voice challenges all to *open the scroll.*

v. 3 No one in all creation (heaven, earth, and under the earth) can disclose the contents of the scroll and reveal God's purpose in creation. God's ways can never be known to man except by revelation. Therefore, is the will of God expressed in creation to be an insoluble riddle?

v. 4 John weeps because he sees no way by which the seals of the scroll can be broken and God's will and purpose for humanity unfolded. God's purpose and will is of great importance to the church, because the church is the divine agency for the accomplishing of his will.

b. The Lion-Lamb (5:5-7)

⁵ Then one of the elders said to me, "Weep not; lo, the Lion of the tribe of Judah, the Root of David, has conquered, so that he can open the scroll and its seven seals."
⁶ And between the throne and the four living creatures and among the elders, I saw a Lamb standing, as though it had been slain, with seven horns and with seven eyes, which are the seven spirits of God sent out into all the earth; ⁷ and he went and took the scroll from the right hand of him who was seated on the throne.

v. 5 In this verse, one of the twelve elders, representing the church, speaks a word of encouragement to the prophet. Only a redeemed person can know the meaning of salvation. There is One, **the Lion of the tribe of Judah, the Root of David** (Gen. 49:9; Isa. 11:1,10; 53:2 f.; Rom. 15:12; Heb. 7:14; Rev. 3:7; 22:16), who, because of a former act of victory, is worthy to open the seals on the scrolls. The Lamb that has been slain is the only one with lion-like strength who is able to break the seals of the scroll. This anomaly is not difficult to accept when one realizes that he conquers through self-sacrifice (Isa. 53:7-12).

The right to open the scroll is made to turn upon his victory over sin, death, and the grave. The powers of darkness, which have held sway over this world age have been defeated. In Christ's death and resurrection, the ultimate triumph of good over evil was potentially achieved. He conquered and yet the victory is a continuing process. "Evil overreached itself when it crucified Jesus Christ, and God's Easter-event proclaimed the promise that is how evil will be destroyed. In Christ, God triumphed over principalities and powers; in Christ, that triumph at last will be made secure and complete" (Niles, p. 167).

The incarnation was not only an event in history, it is an abiding reality. To open the seals means not merely to reveal but to carry out God's will and purpose. It is to reveal and to put into effect God's plan of history. In the Revelation, the scroll is never read. The breaking of each of the seals is accompanied by its own phenomena, which seem to indicate the nature of its contents. These visions of the breaking of the seals represent, not the content of the scroll, but the gradual steps of access to them.

v. 6 The dramatic symbolism of this verse pictures a little lamb instead of a lion. From time immemorial the lamb has been used in religious sacrifice. This title, **Lamb**, for Christ explains nothing; it merely states something. It symbolizes his boundless love which prompts his self-sacrifice to the uttermost. The living Lord is also the slain Lamb. He has suffered death to redeem the people of God. Men look to strength and power to win victories, but it is self-sacrificing love that wins. The Jews expected a warring Messiah to give them victory; instead, there came a crucified Christ. God's infinite and self-giving love was incarnate in the Lamb in the midst of the throne. The Lamb occupies a central position in the assembly described in the previous chapter. It seems that the Lamb is standing in the space between the throne and the four living creatures (creation) and in the midst of the circle formed by the twenty-four elders (the church). He holds the center of attention. He bears the marks of his past death wounds, but he is not dead. These mutually antagonistic metaphors are intended to convey the truth that though he died, he is alive. The voluntary sacrifice by the Lion-Lamb of his life is the key to the whole divine plan. From the signs of death and life, the vision passes to the signs of strength and wisdom in the Lamb.

Horns throughout the Bible and apocalyptic writings are used as emblems of power (Deut. 33:17; 1 Sam. 2:1; Pss. 89:24; 148:14, etc.). The number *seven* denotes perfection. His *seven horns* means that he is the All-powerful one. The *seven eyes, which are the seven Spirits of God* are symbolic of the Lamb's all-inclusive and searching vision from which nothing can be hid (Deut. 11:12; 1 Kings 8:29; 2 Chron. 16:9; Prov. 15:3; Pss. 33:18; 34:15; Zech. 4:10). In other words, the Lamb possesses fullness of power, omniscience, and the Holy Spirit. His power is available to the believer through the Holy Spirit. The Holy Spirit brings the living Christ to the believer.

The mission of the Lamb's Spirit is poetically represented and declared to be universal in scope. He is fully present everywhere. He is as much present in the less seemly places as in those that are recognized as fitting temples for him to dwell in. He is present with those who do not recognize him, as well as with the Christian all through his pilgrimage. It is almost unnecessary to say that the Lamb represents Jesus Christ as God's Mediator with his creation. The Greek word *arnion* used here for little lamb is used twenty-nine times as a title for Christ in Revelation and nowhere else in the New Testament. There is another Greek word *annos* for lamb which is used for Christ four times in the New Testament.

(John 1:29,36; Acts 8:32; 1 Pet. 1:19). Christ only resembles a lamb in his moral attributes and in his sacrifice. In the prophet's mind, he sees a picture of a hidden mystery which he expresses in figurative symbolism. It is through sacrificial self-giving that the Lamb conquers (Stagg, *New Testament Theology*, p. 75). He unfolded the eternal and unchangeable divine plan by his obedience even to the death on the cross (Phil. 5:5). The truth which John sees is Christ's sacrifice upon the cross for the sin of the world and his resurrection as the means of reconciling man to God.

The true Lord of heaven is the Crucified One. The convincing credential of his right to reign is the fact that he was faithful to God even unto dying. The death which the believer dies with Jesus is also death to self, a yielding up of one's life to another (Stagg, *New Testament Theology*, p. 224).

v. 7 God's **right hand** indicates power and honor. The Lion-Lamb (Christ), to whom "all authority in heaven and on earth has been given" (Matt. 28:18), is the only one who can dispense the power of God's right hand and show how God relates himself to his creation. The divine government of the universe and the realm of heaven have been given to the Lion-Lamb. Jesus Christ reveals God and his will. Paul expressed this same idea when he said that Christ at God's right hand was "far above all rule and authority and power and dominion, and above every name that is named, not only in this age but also in that which is to come; and he [God] has put all things under his [Christ's] feet" (Eph. 1:21-22; cf. Phil. 2:8-11; Heb. 2:9; 1 Pet. 1:21).

The Lamb is said to send forth the seven Spirits, because it is by Jesus Christ that the gifts of the Holy Spirit are sent and spread abroad in the world (John 14:26).

c. The Adoration of the Lamb (5:8)

[8] And when he had taken the scroll, the four living creatures and the twenty-four elders fell down before the Lamb, each holding a harp, and with golden bowls full of incense, which are the prayers of the saints;

v. 8 The whole creation (Rom. 8:22) and the church are interested in the meaning of life which the Lion-Lamb holds in his hand. The verbs in the original indicate that the adoration offered coincides in point of time with the act of taking the scroll. The *four living creatures* (all creation) *and the twenty-four elders* (church) prostrate themselves before *the Lamb* and offer acts of adoration and worship, commemorating their redemption by him. The bowls, which hold the incense (Ex. 30; Mal. 1:11), and the harps were instruments used in the service of God. In simple symbol, the incense represents the prayers of the church (Ps. 142; Luke 1:10). These symbols are emblems of the worldwide and age-long offering of prayer and praise by the elders (church) for redemption. The prayers of agonizing saints come up to God's throne, and in answer, the Lion-Lamb has taken the scroll to reveal to them that God will lead his church to triumph.

d. The New Song (5:9-10)

⁹ and they sang a new song, saying,
"Worthy art thou to take the scroll and to open its seals, for thou wast slain and by thy blood didst ransom men for God from every tribe and tongue and people and nation,
¹⁰ and hast made them a kingdom and priests to our God, and they shall reign on earth."

v. 9 The Christ-event was the breaking into history of a qualitative "new." The song is "new" because it has a new theme, victory. Thus, the *new song* telling of the redemptive work of Christ concerns first those who have been liberated. At the price of his life, he ransomed the redeemed from the enslaving and hostile power of sin. The basic idea in the word "redemption" is release or liberation. He broke the bondage of sin, self-will, self-love, and self-worship. He liberated man for God and for the church (Stagg, *New Testament Theology*, p. 139). He liberates men from the power of darkness and translates them into the kingdom of Christ. The redemption wrought by Christ establishes God's kingdom in power. God loves his creatures so much that he sacrificed his Son to save them (John 3:16). It is the great victory in suffering and death which points to a particular act performed at a definite time which inspires the song. The Lamb is worthy of the adoration, because he purchased a community (see 1 Cor. 6:20; 7:23; 1 Pet. 1:18-19; 2 Pet. 2:1) for God out of mankind (tribe, tongue, people, nation, i.e., the fourfold classification of mankind) by the shedding of his blood. This fourfold enumeration shows that the redeemed come from all over the world. Only the self-sacrificing love of God for the redemption of man can reveal God. The general fact of redemption is stated.

v. 10 As an outcome of the Lamb's work, the saints become a realm (kingdom) of priests. (The better text has kingdom instead of kings.) Already they reign (present tense) upon the earth. John's declaration of the reign of the saints is in line with the current Jewish apocalyptic writing of his time. The reign of the redeemed is a present spiritual reign (Matt. 5:3,10; Luke 12:32; 22:28-30; Rom. 5:17; 1 Cor. 3:21-23; 4:8; Eph. 2:6; 2 Tim. 2:11-12; 1 Pet. 2:9) with and in Christ (cf. Ex. 19:5-6). As the old Israel, having been redeemed from Egypt, was made a people subject only to its divine King, so the church of Christ the new Israel, has become a people under God as King (Richardson, p. 88). There is a new theocracy, but it is a theocracy of the whole Christian body. It is a divine rule exercised through the saints who are the true sovereigns of earth. This is in line with the other apocalyptic writers who expected an enduring kingdom to be administered by the saints. The Lion-Lamb revealed the contents of the scroll. The unifying theme of the whole Bible is the "theme of redemption, of salvation; and it is caught up particularly in those concepts which revolve about the idea of a people of God, called to live under his rule, and the concomitant hope of the coming Kingdom of God" (Bright, p. 10).

The kingdom and the church are not the same, as Stagg well says, "a common error is that of equating the kingdom of God with the church. There is a close relationship between the kingdom of God and the church, but they are not identical. Whereas the kingdom is the sovereignty of God, the church is the fellowship of persons made one people under that sovereignty" (Stagg, *New Testament Theology,* p. 154).

e. The Redeemed Worship the Redeemer (5:11-14)

> [11] Then I looked, and I heard around the throne and the living creatures and the elders the voice of many angels, numbering myriads of myriads and thousands of thousands, [12] saying with a loud voice, "Worthy is the Lamb who was slain, to receive power and wealth and wisdom and might and honor and glory and blessing!" [13] And I heard every creature in heaven and on earth and under the earth and in the sea, and all therein, saying, "To him who sits upon the throne and to the Lamb be blessing and honor and glory and might for ever and ever!" [14] And the four living creatures said, "Amen!" and the elders fell down and worshiped.

v. 11 The chorus of the redeemed is followed by a vast chorus of angels (Dan. 7:10). This innumerable company encircles the throne, the Lamb in the midst before the throne, the four living beings, and the twenty-four elders. The numbers vary in the different texts though the sense of the passage is not affected. The numbers are not to be taken literally, but they are used to express the idea of an exceeding great throng who join in antiphonal singing and the worship of the Redeemer.

v. 12 This second song of praise again gives the reason for considering the Lamb worthy to receive adoration. This song of praise is a sevenfold doxology to the Lamb by the angels. This doxology provides the background of the whole service of worship. The sevenfold blessing is probably indicative of its complete and perfect nature. Christ has won this honor of such praise, because his self-giving self-sacrifice is at the very center of the being of God. Christ went to his cross like a King to his crowning.

v. 13 The whole creation now joins in the glad antiphonal acclaim (Rom. 8:20-22). This song of praise is addressed to the Throned-One and the Lamb. Christ is adored in complete equality with God the creator. This is a fourfold doxology which emphasizes the complete creation. This great universal confession is the fulfilling of Philippians 2:9-11.

v. 14 The four living creatures (creation) and the twenty-four elders (church) now conclude the song of praise. God is worthy of all worship, because of the double author of creation and redemption. All other worship is false. In dramatic presentation, the whole universe is represented as worshiping God (the One on the throne) and Christ (the Lamb), and waiting for the developments to follow on the breaking of the seals on the mysterious scroll.

2. The Opening of the Seals (6:1 to 8:1)

Through chapter five there is very little difference in the interpretations. Most of the commentaries agree up to this point. However with chapter six, the multitudinous interpretations start. There are two major causes for these problems of interpretation. Most of the interpreters agree at least in general terms with *what* is happening, but the major problem is deciding *when* it is happening, whether it is past, future, present, synonomous, parallel, etc. Charles has tried to solve this problem of time by excisions and rearrangements. These efforts have not been very successful. John's prophecy canno be forced into any chronological framework. It is not so much chronological as it is logical.

The second problem is in the movement from the earthly sphere into the heavenly sphere. Because of our cosmology, we always think of heaven as being up. So when the writer in a vision goes to heaven, we think that he must go up and leave the earth. John was a prophet and to him spiritual reality is applicable at any time, at all times. Truth does not vary with time. That is, it was true then, it is true now, and it will always be true. Since the writer is a prophet then the spiritual reality which he portray is wherever man is. So heaven is not *just* a place; it is also a condition—where God is. At least four times in Ephesians the write says, "In the heavenly," referring to being in Christ Jesus (Eph

1:3; 2:6; 3:10; 6:12). That is, when one comes into salvation, he comes into the new realm created by Christ Jesus. That one is already experiencing heaven. Heaven is not limited by time or space. If these two problems can be solved, most of the difficulties from this point on will be removed. If it is spiritual truth, then it is applicable at any time. It has always been applicable and always will be.

Did John see the truth of the ultimate victory of the cross and use these symbols to present it to his people or did he see both the truth *and* the symbols?

Up to this point, the revelation has been more or less introductory. There was an inaugural vision of Christ and a description of the conditions within the churches. This was followed by visions of God as Creator and Redeemer. Now the writer presents the picture of the sufferings of the church with the divine judgment upon his people and the people of the world with the final victory of Christ. The first cycle in this section shows a series of events which follow the successive opening of the seven seals on the scroll that the Lamb took out of the right hand of God. The events which the prophet records are historical-prophetical. They happened in history, and they will happen any time when circumstances are the same or similar. The writer pictures the breaking of each seal as revealing the means of divine judgment. This is the way by which God deals with rebellion against his purpose (Lev. 26:18,21,24,28). These are the means he uses in judgment. These forces of judgment are still in God's hand. They have been let loose on the earth, but they are still subject to God. Although apparently destructive, they are for the accomplishment of his will (Calkins). As the seals are broken, the writer does not read anything, but events take place with the breaking of the seals. So the truth is translated into action. When the seal is broken, out comes the horse and the rider.

The background for these first four seals can be found in Zechariah 1:7-17. In this Old Testament passage, God sent forth these horsemen to patrol the earth, symbolic of the return of the Jews from Jerusalem. Also, this vision of Revelation 6:1-8 is supplemented by a vision in Zechariah 6:1-8. The Revelation passage is the combination of these two Old Testament passages. Those first four horsemen personify the four powers of evil which are the agents of God for punishing the world for its sin (Jer. 15:2-3; 24:10; 29:17-18; 42:17; 44:13; Ezek. 5:12,17; 14:21; 33:25). These first four seals typify various phases of the scourges of the earth which are permitted by God to afflict mankind, including the church. Each of these four dramatic goings-forth is preceded by a call from one of the four living creatures. These four living creatures stand for all creation. So these first four seals opened are the judgments upon creation including the church, as much as the church is a part of the world. Again the space problem comes in. Is a Christian in the world and in Christ at the same time? Yes. To the extent that his life is a projection of Christ, he is in but not of the world (John 17:14-18). To the extent that the Christian is of the world, these judgments are on him. So these visions are divine judgments within history upon the world.

(1) The First Seal Opened—A White Horse (6:1-2)

Now I saw when the Lamb opened one of the seven seals, and I heard one of the four living creatures say, as with a voice of thunder, "Come!" ² And I saw, and behold, a white horse, and its rider had a bow; and a crown was given to him, and he went out conquering and to conquer.

vv. 1-2 These verses describe the opening of the first seal on the scroll. The unsealing simply indicates that the contents are made visible (10:4; 22:10; cf. Isa. 29:11 f.). When the seal is broken, one of the four living creatures (representing all creation) cries aloud, *Come,* and there comes forth a white horse with a rider armed with a bow. The white horse is a symbol of victory. The white horse and the rider represent a conquering invader. The bow and arrow are used as symbols of power by Old Testament writers (Zech. 9:13; Hab. 3:8-9). Probably this figure is taken from the prevalent idea of the Parthians in the first century. A crown of victory is given to him, and he goes forth to conquer. There have been many interpretations to this symbolism. On a consideration of the whole of the vision attending the opening of the seals, it seems best to interpret this vision as a symbolic representation of the personification of evil—the Antichrist. Only in the Johannine epistles is the word "antichrist" used in the Bible (1 John 2:18,22; 4:3; 2 John 7). The word is used to describe corrupt power and hostile influences at work impeding, counterfeiting, and contradicting the work of Christ. The antichrist opposes and apes Christ. There could not be antichrists unless the Christ had come (1 John 4:3). In 1 John 2:18, the writer uses the fact that there have arisen many antichrists as evidence that the Christ has come and has ushered in "last hour," that is, End time. The antichrist so resembles the real Christ that he deceives many people. There are two reasons for holding to the interpretation that the white horse and the rider symbolize the antichrist. John usually divides the number 7 into 4 and 3; or 3 and 4. If the white horse and rider represent some aspect of righteousness (Christ, Gospel, Word of God, Holy Spirit, etc.), then this pattern is broken in the opening of the seals, because the writer identifies the contents of the opening of the next three seals as evil. Another reason for identifying the white horse and the rider with the antichrist is because in the Revelation evil always tries to imitate good, (slain-Lamb: standing 5:6; beast with death-stroke: healed 13:3; woman-church 12:1; great harlot 17:1,5). The thing that is false gains its influence over men's minds because it resembles the true. The counterfeit circulates because it seems like the genuine. This white horse and its rider, if this interpretation is correct, represent the way of spiritual evil in history. It is dangerously successful when disguised as an angel of light—even as Christ himself.

(2) *The Second Seal Opened—A Red Horse (6:3-4)*

[3] When he opened the second seal, I heard the second living creature

say, "Come!" ⁴ And out came another horse, bright red; its rider was permitted to take peace from the earth, so that men should slay one another; and he was given a great sword.

vv. 3-4 The scenic representation of these verses accompanied the act of opening the second seal. The red horse and its rider take peace from the earth. There is general agreement that the red horse and its rider represent war, carnage, discord, and bloodshed (Matt. 10:34). The sword was given to him as an emblem of what he was to do. War is one of the great afflictions from which the human race suffers. The truth of this dramatic symbolism indicates that war is one of the great afflictions of the world.

(3) The Third Seal Opened—A Black Horse (6:5-6)

⁵ When he opened the third seal, I heard the third living creature say, "Come!" And I saw, and behold, a black horse, and its rider had a balance in his hand; ⁶ and I heard what seemed to be a voice in the midst of the four living creatures saying, "A quart of wheat for a denarius, and three quarts of barley for a denarius; but do not harm oil and wine!"

v. 5 It is generally agreed that the rider on the black horse with the pair of scales signifies scarcity, famine, hunger, distress, and calamity (Jer. 4:28; 14:2; Lam. 5:10; Ezek. 4:10; 32:7; Joel 2:6; Nah. 2:10; Mal. 3:14). The scales are a symbol that signify that food was to be accurately and carefully weighed out. Food is not weighed in the time of plenty. The voice from among the four living creatures stressed two things: first, the price or value of wheat and barley, and second, that care should be taken not to injure the oil and wine.

v. 6 The quart (*choenix*) was the amount of food to support a man for a day and no more. The denarius (*dēnarion*) was the usual day wage for a soldier and a laborer (Matt. 20:2). The prices given were exorbitant, perhaps ten times the usual rate, and denote great scarcity. This famine is not of the luxuries of life but of the necessities. This symbolism describes the poverty, oppression, hardship, and injustice that the church suffers along with others while the church remains in the world. The chaos and evil of the world are to be seen as God's judgment upon sin.

(4) The Fourth Seal Opened—An Ashen Horse (6:7-8)

⁷ When he opened the fourth seal, I heard the voice of the fourth living creature say, "Come!" ⁸ And I saw, and behold, a pale horse, and its rider's name was Death, and Hades followed him; and they were given power over a fourth of the earth, to kill with sword and with famine and with pestilence and by wild beasts of the earth.

v. 8 The breaking of the fourth seal reveals another sore judgment upon the earth (Ezek. 14:21). The writer identifies the rider of this *klōros* (pale, yellowish, greenish-white, livid) horse. Death rides and his inseparable companion, Hades, follows (Swete). The destructive forces of Death and Hades are combined and personified. In the New Testament, Hades is the abode of the dead. So Death is pictured as riding along as his servant Hades follows him and gathers unto himself the slain. Only a part (one fourth—this indicates the extent of the destruction, wherein there is still a limitation) of mankind will be thus afflicted. These first four opened seals depict troubles which all mankind, including Christians, undergo in the course of the world's judgment (John 12:31). These symbols point to events which have happened, and are happening, and will continue to happen to the world and the church until the end of time. The warfare, famine, pestilence, and death by wild beasts show that the course of world history is also the course of the world's judgment.

(5) The Fifth Seal Opened—The Martyred Souls Under the Altar (6:9-11)

⁹ When he opened the fifth seal, I saw under the altar the souls of those who had been slain for the word of God and for the witness they had borne; ¹⁰ they cried out with a loud voice, "O Sovereign Lord, holy and true, how long before thou wilt judge and avenge our blood on those who dwell upon the earth?" ¹¹ Then they were each given a white robe and told to rest a little longer, until the number of their fellow servants and their brethren should be complete, who were to be killed as they

themselves had been.

vv. 9-11 Each of the first four living creatures cry out at the opening of the first four seals. This indicates a break in the grouping between the fourth and fifth seals, dividing the seven into four and three. This is the pattern of the writer. The fifth seal is opened. The first four seals have to do with the world primarily. The other three are more specifically related to the spiritual world. The scene shifts from earth to heaven. Reference is made to the altar in the outer court of the temple. In the temple, the altar had a little trough under the altar which caught the blood of the sacrificed animals (Lev. 4:7).

The writer says that he saw under the altar the souls of the martyrs, that is, martyred persons. This does not indicate the Greek concept of man as a soul temporarily occupying a physical body but the Hebrew understanding of man as a total being (20:12). They are under the altar, because they have been sacrificed (cf. Phil. 2:17; 2 Tim. 4:6). Martyrs are in one sense victims sacrificed unto God. He sees those people who had been sacrificed and hears their blood crying out (Gen. 4:10; Matt. 23:35). The martyrs are crying out not for revenge, but they are crying for a vindication of divine justice. Calkins says, "It was an ancient apocalyptical idea that the day of judgment could be hastened by the prayers of the saints . . . and cries of the martyrs." Their pleadings will have something to do with the vindication of right and the punishment of evil (Blaney). They have on white robes. This means purity and victory. Although they are in the presence of God, yet they long for the ultimate triumph of the kingdom for which they died. This is an eternal truth. They are told to wait, because there is going to be much suffering. More Christians are going to be killed.

(6) *The Sixth Seal Opened—Judgments (6:12-17)*

[12] When he opened the sixth seal, I looked, and behold, there was a great earthquake; and the sun became black as sackcloth, the full moon became like blood, [13] and the stars of the sky fell to the earth

THE SEVENFOLD VISION OF CONFLICT 107

as the fig tree sheds its winter fruit when shaken by a gale; [14] the sky vanished like a scroll that is rolled up, and every mountain and island was removed from its place. [15] Then the kings of the earth and the great men and the generals and the rich and the strong, and every one, slave and free, hid in the caves and among the rocks of the mountains, [16] calling to the mountains and rocks, "Fall on us and hide us from the face of him who is seated on the throne, and from the wrath of the Lamb; [17] for the great day of their wrath has come, and who can stand before it?"

This sixth seal portrays a world-wide cataclysm showing the confusion of the foes of Christ (Matt. 24:29,30; Mark 13:24-26; Luke 21:20-36). This is apocalyptic. In this scene, nature becomes the instrument of God's judgment and is itself affected by its unleashed powers, along with mankind. The forces of nature are instruments of their Creator in the conflict of good and evil. This is just as present as the preceding scene, and he is not just talking about the end of time. He is talking about the *end;* he is talking about the *past;* he is talking about the *present;* he is talking about *any time.* John represents these cosmic upheavals and natural calamities as God's way of punishing evil men and nations. This is present reality. This sevenfold accumulation of calamity seems to enumerate the all-inclusiveness of God's judgment. When people sin, they suffer the consequences. The sevenfold calamity affects seven classes of people (that is, all people). The judgment is complete upon all men. There is not one who will get by. All sins have their consequences, and all people are judged. The writer of the Fourth Gospel says that the ones who have faith have passed out of judgment into life (John 5:24). In the New Testament, all sins are expressions of a lack of faith. So to the extent that a person "faiths," he has passed out of judgment, because he is lifted out of these things.

If sin brings evil consequences (as it must in any morally ordered world), and if God's nature is fully revealed in Christ, then those who sin are sinning against Christ and the world and are suffering the consequences. God is ruling in his world through Christ, and his faithful people have nothing to fear since evil itself is opposed by destructive agents in the hand of God. In a sense, it is Christ who brings disaster upon people, because it is defiance of all that he stood for that produces its own inevitable consequences. Notice the sevenfold calamity that is in verses 12-15. All of these signs have their parallels in other apocalyptic writings. They appear too regularly in apocalyptic writings for them to be taken literally. These apocalyptic figures are used to express spiritual truths, and when these calamities in nature happen, they are representing a consequence of sin in the world. One does not have to go outside of the New Testament to find this. At Pentecost, Peter preached this. The people accused the believers of being drunk because a great spiritual upheaval happened. Peter denied that they were drunk and said that what had happened was what Joel had spoken (Acts 2; Joel 2). Joel said: "The sun shall be turned into darkness, and the moon into blood, before the great and terrible day of Jehovah cometh." Peter saw that what Joel had in mind had now become their own experience. In the same way, John here is talking about the consequences of sinning in man's life any time he sins.

vv. 12-14 *A great earthquake.* Out of the seven consequences come another series of seven, a series of seven different people.

v. 15 There is a sevenfold classification of men in this verse: *... kings ... great men ... generals ... rich ... strong ... slave ... free.* No one is excluded. Sin brings its consequences; consequences to every person. That is what this chapter says. Verses 15-17 picture a frightened human race horrified at the results of their own actions and seeking to escape from the sovereign God on his throne and *from the wrath of the Lamb.* Wrath is not hatred. It is a just reaction to evil. It is an overflow of love. The wrath of the Lamb indicates that he cares. Paul said, "God appointed us not unto wrath, but unto the obtaining of salvation through our Lord Jesus Christ (1 Thess. 5:9). In this passage, John says that men are seeking to escape from a guilty conscience, a holy God, and a rejected Savior. These verses give a description of the shrinking of unbelievers from the presence of the divine Judge

(Matt. 22:12). What is this truth about? The end of the world? Yes. In 96? Yes. In 1840? Yes. In 1971? Yes. Anytime! When Paul says that "all have sinned and fall short of the glory of God" (Rom. 3:23), he states a universal truth. It was true then, and it is always true. What John is mentioning here is that the judgments of God inevitably come upon those who sin. This is sin and its consequences. This is not just a picture of the end of the world. It will be true at the end of the world, but these same principles that will operate then are operating now. It is not then *or* now but then *and* now.

(7) First Interlude: God's Care for the Faithful (7:1-17)

This chapter is evidently a complement of the incidents narrated in the closing events of the preceding chapter. What is the fate of the church during the terrible judgments just described? This interlude between the opening of the sixth and seventh seals is intended to reassure the church. The servants of God are under his special care. Chapter 6 closes with the words, "who can stand?" The oppressed church, with the symbolism of the six seals, has been assured that God is judging the world. These judgments include Antichrist, warfare, famine, death, persecution, and inner guilt and conflict. The realization that the church is still a part of the world and the very terrors of this judgment suggest the cry, "who can stand?" (cf. 1 Pet. 4:18). This chapter is intended to answer this question.

There are some who "can stand" through all the disturbances of life. This chapter shows the safety of God's people and the protective care with which he watches over his church (Luke 21:18). The imposition of the divine seal protects the righteous against the plagues which the breaking of the first six seals have let loose upon the wicked. The righteous are secure because God has enabled them to overcome the sins which produce these judgments. The "sealing" symbolizes what has gone on, is going on, and will go on, while the church is on the earth. It tells that which is true at all times. This vision was given to encourage the people of God amidst the judgments which surround them. It would give encouragement and assurance to the suffering saints on earth.

a. The Church Militant, Assured Safety in the Midst of Judgment (7:1-8)

After this I saw four angels standing at the four corners of the earth, holding back the four winds of the earth, that no wind might blow on earth or sea or against any tree. ² Then I saw another angel ascend from the rising of the sun, with the seal of the living God, and he called with a loud voice to the four angels who had been given power to harm earth and sea, ³ saying, "Do not harm the earth or the sea or the trees, till we have sealed the servants of our God upon their foreheads." ⁴ And I heard the number of the sealed, a hundred and forty-four thousand sealed, out of every tribe of the sons of Israel, ⁵ twelve thousand sealed out of the tribe of Judah, twelve thousand of the tribe of Reuben, twelve thousand of the tribe of Gad, ⁶ twelve thousand of the tribe of Asher, twelve thousand of the tribe of Naptali, twelve thousand of the tribe of Manasseh, ⁷ twelve thousand of the tribe of Simeon, twelve thousand of the tribe of Levi, twelve thousand of the tribe of Issachar, ⁸ twelve thousand of the tribe of Zebulun, twelve thousand of the tribe of Joseph, twelve thousand sealed out of the tribe of Benjamin.

v. 1 In this vision, John saw four angels standing at the four corners of the earth. This was John's way of saying that these angels overshadowed the whole earth. It is hardly necessary to be reminded that this is a symbolical representation. John accommodated his presentation to the prevailing manner of speaking of the earth by the Hebrews. He was a prophet delivering God's message; not an astronomer, describing the earth. The emphasis upon the *four* indicates that the judgments about to fall are universal. None of the earth is beyond the judgments of God. The angels are the agents of divine judgment (2 Sam. 24:16; 2 Kings 19:35). The winds are clearly emblems of judgment (Job 38:24; 1 Kings 19:11; Job 1:19; 21:18; 30:15; Pss. 29; 106:27; Isa. 11:15; 41:16; Jer. 4:11-12; 10:13; 18:17; 49:32,36; Ezek. 5:2; 12:14; Dan. 7:2). Trees were often used by the Jews as visible signs of storm or calm. This simply means that all the agencies of nature, all the instruments of judgment, are in God's hand. Some Jews believed the winds from due north, east, south, or west were favorable, while those from the angle were unfavorable (Charles). The angels are holding back the winds. This is a picture of restrained destruction. This symbolism seems to mean that the judgments of the first six broken seals are held in complete suspension, as if by some restraining power not their own, until the safety of the people of God has been made secure (2 Thess. 2:6). The judgments are God's judgments, and they are in the controlling power of God.

vv. 2-3 The meaning of the symbolism of these verses is that something is done to the church as if an angel does it. Another angel brings "the seal of the living God." God is referred to as the "living" God because by this sealing, life is imparted. In Jewish thought, the "east" (literally, "the sunrising") was the place from which God's special manifestations were expected (Isa. 41:2; Ezek. 43:2). The mission of this angel is to render secure the people of God, that is, the entire redeemed community on the earth. A seal was used to give validity to documents. It was a mark of ownership. This is an authenticating seal. A steward in the first century who was committed the oversight of the estate wore the signet ring of the master. To authenticate a document he pressed this signet into wax. Jesus used the same example in the discussion with the Jews after the feeding of the five thousand (John 6:27). Believers are "sealed" with the Holy Spirit unto the day of redemption (Eph. 4:30; cf. Rom. 4:11; 2 Cor. 1:22; Eph. 1:13). This angel *from the rising of the sun* has been given God's authority to apply some conspicuous sign or token by which the redeemed would be known as the true servants of God. This is a vision. The seal is God's mark, not man's.

With the seal of the living God means that the angel anthenticates in the name of God. He tells the winds to do no harm until he has sealed the servants of God. The mystical seal signifies identification, protection, and security (Ezek. 9:1-8; Rev. 14:1; John 6:27; Eph. 1:13; 4:30; Rom. 4:11; 2 Cor. 1:22). According to the

Psalm of Solomon 15:8, at the exodus the righteous were given a distinct mark on their foreheads, and this mark was to protect them from famine, war, and pestilence. This seems to be the background.

God sent this angel to seal his servants with the sign and pledge of their salvation. They are thus all preserved from the destructive agents of divine judgment (cf. Ezek. 9:1 ff.). The seal is here impressed as the mark in Ezekiel 9:4-5, that those who bear it may be protected. They are "hid with Christ in God" (Col. 3:3). This does not mean that the people of God will be exempt from suffering; sometimes it increases their suffering. However, for them there are two things of which they cannot be deprived; namely, the assurance of the union with Christ, and the daily new experience of his love amidst all distress and trouble. The assurance is that all things work together for their good, not for their hurt (Rom. 8:28). This assurance has no chronology. The truth here illustrated is always true.

Nowhere does the prophet ever describe the sealing or tell what the seal was. He only heard the number who were sealed. The servants are sealed on their foreheads because that is the most conspicuous part of man. One thousand is usually used to denote a large and complete number. Twelve is the number of the church. This square of 12 multiplied by 1,000 is typical of a large perfect number. It suggests totality, completeness, or fullness as well as diversity within an essential unity. The 144,000 stands in the vision for God's elect, the entire congregation of the redeemed on earth during End time. It is an ideal number denoting that the group is complete, yet unlimited. Not one was missing. The twelve tribes symbolizes the true Israel which is made up of all peoples and nations and languages. The struggling church is consoled by being shown how God will preserve it in trouble, by being assured that each member will have divine care. The true Israel is sealed but is not removed from the world (John 17:15). Each one of these one hundred and forty-four thousand is "sealed permanently" to protect him from the impending calamities.

vv. 5-8 In Israel there were thirteen tribes, including Levi (Num. 1; Josh. 14—21). There are some irregularities in Revelation in the listing of the tribes. The explanations for these irregularities have been many and varied. Twelve tribes are probably listed to signify the whole nation (Acts 26:7). It is a family roll call. The twelve tribes are representative of the people of God. Several writers of the New Testament understood that the church was the new Israel (Rom. 2:29; Gal. 3:29; 6:16; Phil. 3:3; 1 Pet. 1:1; Jas. 1:1). John not only uses the Old Testament "my people" for the church (18:4; 21:3) but also the twelve tribes as well (Rissi, p. 89). All the tribes are listed to emphasize the inclusion of all of God's people. The writer's purpose here is to show that all the church on earth has divine protection. Whatever judgments may come upon the earth, the people of God on the earth are safe in the most meaningful sense.

b. The Church Triumphant, Assured Safety Above Judgment (7:9-17)

⁹ After this I looked, and behold, a great multitude which no man could number, from every nation, from all tribes and peoples and tongues, standing before the throne and before the Lamb, clothed in white robes, with palm branches in their hands, ¹⁰ and crying out with a loud voice, "Salvation belongs to our God who sits upon the throne and to the Lamb!" ¹¹ And all the angels stood round the throne and round the elders and the four living creatures, and they fell on their faces before the throne and worshipped God, ¹² saying, "Amen! Blessing and glory and wisdom and thanksgiving and honor and power and might be to our God for ever and ever! Amen."

¹³ Then one of the elders addressed me, saying, "Who are these, clothed in white robes, and whence have they come?" ¹⁴ I said to him, "Sir, you know." And he said to me, "These are they who have come out of the great tribulation; they have washed their robes and made them white in the blood of the Lamb.

¹⁵ Therefore are they before the throne of God, and serve him day and night within his temple; and he who sits upon the throne will shelter them with his presence.

¹⁶ They shall hunger no more, neither thirst any more; the sun shall

not strike them, nor any scorching heat.
¹⁷ For the Lamb in the midst of the throne will be their shepherd, and he will guide them to springs of living water; and God will wipe away every tear from their eyes."

v. 9 The preceding vision represented the assured safety of God's people in the midst of tribulation upon the earth. The vision in 7:9-17 represents the triumph of the redeemed who have passed through tribulation and have been caught up out of it. Not only is the church sealed and protected on earth, it is vindicated and triumphant in heaven. In this paragraph, the scene changes from earth to heaven. This great innumerable multitude may be regarded as the redeemed in heaven who have rest after conflict. The phrase "after this," marks a logical rather than a chronological sequence. The "great multitude" here shows the impossibility of counting the redeemed. The white robes are emblems of victory and purity, the characteristics of all saints. The palm branches are emblems of triumph, victory, and peace. The imagery is drawn from the Feasts of Passover and Tabernacles which commemorated God's deliverance from Egyptian bondage and his care over Israel in the wilderness (Ex. 12-18; 23:16; Lev. 23:43; Neh. 8:14-17). The fourfold classification of humanity is symbolical of completeness. The lessons of his vision are that the eternal salvation of all of God's people is sure and that triumph comes through trust in God.

vv. 10-11 The redeemed ascribe (present tense) their salvation (victory) to God and to the Lamb. The figure of the Lamb represents in a special manner the sacrifice of Christ. Deliverance comes from the sovereign act of God in Christ. Their victory was the result of redemptive love manifested at Calvary. They attribute their victory entirely to him. God and the Lamb are entitled to equal praise. The angels (5:11) in a great circle around the throne and the four living creatures (creation) join the elders in the adoration and praise of God. In the symbolism, the elders (church) occupy the inner circle, near the throne. There is also a cosmic redemption (Rom. 8:18-22). Redemption is never complete without it. Worship is the natural expression of all life toward God.

v. 12 This sevenfold ascription of praise is substantially the same as that of 5:12. It denotes the universal and all embracing character of the praise. The general idea of the doxology is that the highest kind of praise, complete praise, is to be ascribed to God because of redemption.

vv. 13-14 The elder speaks here because he represents the church. The elder knows by experience how the multitude obtained their white robes, the emblems of holiness. *These are they who have come out of the great tribulation; they have washed their robes and made them white in the blood of the lamb.* That is, they have undergone that process of death and new life which Jesus by his incarnation inaugurated. This is the prophet's way of stressing the place of grace in salvation. They did not wash their robes by themselves alone. John, though a prophet in the church on earth, did not know the full reward of salvation. The elder, a representative of the church in heaven, knew because he is participating in it. The "great tribulation" is a general designation which includes all of the trials, temptations, afflictions, hardships, sufferings, and persecutions of the church on earth. It is the constant trial of life which is the result of evil's warring against God. These who make up the multitude are not just "martyrs" but the whole number of the elect. They are arriving safe out of their tribulation into their triumph. In the original text, the verb is in the present tense and should be translated, "these are they which are coming." There is a continuous coming from the tribulation. All that the redeemed have passed through in their life on earth is now completed and past. During their life of struggle and crossbearing, they "washed their robes (3:4-5; 22:14) and made them white in the blood of the Lamb" (Rom. 3:25; Eph. 1:7; Col. 1:20; Heb. 9:14; 1 Pet. 1:2; 1 John 1:5). It is because of their triumphant faith and the purity of their lives by divine cleansing during the whole struggle of life on earth that they are *before the throne of God.*

v. 15 The redeemed who have passed out of the great tribulation not only enjoy ceaseless worship which night does not interrupt but also an unbroken vision of the divine glory. God's dwelling-place is with them, and his presence overshadows and protects them (Ps. 23; Ezek. 37:27; John 1:14; 14:23; Rev. 21:3; Eph. 5:25-27).

v. 16 The allusion seems to be to the tabernacle in the wilderness (Ex. 35—40). It was regarded as the peculiar dwelling place of God and always occupied a central place among the tribes of Israel. The church triumphant is no longer subjected to hunger, thirst, or the excessive heat of the sun (Isa. 49:10; Ex. 17:3; Ps. 63:1; 2 Cor. 11:27). In contrast to the tribulations and martyrdoms which the church on earth suffers, the church in heaven enjoys eternal blessings. The triumphant church has no unsatisfied need.

v. 17 The members have been delivered from the trials which they suffer on earth. By complex figures Christ is presented as Lamb (5:6) and Shepherd. The climax in this vision of the victorious church shows that every trace of the great tribulation has been removed. In expressions of exquisite tenderness, the prophet represents divine protection for the people of God who have lived in the midst of confusion and destruction. John is seeking to fortify the steadfastness of the church by the assurance of the benevolent guidance of God and its certain victory and reward.

(8) The Seventh Seal Opened—Silence of One-half Hour in Heaven (8:1)

¹ When the Lamb opened the seventh seal, there was silence in heaven for about half an hour.

The sixth chapter ended amid suffering and gloom. The first six seals show that there is a divine power at work though it is hidden. They have portrayed some of the resources of the infinite God in his struggle against evil. When men are left alone in their rebellion, their sins will work out their own judgment (Rom. 1:24,28; Eph. 4:19). Would anyone be able to survive these judgments of God? In the interlude, John has shown the security of the church, sealed on earth (7:1-8) and safe in heaven (7:9-17). Now that God's people are safe from the destructive effects of the judgments, the breaking of the seals is continued. When the seventh seal is broken, there is silence in heaven for about half an hour. An "hour" is a Hebrew idiom for a brief period of time (Dan. 4:19; 5:5; Matt. 26:40; Rev. 17:12; 18:10). The *about half an hour* signifies a very brief period of time. The background for this symbolism of silence seems to be Elijah's experience on Horeb where he heard the voice of God in "a sound of gentle stillness" (1 Kings 19:12, margin). Also in the Jewish Temple at the offering of incense a solemn silence was kept (Pss. 62:1; 65:1). God's actions in judgment are often introduced by a reference to silence (Hab. 2:20; Zeph. 1:7; Zech. 2:13). Also the events which follow show that this silence in heaven is in order to allow the prayers of the saints to be heard. During the "half-hour" (i.e. a brief time) God's people are assured that God will hear their prayers. The prophet wants the people to know that they through prayer can participate in God's purposes and actions.

3. The Seven Trumpets (8:2 to 11:19)

The purpose of the seals was to fortify the patience of the saints by assuring them of God's providence and of their victory and reward. The prophet's mission, however, included another aspect. He was not only to bring a message of encouragement to the faithful but also a warning to the unfaithful and ungodly. Evil is obstinate. Victory is not won by an easy campaign. The new series of visions inaugurated by the opening of the seventh seal, forms a dramatic message of God's judgment upon the ungodly. The number seven indicates the complete nature of the judgment.

The vision of the seven trumpets seems to grow out of the opening of the seventh seal, and it recapitulates and develops the themes already stated in the vision of the seals. This is John's literary method. He proceeds by way of interlocking spirals of material dealing in repetition, emphasizing his main points over and over

(Blaney). The first four trumpets form a series within the complete series, while the last three are included in a separate vision as "woes." As in the seals vision, an interlude is placed between the sixth and seventh trumpets. The first four bring judgments indirectly upon men through nature. They portray troubles affecting man through his environment: the earth, trees, grass, the sea, rivers, fountains, the light of the sun, moon, and stars. Four is the cosmic number. The prophet is saying in these judgments that the forces of nature (all natural phenomena) are all under the control of God. The destruction produced by these judgments is partial—one third. God's mercies always attend his judgments. He is interested in repentance, not destruction. Judgment is not only punitive but also redemptive, and each of the judgments is a call to repentance (9:20). Much of the imagery in these judgments corresponds with the description of the plagues in Egypt (Ex. 7-11).

(1) Preface to the Vision of the Trumpets (8:2-6)

[2] Then I saw the seven angels who stand before God, and seven trumpets were given to them. [3] And another angel came and stood at the altar with a golden censer; and he was given much incense to mingle with the prayers of all the saints upon the golden altar before the throne; [4] and the smoke of the incense rose with the prayers of the saints from the hand of the angel before God. [5] Then the angel took the censer and filled it with fire from the altar and threw it on the earth; and there were peals of thunder, loud noises, flashes of lightning, and an earthquake.

[6] Now the seven angels who had the seven trumpets made ready to blow them.

v. 2 John now saw the seven angels who stand before God. The definite article is probably used, not because the seven angels were previously mentioned, but because it would be sufficiently understood from the common usage of the language that reference was made to the angels of the presence. In apocalyptic writings, these angels of the Presence are named: Gabriel, Michael, Raphael, Uriel, Raguel, Sariel, and Remiel (Enoch 20:7). These seven angels are symbols of the complete and varied messenger force of God.

To each of these angels a trumpet was given. Trumpets were used in Israel to denote the awakening signals of divine visitation. They were used in ceremonial processions (Josh. 6:1-21; 1 Chron. 15:24; Neh. 12:41), to proclaim the accession of a king (1 Kings 1:34,39; 2 Kings 9:13), to summons Israel to repentance in the face of imminent divine judgment (Isa. 58:1; Jer. 4:5; 6:1,17; Ezek. 33:3 f.; Joel 2:1,15), and to announce religious ceremonies and national festivals (Ex. 19:16; Lev. 23:24; Num. 10:1-10; 29:1). In all of these usages, the trumpet symbolized the truth of divine visitation.

vv. 3-4 In this vision, another angel as a ministering spirit is seen performing the priest's function. The golden altar of incense stood in the holy place before the veil in the Jewish Temple (Ex. 30:6; 40:5). On this altar, a priest burned incense every morning. The smoke from the burning incense symbolized the rising prayers to heaven. This is merely a figurative representation of prayer offered to God. The stress is not on the person who offers but on the prayers offered. The prayers of the afflicted saints shall surely be heard and answered. These prayers are for the vindication of the justice of God.

vv. 5-6 The fire cast from the censer upon earth is taken from the golden altar, the same fire with which the incense had been burned. This imagery implies a direct connection between the prayers of God's people and God's actions. The symbols of the ***peals of thunder, loud noises, flashes of lightning, and an earthquake*** indicate that God has heard the prayers of his saints (Ps. 18:6-9). How he answers their prayers by providential interpositions is symbolized by the phenomena disclosed in the vision of the trumpets.

(2) The First Trumpet: Hail and Fire Mingled, Sent in Blood (8:7)

⁷ The first angel blew his trumpet, and there followed hail and fire, mixed with blood, which fell on the earth; and a third of the earth was burnt up, and a third of the trees were burnt up, and all green grass was burnt up.

v. 7 The first trumpet declares God's judgment on men in a similar manner to the seventh plague in Egypt (Ex. 9:22-25). It brings blight upon the land through hail and fire mingled and both together sent in blood. Hail is a symbol of God's displeasure and an instrument in inflicting punishment (Ex. 9:23; Job 38:22-23; Pss. 18:13; 78:48; 105:32; Isa. 30:30; Ezek. 13:11; 38:22; Hag. 2:17). The other two figures are also emblems and instruments of destruction. All of them wrought by nature turned the earth against itself. The vision, like all the others, is symbolical. It represents the true, not the apparent, effects of the destruction upon the earth. The figurative character of the vision must be maintained. The phrase, *third of the earth* is designed to emphasize that in judgment God remembers mercy. God gives opportunity in judgment for repentance. These plagues symbolize God's judgment on human sin.

(3) *The Second Trumpet: A Great Burning Mountain Cast into the Sea (8:8-9)*

⁸ The second angel blew his trumpet, and something like a great mountain, burning with fire, was thrown into the sea; ⁹ and a third of the sea became blood, a third of the living creatures in the sea died, and a third of the ships were destroyed.

vv. 8-9 Mountains are used as the prophetic symbol of a kingdom (Jer. 51:25; Dan. 2:35), as symbols of strength and great power (Isa. 2:2; 41:15; Amos 4:1), and to denote something remarkable and awe-inspiring (Judg. 5:5; 1 Kings 19:11; Job 9:5; Ps. 46:2; Isa. 34:3; 54:10; Ezek. 38:20; Mic. 1:4; Nah. 1:5). Here a blazing mass as large as a mountain is used as the instrument of the punishment of the ungodly world (Ex. 7:17). The sea in apocalyptic writings often represents people in a state of confusion. Ships represent commerce and wealth. The meaning of the vision is evident. The "fish" and the *ships* are natural parts in a figure where the mountain and the sea are used to symbolize agitation and destruction. The vision is designed to describe great trouble and commotion. It is not to be understood literally.

(4) The Third Trumpet: A Blazing Star Falls on the Waters (8:10-11)

¹⁰ The third angel blew his trumpet, and a great star fell from heaven, blazing like a torch, and it fell on a third of the rivers and on the fountains of water. ¹¹ The name of the star is Wormwood. A third of the waters became wormwood, and many men died of the water, because it was made bitter.

vv. 10-11 In prophetic language, a star symbolizes one in an exalted position (Isa. 14:12). The figure here is patterned after the first Egyptian plague (Ex. 7:17 f.). It symbolizes troubles inflicted by God upon the guilty world. Judgment is an act of God and is not to be attributed to merely natural circumstances. This metaphorical language is used to show and assure men that there is a divine power at work though it be hidden. *Wormwood.* The artemisia is an aromatic desert plant having a bitter taste; it symbolizes bitter sorrow (Deut. 29:18; Prov. 5:4; Jer. 8:14; 9:15; 23:15; Lam. 3:19). The ungodly are reaping the bitter fruits of sin. For the faithful, God makes the bitter waters sweet; for the unfaithful he makes the sweet water bitter (cf. Ex. 15:23). "In symbolism he is simply saying that the sin of the world carries moral and spiritual poison into the very springs of life; and that the waters of the world become bitter to the enemies of God" (Richardson, p. 97).

(5) The Fourth Trumpet: Darkening of Sun, Moon, Stars (8:12)

¹² The fourth angel blew his trumpet, and a third of the sun was struck, and a third of the moon, and a third of the stars, so that a third of their light was darkened; a third of the day was kept from shining, and likewise a third of the night.

v. 12 This catastrophe corresponds with the ninth Egyptian plague (Ex. 10:21-23). Darkness in apocalyptic writings symbolized tragedy, calamity, disaster, distress, and gloom. The mention of the *third* simply means that the plague was limited. The darkening of the sun, moon, and stars was not to show the effect upon these heavenly bodies but to show that their light was withdrawn from the earth. This is another sign of God's wrath. Time brings forth its consequences, but these consequences are circumscribed by the mercy of God. The plague is designed to warn and not to destroy. Every temporal judgment of God is a call to repentance.

(6) The Eagle's Warning (8:13)

¹³ Then I looked, and I heard an eagle crying with a loud voice, as it flew in midheaven, "Woe, woe, woe to those who dwell on the earth, at the blasts of the other trumpets which the three angels are about to blow!"

v. 13 The last three trumpet visions announce judgments that affect men directly. The sounding of these trumpets is preceded by a vision in which a "vulture" or *eagle* (according to the best manuscripts) is seen flying in midheaven screeching three coming woes. The vulture or eagle in midheaven, plainly visible and audible to all, is a symbol of swiftness and unerringness (Matt. 24:28). It symbolizes judgment descending from on high. In Jewish apocalypses, the eagle is also used as a messenger (Calkins). This vision announces the swiftness and certainty of the coming woes (Deut. 28:49; Hos. 8:1; Hab. 1:8). The threefold repetition of the word *woe* is intensive, and it indicates that the three remaining trumpet judgments are particularly terrifying and tormenting. These remaining judgments are spiritual rather than material in kind. These "woes" are directed *to those who dwell on the earth,* i.e., the world in distinction from the church. They are given as warnings and are intended to bring repentance (9:20). The first *woe* is described in 9:1-11. The second *woe* is described in 9:12-21, and the third is described in 11:15-19.

(7) The Fifth Trumpet: Swarms of Locusts (9:1-12)

a. Smoke from the Abyss (9:1-2)

¹ And the fifth angel blew his trumpet, and I saw a star fallen from heaven to earth, and he was given the key of the shaft of the bottomless pit

² he opened the shaft of the bottomless pit, and from the shaft rose smoke like the smoke of a great furnace, and the sun and the air were darkened with smoke from the shaft.

vv. 1-2 When the fifth trumpet sounded, a fallen star, the symbol of Satan, was seen on the earth. This star was a person as the word "him" denotes. This fallen star was given the key, that is, the authority (1:18; cf. Matt. 16:19), to open the door to the shaft, leading into the abyss (bottomless pit) (Job 28:22; 31:12; Pss. 71:20; 107:26; Luke 8:31; Rom. 10:7). This vision is a parody of the vision of the risen Christ with the keys of death and Hades (1:18). The abyss evidently means the abode of the dead, equivalent to the Hebrew *Sheol*. This region is the abode of Satan and demons; it represents hell before the final judgment (Luke 8:31). The fallen star (Satan) unlocks and removes the covering of the abyss, and there pours out a dense volume of smoke which darkens the air and obscures the sun. This image was probably taken from the destruction of Sodom and Gomorrah (Gen. 19:24). This dense smoke symbolizes a demonic force of evil from the underworld, which clouds men's minds and darkens their understanding. God allows the powers of evil to be let loose to execute his judgment upon the world. This vision of the smoke from the abyss is a parody of the smoke of the incense which symbolizes the prayers of the saints ascending to God. (8:4). The purpose of this vision was to indicate the origin of the plague which is described in the following verses.

b. The Plague of Locusts (9:3-6)

³ Then from the smoke came locusts on the earth, and they were given power like the power of scorpions of the earth; ⁴ they were told not to harm the grass of the earth or any green growth or any tree, but only those of mankind who have not the seal of God upon their foreheads; ⁵ they were allowed to torture them for five months, but not to kill them, and their torture was like the torture of a scorpion, when it stings a man. ⁶ And in those days men will seek death and will not find it; they will long to die, and death flies from them.

v. 3 The prophet now sees coming out of the smoke a swarm of locusts more terrible than those of Egypt. Locusts were the most dreaded and destructive creatures of the ancient world. They are used in the Old Testament as an emblem of desolation and destruction (Deut. 28:38,42; Judg. 6:3-6; 7:12; Ps. 78:46; Jer. 46:23; Joel 1; 2; Amos 7:1; Nah. 3:15,17). These locusts are transformed into supernatural creatures, whose characteristics are in part taken from exaggeration of natural locusts. They depict a visual representation of demonic creatures. John uses this demonic incursion to symbolize a force of an immoral type. He shows how God uses evil, which he has not engineered, for his own purpose. He uses demonic forces to bring plagues of a mental and spiritual nature upon godless men (Blaney).

v. 4 These locusts were told that they should not hurt the grass or any green growth or any tree, the normal diet of locusts, but only men who have not the seal of God in their foreheads (7:1-3; cf. Eph. 1:13; 4:30; 2 Cor. 1:22; 2 Tim. 2:19). The truth stated by this symbolism is that God controls and limits the process of retribution. Just as Israel was preserved from the plagues in Egypt, so the "sealed" of God are protected from the plague of locusts by God's love and power (Swete). Because this affliction comes from an evil spirit, it does not injure the saints. They have been marked with the seal of divine ownership and protection and are, therefore, safe from demonic powers. This fact is consolatory to faithful Christians.

v. 5 These demonic creatures were not permitted to kill people but to torment them painfully for five months. The five dry months of the spring and summer is the ordinary time for the duration of a locust-plague in the East. In apocalyptic language, it means a long time, and yet of limited duration. This demonic host is limited in its license and duration. The torment is compared to that when a scorpion stings a man. The pain and suffering caused by such a sting is usually very intense and excruciating. The stings torment by poisoning. John seems to be saying that the distressing torment of sin lasts during the entire life of the ones who do not have *the seal of God upon their foreheads.*

v. 6 The distressing torment discussed in the preceding verse is described further in this verse. It is a picture of the extreme anguish. It is an anguish where the distress is so great that the victims consider death a relief and anxiously look to the time when they may be released from their suffering by death (Job 3:20-22; 7:15; Jer. 8:3; Luke 23:30). "Such a death as they desire, a death which will end their sufferings, is impossible; physical death is no remedy for the *basanismos* of an evil conscience" (Swete). This graphic picture represents a divine judgment upon wicked men by the use of demonic powers. The judgment is in reality internal and spiritual, the affliction of mind and spirit by inner decay.

c. A Description of the Locusts (9:7-10)

⁷ In appearance the locusts were like horses arrayed for battle; on their heads were what looked like crowns of gold; their faces were like human faces, ⁸ their hair like women's hair, and their teeth like lions' teeth; ⁹ they had scales like iron breastplates, and the noise of their wings was like the noise of many chariots with horses rushing into battle. ¹⁰ they have tails like scorpions, and stings, and their power of hurting men for five months lies in their tails.

vv. 7-10 The additional features of the locusts enumerated in these verses make it clear that the prophet is simply portraying the ghostly demonic character of the destructive forces of evil. Many details of the description corresponds with those given in Joel chapter 2. The details of the description are calculated to arouse intense feelings of terror. These loathsome creatures are really malicious spirits whose mission is destruction and spiritual devastation. They are cruel creatures. Their description is grotesque because they are devilish in origin and nature. In whatever spirit moral evil exists, it gives pain and works destruction. Dire consequences befall people who ignore the moral universe created by God. Evil is in its nature self-destructive, but God in his mercy limits its effects in order to bring men to repentance.

d. The Ruler of the Locusts (9:11)

¹¹ They have as king over them the angel of the bottomless pit; his name in Hebrew is Abaddon, and in Greek he is called Apollyon.

v. 11 Real locusts have no king (Prov. 30:27). However, these locusts have as their king Abaddon, or to use the Greek, Apollyon. *Abaddon* in Hebrew means "destruction," or the "place of destruction." *Apollyon* in Greek means "destroy" or "destroyer." The name sums up and personifies the character of him who bears it. The titles **king** and **angel of the bottomless pit** probably are new designations for the "star" in the beginning of the chapter who was given "the key of the shaft of the bottomless pit." The king then, who marshals the malicious spirits for their work of destruction, is Satan (John 8:44). This does not mean that he marches at their head, but that they are his subjects and belong to his kingdom. The conflict involves spiritual principles, the conflict between good and evil. The picture is forceful and vivid, but it describes how moral evil, which is really rebellion against God, becomes his instrument in working out his purposes. The awesome combination of the qualities of men and beasts in the description of the locusts depicts the fearful character of the instruments of divine judgment for the oppressors of God's people.

(8) *Announcement of Two More Woes (9:12)*

¹² The first woe has passed; behold, two woes are still to come.

v. 12 In 8:13, three "woes" were announced. In 9:1-11, the first *woe* has been described. Fearful as is the torment inflicted by the first "woe," it is only the first of three great "woes." The retributions for sins pass and give place for more intense demonstration. The powers of evil do not exhaust themselves in one kind of manifestation. There are *two woes* remaining to be announced with increased dramatic vividness.

(9) *The Sixth Trumpet: External Enemies (9:13-21)*

THE SEVENFOLD VISION OF CONFLICT

a. The Releasing of the Agents of Divine Judgments (9:13-15)

¹³ Then the sixth angel blew his trumpet, and I heard a voice from the four horns of the golden altar before God, ¹⁴ saying to the sixth angel who had the trumpet, "Release the four angels who are bound at the great river Euphrates." ¹⁵ So the four angels were released, who had been held ready for the hour, the day, the month, and the year, to kill a third of mankind.

vv. 13-15 When the sixth angel blew his trumpet, the prophet heard *a voice* which he describes as coming *from the four horns of the golden altar before God.* The voice comes from the same altar where the prayers of the saints and the incense were offered (8:3-4; Ex. 30). The prayers of the saints are being answered though in strange and painful judgments (Charles). The voice tells the sixth angel who had the trumpet to *release the four angels who are bound at the great river Euphrates.* Four is the cosmic number denoting universality in things of the world. The number implies that the power of the angels is of universal extent. The four prepared angels are released at the precise predestined time to kill a third of mankind; that is, a great part, though not the larger. The releasing of these angels of judgment is the preparation for a great invasion of hostile armed forces. To the Jews the Euphrates was the northern frontier of Palestine, and to the Romans it was the eastern frontier. To Jew and Roman it was the last natural barrier for the invasion of dreaded hordes out of the earth. Most Hebrew prophets interpreted the invasions from the East as God's judgments upon the ungodly and idolatrous people (Isa. 14:29-31; 28:1-29; Jer. 1:13-16; 4:11-13; 6:1-26; 10:22; 13:20; 25:1-11,26; 46:20,24; 47:2; Ezek. 6:1-9; 8; 21:18-32; 26:7; 38:6,15; 39:2; Dan. 9:1-14; Joel 2; Amos 5:18-27; 7:1-9; 8:1-3; 9:1-10; Mic. 1; Hab. 1; Zeph. 3:1-8; Zech. 1:12; 7:8-14). In the same way, in this dramatic metaphor, John signifies that God's restraint is removed and partial judgment is allowed to come to the idolatrous people who refuse to respond in repentance (vv. 20-21).

b. A Description of the Invading Army (9:16-19)

> [16] The number of the troops of cavalry was twice ten thousand times ten thousand; I heard their number. [17] And this was how I saw the horses in my vision: the riders wore breastplates the color of fire and of sapphire and of sulphur, and the heads of the horses were like lions' heads, and fire and smoke and sulphur issued from their mouths. [18] By these three plagues a third of mankind was killed, by the fire and smoke and sulphur issuing from their mouths. [19] For the power of the horses is in their mouths and in their tails; their tails are like serpents, with heads, and by means of them they wound.

vv. 16-19 John next envisioned an immense host, two hundred million horsemen, who go forth at the command or under the leadership of the four angels. In describing the terrifying invading army, the prophet's chief interest is upon the destructiveness of the horses. The destruction is apparently executed by the horses themselves, not by the horsemen. These horses destroy in front and behind, coming and going. The prophets used horses to symbolize strength, destruction, and ruthless conquest (Deut. 17:16; Hos. 14:3; Hab. 1:5-10). Like the locusts in the preceding vision, these horses are not an earthly cavalry but are demonic forces, hideous monstrosities. The features of the horsemen and the horses are intended to symbolize their satanic natures. The description mingles the elements of the natural and the supernatural in such a way as to make them indistinguishable. It is these demonic powers, malicious, mighty, and relentless, which God allows to be released against the oppressors of his people, the unrepenting world.

c. The Response of the Stubborn to These Judgments (9:20-21)

> [20] The rest of mankind, who were not killed by these plagues, did not repent of the works of their hands nor give up worshiping demons and idols of gold and silver and bronze and stone and wood, which cannot either see or hear or walk; [21] nor did they repent of their murders or their sorceries or their immorality or their thefts.

vv. 20-21 The purpose of the judgment of the sixth trumpet was to bring about repentance, but the godless did not repent. Such is the dreadful hardness and depravity of the human heart. These retributions did not lead to an abandonment of sins; there was no change in their idolatry, their vices, or their crimes. It is a tragic and familiar fact that men are not long sobered by even the most terrible calamities (Calkins). Men continue to worship the gods of their own making rather than the God who made them.

In these symbolic pictures, John has shown that the very forces of evil are turned by God to the destruction of evil. He has shown people caught in this tragedy with no moral understanding of its meaning and no turning to God in repentance and with no power to repudiate their evil ways. John is saying that there is no power which is not under the control of God. Those who reject God and his moral principles and power find that everything which goes to make up the pattern of their lives is against them. The ones who would destroy God's will are destroyed by it. The ones who defy God are impotent in their opposition. Their very rebellion is turned to his purposes. They are unwilling servants, but they are his servants still (Rist).

In the first six trumpet-judgments, three instruments have been used to symbolize the law of sin and retribution: natural calamity, 8:7-12; internal decay, 9:1-12; and external enemies, 9:13-21. Even under such judgments men are still capable of hardening their hearts. These plagues are for the unrepenting world, the enemies of God and his church. However, redemption is implicit in each judgment. These visions have been given to bring comfort and reassurance to the church and warning to the ungodly persecuting world. In a morally ordered universe, the evil world would not triumph over the people of God.

These six plagues symbolize the continuous operation of the effects of sin and evil. They are in answer to the cry of the saints to God. They portray how men forever suffer from their disobedience to God. They also show how in men's rebellion and blindness they will not recognize the results of their sin and repent. Instead of repenting, they grow more and more reckless with nothing to expect except the heavier judgments of God. If they refuse to respond in repentance, the natural decay caused by further sin will cause defeat. Before the prophet sets forth the last trumpet of dreadful judgment, he places a second interlude in the writing to emphasize the opportunities which God affords men of escaping.

(10) The Second Interlude (10:1 to 11:14)

As an interlude was inserted between the opening of the sixth and the seventh seals, so there is one introduced between the sixth and seventh trumpets. Both of these interludes are designed to comfort the people of God.

a. The Strong Angel (10:1-7)

¹ Then I saw another mighty angel coming down from heaven, wrapped in a cloud, with a rainbow over his head, and his face was like the sun, and his legs like pillars of fire. ² He had a little scroll open in his hand. And he set his right foot on the sea, and his left foot on the land, ³ and called out with a loud voice, like a lion roaring; when he called out, the seven thunders sounded. ⁴ And when the seven thunders had sounded, I was about to write, but I heard a voice from heaven saying, "Seal up what the seven thunders have said, and do not write it down." ⁵ And the angel whom I saw standing on sea and land lifted up his right hand to heaven ⁶ and swore by him who lives for ever and ever, who created heaven and what is in it, the earth and what is in it, and the sea and what is in it, that there should be no more delay, ⁷ but that in the days of the trumpet call to be sounded by the seventh angel, the mystery of God, as he announced to his servants the prophets, should be fulfilled.

v. 1 The description of the angel shows the celestial dignity and heavenly glory of the messenger (cf. 5:2). God's glory is reflected in his messenger, as formerly it was of Moses. The fact that he is seen *coming down from heaven* indicates that he is God's messenger.

v. 2 *Foot on the sea . . . foot on the land.* The firmly planted feet declare that the revelation which is to follow affects the whole world and is not partial in its operation, as were the judgments set forth under the earlier trumpets.

Once again John sees himself as an actor in the great drama

(cf. court of heaven and book with seven seals, chap. 5). In this vision, John sees himself in relation to a book that is his own. It is a little book (*biblaridion*) and is not to be confused with the scroll (*biblion*) with the seven seals (5:1). John is struggling for his message, and as his vision moves on toward its grand climax, there is impressed upon him more clearly the character of the message he must proclaim and the demands it imposes upon the messenger. In this little book is contained a mere fragment of the counsels of God which are to be revealed by the prophet, yet the contents are of deep significance. This little scroll contained the redemptive purpose of God as it is made effective through the martyr witness of the church and completes "what remains of Christ's afflictions" (Col. 1:24).

v. 4 *Seven thunders.* The seven thunders symbolize the full heavenly testimony which has been so forcibly impressed upon the author in the visions of the horsemen and of the six trumpets. God's judgment can be revealed in symbol, but the spiritual forces that lie behind it cannot be revealed to human comprehension. So, before the prophet receives his commission, he must learn that his knowledge of God is incomplete. Enough for his guidance and needs God does reveal to him, but the voices that speak his inner counsels are inarticulate to human ears. The deepest truths of life can only be partially understood, because they overflow man's capacity. Evidently the prophet indicates that he had received in his vision more than he is permitted to reveal, or that it is now too late to record the possible warnings of coming judgment which the "thunders" expressed. Whatever the thunders said, it was not for the record (cf. Dan. 12:4; 2 Cor. 12:4).

vv. 5-6 It was customary to lift up the right hand towards heaven, appealing to the God of truth, in taking a solemn oath (Ezek. 20:5; Dan. 12:7 f.). God's eternity and omnipotence are referred to in order to demonstrate the certainty of the fulfillment of the prophecy which follow.

That there should be no more delay (cf. Matt. 24:48; Heb. 10:37).

The visions of the first six trumpets have shown how in the world the ungodly do not escape judicial retribution. But the six judgments did not bring repentance. Therefore, there can be no more delay in the fulfillment of the seventh trumpet (cf. 6:10). The last judgment is for eternity (cf. 11:18).

v. 7 *Mystery of God.* The "mystery of God" is the whole purpose of God in human history (contrast 2 Thess. 2:7). It includes all that man does not now understand in connection with God's dealing with humanity, that is, the existence of evil and God's modes of dealing with it, and all mankind (Rom. 16:25; 1 Cor. 2:7; Eph. 3:4 f.). God's plans are being steadily and surely worked out, though we are not able to comprehend them (cf. Amos 3:7). The fact that the future is as certain as if it were past is consolation to the suffering saints.

b. The Little Scroll (*Book*) (10:8-11)

⁸ Then the voice which I had heard from heaven spoke to me again, saying, "Go, take the scroll which is open in the hand of the angel who is standing on the sea and on the land." ⁹ So I went to the angel and told him to give me the little scroll; and he said to me, "Take it and eat; it will be bitter to your stomach, but sweet as honey in your mouth." ¹⁰ And I took the little scroll from the hand of the angel and ate it; it was sweet as honey in my mouth, but when I had eaten it my stomach was made bitter. ¹¹ And I was told, "You must again prophesy about many peoples and nations and tongues and kings."

vv. 8-9 This paragraph opens in a very vivid way for John, who thus far has merely recorded what he heard and saw, now becomes an actor in the drama. His part is to eat the *little scroll.* This idiomatic language is taken from Ezekiel 2:9 to 3:3. The taking of the little scroll represents the deliberate acceptance by the prophet of the commission to which he was called. As the scroll in chapter 5 represents the whole counsel of God, as it was made effective by Christ, so the little scroll represents that part which is made effective through the witness of the church. The eating of the scroll indicates the necessity of personally assimilating his message, of making his message a part of himself, as prerequisite to its delivery. The message was to become so much a part of the man that it would be impossible to separate the prophet from his prophecy.

v. 10 John's commission was much to his liking, and he became personally involved in presenting it to the people. However, he soon found that the *sweet* message in his mouth became *bitter* after he had eaten it. The mercies and judgments of God are included in the same message. The message is a two-edged sword (1:16). It is a message of the uncompromising sovereignty of God in Jesus Christ. To be admitted to the knowledge of the purpose of God in redemption is sweet (Jer. 15:16), but it is bitter to carry to men a message of judgment. "Every revelation of God's purposes, even though a mere fragment, a *biblaridion*, is 'bitter-sweet' disclosing judgments as well as mercy" (Swete). Also it is "bitter-sweet" to learn that the cross must be borne before the crown can be worn.

v. 11 There will be much more to disclose which will not concern his people alone, but in which their fate will be involved. This fourfold enumeration means the whole of mankind (cf. 5:9).

c. The Measuring of the Temple and the Two Witnesses (11:1-14)

The first part of this chapter continues the interlude between the sixth and seventh trumpets. It is easily divided into two sections, the former describes the measuring of the temple (11:1-2), and the latter gives an account of the appearance and murder of two witnesses (11:3-14). These two sections show that nothing can violate the dwelling place of God and that nothing can destroy his witnesses until their testimony is complete. John uses these two events by employing biblical persons, objects, and incidents for the purpose of conveying spiritual truths applicable to all times. He sets forth in symbolic language truth that is eternal.

(a) The Measuring of the Temple (11:1-2)

¹ Then I was given a measuring rod like a staff, and I was told: "Rise and measure the temple of God and the altar and those who worship there, ² but do not measure the court outside the temple; leave that out, for it is given over to the nations, and they will trample over the holy city for forty-two months.

v. 1 The *temple* referred to is not the Jewish Temple; it had been destroyed some twenty-five years before. The *temple* is a symbol of the church, called by Paul "God's temple" (1 Cor. 3:16), "a holy temple" (Eph. 2:21), "the temple of the living God" (2 Cor. 6:16), "the household of God" (1 Tim. 3:15), and "a dwelling place of God" (Eph. 2:22). The *temple* (*naos* i.e., sanctuary) is the dwelling place of God, the place in which he is worshiped, the true believers, or the faithful church. The measuring of the temple of God is an apocalyptic literary technique for marking out or distinguishing the true church, the faithful Christians from those by whom they are surrounded. The measuring implies preservation (Charles). The basis of the vision is in Ezekiel 40—43 and Zechariah 2:1-5 (cf. 20:15 f.). It is like the sealing of the faithful in 7:1-8. The temple, altar, and worshipers, everything necessary to the worship, are measured. This measuring is continually going on. When everything else falls into the hands of the enemy, these are spared. It means that the true church will be protected, preserved inviolable and intact, during persecution and in the judgments of God. It assures the true church of safety. God will protect and preserve his people in their trials and troubles.

v. 2 John is told not to *measure* the *court outside the temple.* Those who are in the Court of the Gentiles, that is to say, those who are not of the true Israel, do not have God's protection. The outer court is to be left out, symbolizing the part of the professing church that is still "of the world." In this symbolical picture, John points to a struggle between genuine Christianity and worldly professing religion. "The outer court may be destroyed, but the inner shrine is indestructible" (Calkins). The outer court is grouped with the nations and those who *trample over the holy city for forty-two months*. The true church is trampled but not destroyed. The *holy city*, that is, Jerusalem (Neh. 11:1,18; Isa. 48:2; 52:1; Dan. 9:24; Matt. 4:5; 27:53) is now pointed to its heavenly counterpart, that is, the "New Jerusalem" (21:2,10). Those who trample the outer courts, who are only nominal Christians, are omitted from the measurement and from the protection which the measurement symbolized. World power is allowed to prevail in parts of the professing church and to persecute the "holy city." However, the true church, the inner court, is secure and victorious, even in persecution, over the world. It is placed in antithesis to the outer court, faithless portion of the church, which is given over to the Gentiles, the type of all that is worldly.

The terrible persecution of the Jews by the King of Syria, Antiochus IV Epiphanes, lasted for approximately three and one half years. During this period an image of the Greek god Zeus was situated on the altar in the Temple. The Temple was forsaken by the faithful Jews. Daniel calls these actions by Epiphanes "the abomination that maketh desolate," or some such expression (Dan. 9:27; 11:31; 12:11). References to the length of this period are found in Daniel 7:25; 12:7. In apocalyptic literature, this period became a conventional stereotyped expression to indicate an indefinite period of evil, bitter persecution, hardships, uncertainty, restlessness, turmoil, or unrestrained wickedness, regardless of its actual calendar duration. Sometimes the interval of time is computed by months (11:2; 13:5), or days (11:3; 12:6), or years (12:14).

These numbers are used as symbolical of limitation and incompleteness. The enigmatic three and one half is one half of the perfect number seven. The period is indefinite, but it will come to an end. In Revelation, all of these terms refer to the same period of time. The duration of the prophesying is to correspond with the duration of the trampling under foot. John is told that the Gentiles, the unregenerate, the unbelievers were to *trample over* the court outside for an indefinite period. This period covers the entire duration of the church's history on earth. John expresses his confidence that throughout the course of the history of the church, the believing community will be supernaturally protected. In this march of progress, the church itself will suffer through unfaithfulness and worldliness, but the true church will be kept safe.

(b) The Power and Authority of the Two Witnesses (11:3-6)

³ And I will grant my two witnesses power to prophesy for one thousand two hundred and sixty days, clothed in sackcloth."
⁴ These are the two olive trees and the two lampstands which stand before the Lord of the earth. ⁵ And if any one would harm them, fire pours from their mouth and consumes their foes; if any one would harm them, thus he is doomed to die. ⁶ They have power to shut the sky, that no rain may fall during the days of their prophesying, and they have power over the waters to turn them into blood, and to smite the earth with every plague, as often as they desire.

v. 3 The position of the true church is not one of idle security. Christ must be proclaimed. The task of the church is to publish the gospel even in the face of calamity. The number "two" in apocalyptic symbolism signified strength. The Jewish law required that there should be two witnesses on a trial (Num. 35:30; Deut. 17:6; 19:15; cf. Matt. 18:16; John 5:30-33). Two witnesses were deemed competent and confirmatory. The *two witnesses* are patterned after the biblical pictures of Moses and Elijah, on account of the conspicuous witness they have and the hardships they suffered, as well as their persecution and vindication. The Jews expected Moses (Deut. 18:15) and Elijah (Mal. 4:5) to reappear before the End time. Jesus interpreted Elijah's return as fulfilled by John the Baptist (Matt. 17:9-13; Mark 9:9-13). The time of their witness coincides with the time of the persecution mentioned in the preceding verse. The number and variety of interpretations that have been given to the *two witnesses* are bewildering. However, in the light of John's use of the Old Testament and apocalyptic literature, it seems that these two competent, confirmatory witnesses symbolize the true church (Luke 24:48; John 15:27; Acts 1:8). They refer to the missionary activity of the whole church. The church is called to bear its testimony during the *one thousand two hundred and sixty days.* These two witnesses are to prophesy, that is, to proclaim God's message of salvation and judgment. The witnesses would prophesy in the midst of grief, that is, while being trampled over by the world (Matt. 5:4). In heaven the witnesses wear white robes (3:5; 6:11; 7:9) but on earth they wear sackcloth (Swete).

v. 4 The symbolism for this verse comes from Zechariah 4:2-14. In Zechariah, the account says that the prophet had a vision of two olive trees standing one on each side of the golden lampstand of the temple to supply it with a perpetual stream of oil (1:20). He was told that they were the anointed ones that stand before God. In Zechariah the trees symbolize Joshua and Zerubbabel, the anointed religious and civil leaders. This vision was intended to encourage the weak and restored exiles in their work of rebuilding the temple. They were shown that there is divine strength, like a stream of oil which would make them victorious over all their enemies. John uses the same theme by reminding the church that the two witnesses were channels through which divine strength flowed to the people. He calls the "two witnesses" *two olive trees* because they *stand before the Lord of the earth,* "the true position of every prophet of God," firm as pillars of truth, safe under divine protection, supplying continually the stream of spiritual knowledge and power to sustain and invigorate the church. This is a symbolic representation of the truth that God's strength is available to the church when it relies, not on might or power but on God's Spirit (Zech. 4:6).

v. 5 The experience of Jeremiah supplies the background for this verse. As the fire of judgment proceeded from the mouth of Jeremiah devouring God's enemies (Jer. 5:14), so the proclamation by the two witnesses (i.e., the church) will result in the destruction of such enemies. There also may be here a reference to the act of Elijah (2 Kings 1:10). It is the fire of their witness which refines and purifies and convinces some; it is also the fire of judgment which follows those who reject their testimony.

God has given to his witnesses power to execute judgment on the earth, not only to bring about a particular course of events, but also to show the principle by which he deals with men. There is power committed to his witnesses (Luke 10:19). The same power which supported the prophets supports them. God's witnesses are all under his peculiar protection, and the violence and cruelty of their enemies fall back upon themselves. Those who injure God's witnesses suffer for their folly. The protection does not exempt from persecution and even death. Yet, the faithfulness of the Lord assures his protection to those who trust in him.

v. 6 This verse continues and reinforces the truth presented in the preceding verse. The histories of Elijah and Moses supply the background. Like Elijah (1 Kings 17:1), the two witnesses can close the sky to prevent rain; like Moses (Ex. 7:20 ff.), they can turn water into blood and summon down every plague. In John's vision, the miracles mentioned were truths that people witnessed. People may not oppose or injure the two witnesses (that is the church, which has God's Spirit and power) without punishment. These witnesses wield a spiritual power which it is not safe to provoke. When God's message is proclaimed, its judgments are God's judgments (Matt. 16:19; 18:18 f.; John 20:21-23). Those who oppose the gospel witness will thereby be destroyed (2 Cor. 2:15-16).

(c) The Two Witnesses' Temporary Defeat but Ultimate Triumph (11:7-14)

⁷ And when they have finished their testimony, the beast that ascends from the bottomless pit will make war upon them and conquer them and kill them, ⁸ and their dead bodies will lie in the street of the great city which is allegorically called Sodom and Egypt, where their Lord was crucified. ⁹ For three days and a half men from the peoples and tribes and tongues and nations gaze at their dead bodies and refuse to let them be placed in a tomb, ¹⁰ and those who dwell on the earth will rejoice over them and make merry and exchange presents, because these two prophets had been a torment to those who dwell on the earth. ¹¹ But

after the three and a half days a breath of life from God entered them, and they stood up on their feet, and great fear fell on those who saw them. ¹² Then they heard a loud voice from heaven saying to them, "Come up hither!" And in the sight of their foes they went up to heaven in a cloud. ¹³ And at that hour there was a great earthquake, and a tenth of the city fell; seven thousand people were killed in the earthquake, and the rest were terrified and gave glory to the God of heaven.
¹⁴ The second woe has passed; behold, the third woe is soon to come.

v. 7 The sufferings of the two witnesses follow the pattern of Jesus' suffering (Matt. 10:24,25). When he had finished his work (John 17:4; 19:30), the power of evil seemed to prevail. Like Jesus (John 2:4; 7:6,8,30; 8:20), the two witnesses are secure, indestructible, and invincible until their work of bearing full witness for God is accomplished (Acts 20:27). The two witnesses are opposed by *the beast.* "The beast" was a stock figure in apocalyptic literature concerning the End time. The origin of the symbol comes from Daniel 7. John uses it as a symbolical representation of concentrated evil spiritual forces. It is satanic authority expressed in world power. In 1 and 2 John, this consummate opponent of Christ is called antichrist (see 6:2 above). This *beast* has a spirit of irreconcilable antagonism to Christ and the church. It had its origin in the abyss, the place of demons and the damned (cf. 9:1 ff.), and it has a permanent cast of character which shows that it is from beneath. John uses the present tense of the verb *ascends* or "comes up," thus giving the impression that rising from the abyss was a permanent attribute of the beast's character rather than a single episode in his career (Caird, p. 216). The beast vigorously opposed and conquered the two witnesses after they had preached the full message of the gospel. The death of the witnesses signifies the triumph of the antichristian power and the silencing of the testimony of the witnesses. However, the assault and victory on the witnesses by the beast gains a short-lived triumph. The intention of the vision is to convey the idea that the church in her witness for God will experience opposition from the power of Satan. The "beast" made war against Christ and for a time seemed to have

killed him. John's words "cover in effect all the martyrdoms and massacres of history in which brute force has seemed to triumph over truth and righteousness" (Swete).

v. 8 The fact that the two witnesses' one "dead body" lies in the street unburied and the world makes merry over its death demonstrates and emphasizes the scorn, contempt, and disgrace to which the church is subjected by world power. The Jews buried the body on the same day of death. The ***great city*** (16:19; 17:18; 18:10,16,18-19,21) is always the symbol of what is ungodly and of the world, and is always consigned to punishment. It symbolizes world power, and no particular earthly city is meant. It is characterized by acts of oppression and wrong toward God's people. It is a recurrent feature of human history. John plainly says that the nature of the city is spiritual, that is, symbolical. John identifies it in three ways. First, it is allegorically called Sodom. This name was proverbal in Hebrew writings for wickedness (Deut. 32:32; Isa. 1:9 f.; Ezek. 16:46,55). Second, it is allegorically called Egypt. This name was proverbial in Hebrew writings for oppression (Ex. 1—15; Ezek. 20:7; 23:8). Third, it is the place where Jesus was crucified (Matt. 27; Mark 15; Luke 23; John 19). The same spirit of slavery, wickedness, oppression, and murder which have characterized world power is alive to persecute the church.

v. 9 See 11:2-3 above for the ***three days and a half.*** This period represents "a short triumph in point of fact, but long enough to bear the semblance of being complete and final" (Swete). The fourfold enumeration symbolizes the worldwide distribution of the people who are representatives of all ungodly men. This is sufficient to demonstrate that the two witnesses are not two individuals. John emphasizes the indignity and dishonor shown toward the two witnesses by repeating the fact that they were denied decent burial. This describes symbolically, but graphically, the scorn and contempt to which the church is subjected by world power.

v. 10 In this verse, John continues to describe the reaction of the ungodly to the "death" of the two witnesses. The figures used indicate that the ungodly are filled with joy at the death and dishonor of the witnesses. The exchanging of gifts was a common practice during festal rejoicing (Esther 9:22; Neh. 8:10,12). The two witnesses tormented the ungodly by their testimony to the truth.

v. 11 See 11:2 above for *the three and a half days.* The background of this verse is the vision of dry bones in Ezekiel 37:1-10. As the witnesses are like Christ in his death, they are also like him in his triumph (Rom. 6:4-11; Eph. 2:1-10). "The resurrection here spoken of is properly a communication of spiritual power—a breath of life 'from God' to Christian testimony, so that after an interval of enforced silence, it becomes more outspoken and effective than ever" (Smith). There is a resurrection power in every rejected truth for the strength of truth is undying. Truth that seemed dead is found to be possessed of a new power and life. The church has sometimes "died," but it always rises again when *a breath of life from God* enters it. "Each such resurrection strikes consternation into the hearts of her oppressors" (Morris). The way of defeat for the church is most often the way of victory, and the more complete the defeat, the more full the triumph.

v. 12 The fate of the two witnesses is the same as Christ's. They are triumphantly vindicated and glorified (Rom. 8:17). Just as Christ put to shame all his enemies by rising again and afterwards ascending to heaven, so will the church's witnessing power, which the enemy thought was dead, revive again. The resurrection of the two witnesses is followed by their ascension. Their ascension is in full view of their enemies. By this symbolism, John wanted to show that "even their enemies recognized that it must have been divine power which brought it about. They were victorious; the truth of their message was vindicated as their enemies saw them rescued by God's power" (Summers).

In describing the fate of the church, John seems to have in mind the life of Christ. His witness, the opposition he encountered, his death for a brief time at the completion of his work, his resurrection and ascension, and triumph over the devil, are all here reproduced. John is saying that the same God who transformed Christ's death into life can transform the church's defeat into victory. The church wins through the power of Christ.

v. 13 The hour of victory for the two witnesses is the hour of judgment for the city where they were slain. "In the Apocalyptic symbolism the earthquake indicates the breaking up of some settled order, by sudden providential visitation. Here it indicates such a visitation, in the shattering of great antichristian power" (Smith). The *tenth* and the *seven thousand* are but tokens of the judgment which is to follow. The symbolical meaning of these numbers is *quality* rather than *quantity*. In the Bible, the tenth part invaribly signifies the tithe—the portion due from the community to God or the ruler (Gen. 28:22; Lev. 27:32; Num. 18:21; 1 Sam. 8:15,17). It seems that God was now exacting his due that men who had refused to recognize what was due from them to God were now forced to recognize his sovereignty by the exaction for punishment of a tithe, and as an evidence that all are under his sway. The *seven thousand* indicates that God's judgment overtakes all, and that his judgment is complete, and that none escape.

v. 14 A voice now announces that since two of the "woes" have passed *the third woe is soon to come.* The third "woe" is the trumpet which ushers in the finishing of the mystery of God. It pictures the Redeemer's triumphant reign. This victorious reign implies the overthrow and the passing away of all that which opposes Christ. It is a "woe" involving the defeat and overthrow of all that resist the Messiah's reign.

(11) The Seventh Trumpet: Announcement of the Reign of God (11:15-19)

a. Loud Voices in Heaven (11:15)

¹⁵ Then the seventh angel blew his trumpet, and there were loud voices in heaven, saying, "The kingdom of the world has become the kingdom of our Lord and of his Christ, and he shall reign for ever and ever."

v. 15 The opening of the seventh seal was followed by silence in heaven (8:1). The sounding of the seventh trumpet was accompanied by voices *in heaven.* However, there is silence as to the fate of the wicked, with whom the trumpet visions have been chiefly concerned. In the revelation, the fate of the church as well as the doom awarded to the ungodly always stop short of describing circumstances after death. This was not John's purpose.

When the seventh trumpet sounded, instead of evoking judgment there is heard a chorus of heavenly voices praising God. The unidentified voices proclaim the replacement of the *kingdom* of the world by that of our Lord. The true reading of the text is "kingdom," not "kingdoms." This expresses more clearly the unity of dominion. It is not that a new ruler takes possession of vacant thrones, but all that was once divided is united into one. The kingdoms of the world, as political powers, are not what the reign of God contemplates. The reign of God contemplates the world itself, as a whole. The literal rendering of the Greek text should be, "The kingdom of the world became of our Lord's possession." John uses the past tense because the event is certain. He sees it as having occurred. The reign will not be temporary but will remain *for ever and ever.* In the New Testament, "the kingdom of Christ and the Kingdom of God must be seen as one kingdom" (Stagg, *New Testament Theology,* p. 165). In this verse, John is reaffirming the great eternal reign of God in Christ, the rule of God in the hearts of men. Jesus *proclaimed, realized,* and *offered* this realm to men. With God the Father is associated Christ, by whose means the overthrow of evil is effected, and by whom his witnesses overcome.

b. The Song of the Twenty-four Elders (11:16-18)

[16] And the twenty-four elders who sit on their thrones before God fell on their faces and worshiped God, [17] saying,
"We give thanks to thee, Lord God Almighty, who art and who wast, that thou hast taken thy great power and begun to reign. [18] The nations raged, but thy wrath came, and the time for the dead to be judged,

for rewarding thy servants, the prophets and saints, and those who fear thy name, both small and great, and for destroying the destroyers of the earth."

v. 16 See 4:4 for a discussion of the twenty-four elders. The ascription of praise by the twenty-four elders, representing the church, is given to God because of his reward to his witnesses and his judgment upon the ungodly. The fact that the elders *sit on their thrones* indicates that the church is now participating in the reign of God.

v. 17 The twenty-four elders are peculiarly indebted to God, since the establishment of his kingdom is the victory of the church. *Who art and who wast,*—(not, art to come)—The future is purposely omitted, since God's "coming" is now an accomplished fact. ***Begun to reign*** should be translated "did reign": God never ceased to reign, he never descends from his throne, though for a time he reigns through Jesus Christ. This power is God's power, and the elders thank him for it, for it is the assurance of the victory of the church.

The practical aim of the writer is to assure and encourage the persecuted Christian communities to believe that in Christ God retains the control of history and will work out the divine plan in history. It is also to warn lukewarm Christians that Christ will tolerate no allegiance to any other sovereignty than his own sovereignty over the lives of God's people.

v. 18 *For destroying the destroyers of the earth.* The wicked destroy the earth by corrupting it, which is the force of the verb. The general tone of the song of the twenty-four elders resembles the second Psalm, in which the triumph of the Lord and his Christ over the heathen is told.

c. God's Response—the Open Temple and the Ark (11:19)

¹⁹ Then God's temple in heaven was opened, and the ark of his covenant was seen within his temple; and there were flashes of lightning, loud noises, peals of thunder, an earthquake, and heavy hail.

v. 19 *God's temple* is God's dwelling place, the church (cf. 11:1-2). "Do you not know that you are God's temple and that God's Spirit dwells in you?" (1 Cor. 3:16).

The ark of his covenant. This idea seems to be introduced in order to render more emphatic the steadfastness and unchangableness of God. The ark was a symbol of God's abiding presence and continual help. He who now promises aid to his people, and threatens judgment upon the wicked, is the covenant God of Israel.

This ends the series of trumpet-visions. These visions, evoked by the cry for the vindication of righteousness in 6:10, have demonstrated the need for *patience* and *endurance* on the part of Christians, and have indicated the punishments meted out to the wicked. It also indicates the final triumph of the faithful. The entire scene represents an accomplished victory.

4. The War Between the Woman (Church) and the Dragon (Satan) (12:1 to 14:20)

In the previous chapters, John has proclaimed God's sovereignty over the world in Jesus Christ. He now portrays the manner in which this rule of God has been signally projected and how its projection precipitates the inevitable conflict with the power of the world. The Revelation gives no regularly progressive disclosure of the conflict between good and evil. The same method is followed in the Fourth Gospel, 1 John, and Revelation. In each one, the writer sets forth only a few ideas. He proceeds by way of interlocking spirals of material, dealing in much repetition, emphasizing his main points over and over (Blaney, pp. 451-52). Through chapter 11 in Revelation, each of the series of visions comes to the same general conclusion: toil and trouble end in rest, and conflict ends in victory. The development in Revelation from chapter 12 to the end is the account of the conflict between the sovereignty of God in Jesus Christ and the pretended sovereignty of Satan expressed through world power. The visions which now follow are somewhat different in character from those already related, inasmuch as the supernatural conflict is now described as between the powers of good and evil, heaven and hell, God and Satan rather than between the individual Christian and his oppressors. However, this spiritual strife with the forces of evil is carried on through the church. In chapter 12, John uses numerous parallels to the experiences of Israel escaping from Egypt.

(1) The Dragon Seeks to Destroy the Child (12:1-12)

a. The Woman, the Child, and the Dragon (12:1-6)

¹ And a great portent appeared in heaven, a woman clothed with the sun, with the moon under her feet, and on her head a crown of twelve stars; ² she was with child and she cried out in her pangs of birth, in anguish for delivery. ³ And another portent appeared in heaven; behold a great red dragon, with seven heads and ten horns, and seven diadems upon his head. ⁴ His tail swept down a third of the stars of heaven, and cast them to the earth. And the dragon stood before the woman who was about to bear a child, that he might devour her child when she brought it forth; ⁵ she brought forth a male child, one who is to rule all the nations with a rod of iron, but her child was caught up to God and to his throne, ⁶ and the woman fled into the wilderness, where she has a place prepared by God, in which to be nourished for one thousand two hundred and sixty days.

v. 1 For the first time John describes what is seen as a *portent*, or "sign" (12:3; 15). The word "appeared" is a translation of a Greek word (*ōphthē*) which is used in the Septuagint in a technical way to describe an objectively real yet spiritual manifestation. John says this truth is revealed or manifested to him by God. He says what was seen was *in heaven*. It would probably be better to translate "in the sky" (Swete). No difficulty needs to be felt when the child is caught up to heaven as though from earth, or when the woman flees "into the wilderness." The action he describes takes place on earth, but he sees the actors in the sky first of all. The *woman*, like all of John's other symbols, belongs to the realm of vision. In the Old Testament, Israel is spoken of as daughter of Zion (Isa. 52:2), virgin (Isa. 47:1 ff. cf. Ezek. 16:7), married (Isa. 62:4-5; Jer. 2:2), mother (Isa. 54:1 ff.) and widow (Isa. 54:4; Lam. 1:1).

The **woman** symbolizes the messianic community, true Israel, the ideal church whose singular beauty, charm, splendor, vitality, and glory are described with unimaginable splendor. She is no earthly being but a celestial being. The sun, moon, and stars that adorn her indicate her status. She is clothed in light from head to foot. The sun, moon, and stars are emblems of light. The church represents light in its constant warfare with darkness. The twelve stars on her crown represent the glory of the complete family of God among men. In the New Testament, the church is viewed in its ancestry, environment, and antecedents as continuous with God's chosen community before Christ (Isa. 54:1-3; 66:7-9; Acts 7:38; Gal. 4:26). The church is a new creation, yet in a sense it is reconstituted Israel. In a true sense, it is the fulfillment of Judaism. Abraham, Isaac, and Jacob sit together with Peter, James, and John, as well as with people "from east and west" (Matt. 8:11). The New Testament insists upon continuity as well as discontinuity with Israel (Stagg, *New Testament Theology*, pp. 171,205).

v. 2 The woman, about to give birth to a child, cries out in her birth pangs. The symbolism of Israel as a travailing mother is found several times in the Old Testament (Isa. 26:17-18; 37:3; 54:1,5-6; 66:7-9; Jer. 4:31; Mic. 4:9-10; 5:3). The true Israel is said to bring forth the Messiah because Christ came to the earth as the Son of the Jewish church (Rom. 9:5). John was also stating the law of life for the church. The church must bring forth Christ to the world and this cannot be done without knowing suffering (Carpenter).

v. 3 Apparently at the time when the child was about to be born, John saw another *portent* in the sky. There appeared a red dragon with seven heads and ten horns with seven diadems upon his heads. In apocalyptic literature the portrayal of an evil force as a crocodile, serpent, or dragon, sometime with more than one head, was widespread (Rist and Hough, *The Revelation of St. John the Divine,* p. 453). In the Old Testament, Jeremiah compared Nebuchadnezzar to a dragon which had gulped down Jerusalem

(Jer. 51:34). Ezekiel (29:3) pictured Pharaoh as a great dragon lying in the midst of his streams (Caird, *The Revelation of St. John the Divine*, p. 150). The dragon is identified in 12:9. He is described as **red** because he is a murderer and destroyer. The seven heads symbolize complete wisdom and cunning for the execution of his plans. A horn in apocalyptic literature symbolized strength, so the ten horns symbolized complete human power (cf. 7:7,24). The seven diadems on his head are a sign of his dominion over the empire of evil. This dragon is a composite creature of malevolent spiritual powers arrayed against God made up of special aspects of various earlier models to represent Satan (Rist and Hough, *The Revelation of St. John the Divine*, p. 454). These aspects signify his destructive powers and his sovereignty over the world. All the forces of evil are represented in this dragon (Dana, *The Epistles and Apocalypse of John*, p. 133).

v. 4 John's object in the first part of this verse is to emphasize the size and strength of the dragon. So immense is his size that with his mammoth tail, furiously lashing against the sky he sweeps away and casts one third of the stars to the earth. The *third* denotes a considerable part, a significant minority (8:7-12; 9:15,18; cf. Zech. 13:8-9). The dragon's primary interest is in devouring the child, the preexistent Messiah, when he is born. The people of God are confronted by the epitome of evil at the crucial point of man's redemption, the incarnation of Christ. "This is one of John's most vivid pictures of the age-old conflict between good and evil" (Blaney).

v. 5 In this verse John tells the whole story of the incarnation and its fruits in language that is strong and figurative. In this vision he sums up the entire earthly ministry of Jesus, his crucifixion, resurrection, and ascension because his purpose here is to show that the dragon's power and craft are futile. John indicates at once the absolute immunity of Christ from any harm proceeding from the power of the devil. The words **rod of iron** are taken from the description of the Messiah's rule in Psalm 2:9. The child was destined for world dominion. Satan desired to devour the Child because he regarded the nations as his legitimate prey. Satan was unable to destroy Christ while he was on earth. This symbolism stresses the truth that God in the incarnation has decisively defeated the devil. Jesus' death was the battlefield where God's power had met and overcome the demonic powers and had triumphed over them openly (Col. 2:15). With the incarnation completing itself with the ascension, spiritual evil has been completely defeated and dethroned (John 16:20-22,33). "The Messiah, so far from being destroyed, is caught up to a share in God's throne" (Beckwith).

v. 6 By a quick shift in symbolism, the woman in this verse becomes the personification of the Christian church. Since Satan could not destroy the Christ, he could still persecute the church. The *wilderness* symbolism here comes from the Exodus story (Lev. 16:7 ff.). To the Hebrews escaping from Pharaoh, the dragon in the midst of his streams (Ezek. 29:3), the wilderness was a condition of safety and liberation (Caird, *The Revelation of St. John the Divine,* p. 152). It also was a condition of divine provision and nourishment. In the wilderness, the woman was protected from the dragon just as surely as was her Son but in a different way. The woman's stay in the wilderness lasts *one thousand two hundred and sixty days.* This term is a stereotyped apocalyptical period for the domination of evil and persecution (11:3; 12:12). Like Israel, the church upon earth has been redeemed from bondage but has not yet arrived in the promised land. The church is still in the world, yet not a part of the world (John 17:15; 2 Cor. 6:17; 1 John 2:15). During this indefinite period of trial and persecution (the End time), God protects and provides for the church.

b. The Effect of the Incarnation (12:7-12)

[7] Now war arose in heaven, Michael and his angels fighting against the dragon; and the dragon and his angels fought, [8] but they were defeated and there was no longer any place for them in heaven. [9] And the great dragon was thrown down, that ancient serpent, who is called the Devil and Satan, the deceiver of the whole world—he was thrown

down to the earth, and his angels were thrown down with him. ¹⁰ And I heard a loud voice in heaven, saying, "Now the salvation and the power and the kingdom of our God and the authority of his Christ have come, for the accuser of our brethren has been thrown down, who accuses them day and night before our God. ¹¹ And they have conquered him by the blood of the Lamb and by the word of their testimony, for they loved not their lives even unto death. ¹² Rejoice then, O heaven and you that dwell therein! But woe to you, O earth and sea, for the devil has come down to you in great wrath, because he knows that his time is short!"

This paragraph is a parenthesis in order to account for the implacable hostility of Satan. Evil has an inveterate and apparently an unyielding hostility to good (Eph. 6:12).

In all the realism of apocalyptic method, John pictures a "war" in heaven between Michael and his angels and the dragon and his angels. It will be observed that the "war" here depicted took place after the ascension of Christ. Therefore, this passage does not teach that a battle was waged in heaven before the creation. This idea, which is found in Milton's *Paradise Lost*, Book VI, was taken from old legends in the Middle Ages. There is nothing in the Bible which deals with such a premundane "battle." Such an idea is a perversion rather than an interpretation of the Scriptures. The story of the origin of evil is never related in the Bible. Its presence is assumed. The name "Michael" (who is like unto God?) is the name for a figure which is prominent in apocalyptic literature but is mentioned only twice in the New Testament (12:7; Jude 9). In Daniel 12:1 he is represented as the champion of the Jewish people. In Daniel 10:5-6 he denotes a chief among the angels appointed to watch over and minister to the chosen people. In Daniel 10:13,21 he is represented as the guardian angel of Israel and he fights for her against the guardian angels of other nations (Rist and Hough, *The Revelation of St. John the Divine*, p. 456) In *The War of the Sons of Light and the Sons of Darkness, XVLL* (as found in *The Dead Sea Scriptures*, translated by Theodor Gaster Garden City, N.Y.: Doubleday and Co., 1956), Michael is said to be used by God to aid the redeemed (Laymon, p. 98). In Jewish tradition, Michael is universally recognized as the guardian angel of God's chosen people. Christian thought assigned that place and function to Jesus Christ and to him alone. John here uses "Michael" as a representative of Christ, who appears himself as the leader of his armies in 19:11.

v. 7-8 In this symbolism, John relates the incarnation and its consequences. This is why it is **Michael** and not Christ who is the leader in the war. Everything in heaven is the counterpart of some earthly reality. "Michael's" victory is the heavenly counterpart of the earthly reality of the incarnation. The outcome of the struggle between good and evil is not determined on earth, it has already been settled in heaven. Satan's defeat in heaven assures the victory of the church on earth. The incarnation had a cosmic significance for good (Caird, *The Revelation of St. John the Divine*, p. 153).

As Jesus was approaching the cross and anticipating his victory, he said, "Now is the judgment of this world, now shall the ruler of this world be cast out" (John 12:31). When the seventy disciples reported the success of their preaching mission, Jesus said, "I saw Satan fall like lightening from heaven" (Luke 10:18). In the same kind of language, John says that the incarnation was the staggering blow to Satan's kingdom.

The dragon and his army were routed, and he and his angels were expelled from their former celestial place. This casting down of Satan by no means effects his destruction. His appearance upon the earthly scene is the signal for the continuation of the struggle in the earth. He finds on earth a new stage on which to carry on the conflict against God and all good. Woe comes upon the earth because it is the battlefield, and the wrath of the devil is multiplied because he knows that he has but a short time. God's mighty act in bringing to birth the Messiah is the great and final challenge to the dominion of Satan. The conflict that is set in motion does not involve earth alone; it is cosmic in its extent. The incarnation is a cosmic event. The defeat of evil forces was so complete that "there was no longer any place for them in heaven." In apocalyptic language, this emphasizes complete defeat or frustration. Babylon's defeat is represented in Isaiah 14 as a fall from heaven.

v. 9 The dragon is now identified. He is called *serpent* because he deceives the world of men (Gen. 3:1). He is called ***Devil*** because he accuses and calumniates (devil means "slanderer"). He is called ***Satan*** because he is the great adversary of mankind (Satan means "adversary" or "accuser"). The beginning of the end for the dragon was when he was thrown down (Luke 10:18; John 12:31). The results of this victory are decisive but not final. The dragon is entrenched throughout the whole of human life, and the whole world is deceived by him (1 John 4:1). Satan seeks to injure mankind by slander, open hostility, and by deception (Wernecke, p. 106).

v. 10 In this verse some unidentified heavenly voice celebrates the victory of God over Satan. This doxology is an exclamation of triumph. The heavenly inhabitants recognize the victory of God in the incarnation.

v. 11 John here tells how the accused ones overcome the dragon (John 16:33). They win the victory over him because of ***the blood of the Lamb and by the word of their testimony,*** and because ***they loved not their lives even unto death.*** This victory is the result of the overcoming and victorious life. They value not their lives in this world, even to the extent of meeting death for the sake of giving their testimony of God's victory in Christ (John 12:25).

v. 12 Because the dragon was thrown down (12:9), those in heaven enjoy absolute immunity from all harm which he can work. This does not mean that the place of Satan's warfare is changed, but, as in the vision, his overthrow is represented by his being cast down from heaven. The inhabitants of heaven are completely free from sin and evil. The rage with which Satan endeavors to make up for his defeat is represented by his coming down in wrath unto the inhabitants of earth. "The earth was no new sphere of Satan's working" (Swete). Christ casts Satan from his throne for those who faithfully trust and follow him. Christ's birth and rapture meant the downfall of Satan, and every Christian victory confirms it. Satan is defeated and disbarred, but he still has power to do much harm. His power is not annihilated but is stimulated by defeat. Evil never accepts defeat without a struggle.

In this symbolism, John shows the persistent hostility between Satan and the people of God. He is still permitted to inflict great sufferings on the servants of Christ, but these activities are the final convulsions of a conquered foe (Glasson).

(2) The Dragon Persecutes the Woman Who Brought Forth the Child (12:13-16)

¹³ And when the dragon saw that he had been thrown down to the earth, he pursued the woman who had borne the male child. ¹⁴ But the woman was given the two wings of the great eagle that she might fly from the serpent into the wilderness, to the place where she is to be nourished for a time, and times, and half a time. ¹⁵ The serpent poured water like a river out of his mouth after the woman, to sweep her away with the flood. ¹⁶ But the earth came to the help of the woman, and the earth opened its mouth and swallowed the river which the dragon has poured from his mouth.

v. 13 When God defeated Satan with the incarnation, Satan continued his attack upon the woman, the church. In the same way that Pharaoh pursued the escaping Hebrews (Ex. 14:8), the dragon pursues the woman.

v. 14 The woman is providentially saved from the dragon. The *two wings of the great eagle* seem to refer to the "eagle's wings" on which God bore his people through the wilderness (Ex. 19:4; cf. Deut. 32:11; Isa. 40:31). The woman, like Israel in the wilderness, is tried, instructed, protected, and nourished with food from heaven (Deut. 32:10-11) for *a time, and times, and half a time.* This symbolizes all of End time.

v. 15-16 The onset of enemies is represented in Scripture as a flood of waters (Ps. 124:4-5; Jer. 47:2). The persecution of the woman by the dragon is thus symbolized. The symbolism may also come from the Exodus experience, because the Hebrews were in danger from water when they escaped from Egypt (Ex. 14:1 ff.). The earth is said to help and swallow up the waters of persecution. All the resources of earth and heaven are at God's command. The providences of the world are on the side of the church. The stars in their courses fought against Sisera (Judg. 5:20), which probably refers to the storm that helped Israel win the battle. Here, John says, the earth put forth her helping hand to save the church. This picture well illustrates the spiritual security of the church against all that Satan can do in his attempts to destroy her. The God of the church is the God of nature, and the God of providence; and he can command them in any situation that may arise. Often he uses worldly powers to overthrow the persecutor and thus save the church (cf. Isa. 44:28; 45:1). The stream from the serpent's mouth may symbolize destructive teaching and malicious accusation (Caird, *The Revelation of St. John the Divine*, p. 159).

(3) The Dragon Persecutes the Rest of the Woman's Offspring (12:17)

¹⁷ Then the dragon was angry with the woman, and went off to make war on the rest of her offspring, on those who keep the commandments of God and bear testimony to Jesus. And he stood on the sand of the sea.

v. 17 The dragon, the woman not being vulnerable to his attacks, proceeds to vent his rage on the remainder of her offspring.

The dragon failed to prevent the mission of the child (Jesus Christ). He failed in his attempts to overwhelm the woman (church). He now proceeds to attack the rest of the woman's offspring (individual members of the church). The *war* here refers to persecutions against all individuals of the church who **keep the commandments of God and bear testimony to Jesus.** The methods by which he endeavors to *make war* on the members are related in the following chapters. For this warfare the dragon takes his position at the side of the sea to summon and direct his subordinates. These subordinates symbolize the resource of evil which are brought to bear upon the members of the church. They are Satan's agents on earth to carry on his warfare against the church. It is the same war, but it is regarded from a different point of view.

(4) *The Beast Out of the Sea (13:1-10)*

¹ And I saw a beast rising out of the sea, with ten horns and seven heads, with ten diadems upon its horns and a blasphemous name upon its heads. ² And the beast that I saw was like a leopard, its feet were like a bear's, and its mouth was like a lion's mouth. And to it the dragon gave his power and his throne and great authority. ³ One of its heads seemed to have a mortal wound, but its moral wound was healed, and the whole earth followed the beast with wonder. ⁴ Men worshiped the dragon, for he had given his authority to the beast, and they worshiped the beast, saying, "Who is like the beast, and who can fight against it?"
⁵ And the beast was given a mouth uttering haughty and blasphemous words, and it was allowed to exercise authority for forty-two months; ⁶ it opened its mouth to utter blasphemies against God, blaspheming his name and his dwelling, that is, those who dwell in heaven. ⁷ Also it was allowed to make war on the saints and to conquer them. And authority was given it over every tribe and people and tongue and nation, ⁸ and all who dwell on earth will worship it, every one whose name has not been written before the foundation of the world in the book of life of the Lamb that was slain. ⁹ If any one has an ear, let him hear:
¹⁰ If any one is to be taken captive,
   to captivity he goes;
if any one slays with the sword,
   with the sword must he be slain.
Here is a call for the endurance and faith of the saints.

v. 1 The prophet *saw a beast rising* (present tense) *out of the sea.* The word in the original language for *beast* denotes a fierce, untamed animal of the lower type of being. It implies the predominance of the beast nature. The background of this image is Daniel 7:2-7. The portrayal of demonic powers as beasts was widely used in Jewish apocalyptic writings. The *sea* from which the *beast* comes represents the confused, unstable, disorderly, and rebellious multitudes of the nations, from which rise the enemies of the church. In the Old Testament, the sea is often used to describe a restless nation of people (Ps. 65:7; Isa. 60:5; Jer. 51:42; Dan. 7:2). The sea was often associated with evil in apocalyptic writings. The **seven heads** symbolize universal or complete dominion. The **ten horns** symbolize complete worldly or human power. This beast is an emissary of the dragon and is the concentration of all powers of evil. The dragon has seven heads and ten horns (12:3), as has this beast. This indicates that the beast and Satan are one in nature and function. This beast, this worldly personification of evil, is an embodiment of the dragon. The **ten diadems** are symbols of sovereignty (12:3). The **blasphemous name** [or names?] **upon its heads** refers to the divine honor claimed for itself by the beast. The details of the beast are intended to convey certain ideas and are not intended to describe an actual bodily form.

John does not identify this beast out of the sea. Through the centuries many attempts have been made to identify it. In the light of John's apocalyptic method, it seems that he intended this beast to represent world power. It is the aggregation of powers expressing themselves in opposition to God in Christ. It is an all inclusive term for all those who are in the kingdom of darkness. It is sinful human society estranged from God, organized in hostility to the will of God; but it is also the embodiment of a sad and perilous order of life belonging to the evil age which has in principle been brought to an end by the coming of Christ and is now doomed and is in the process of passing away (1 John 2:17). It is human society under the dominion of the evil one (1 John 5:19; C. H. Dodd, *Johannine Epistles*, p. xxxvii). Satan holds sway over this sinful human society as "the ruler of this world," (John 12:31; 14:30; 16:11). It is his sphere of influence. He also is "the prince of the power of the air" (Eph. 2:2). This "world is in the power of the evil one" (1 John 5:19). Of course, when John wrote, this beast was personified in the Roman Empire. However, he saw that the issue was much larger. Rome was only one in the successive forms of the same God-defying world power.

This same world power had previously expressed itself against

God through Egypt, Assyria, Babylon, Persia, Greece, Syria, and others.

v. 2 In Daniel's vision (7:2-7) he saw four beasts (same Greek word in LXX) come out of an agitated sea. In this verse, John combines and blends the terrifying characteristics of the beasts in the book of Daniel. The qualities that are indicated by the animals' names are very generally agreed upon. The composite beast has the ferocious swiftness of the leopard, the voracity of the bear, and the strength and courage of the lion. He is a vicious antagonist. John's interest is in symbolism. The beast has the same characteristics as the dragon. The dragon is represented as giving the beast his power and his throne. Worship is given solely on the ground of brute force. The dragon is Satan, who works through his instrument, the beast. Satan makes war against the church through this great world power.

v. 3 In this verse, John states that the beast possessed two mutally antagonistic qualities. One of his heads had received a mortal wound, and yet he continued to live and exert his power. The statement that the beast's **_mortal wound was healed_** is a parody of the death and resurrection of Christ (1:18; 5:6). When Christ was victorious over death, he gave the signal defeat of world power. However, the death-stroke is apparently healed. World power continues to exist in spite of its fatal wound. If its dominion is overthrown, contrary to all expectations, it rises again. Given a deathblow, it lives on under new forms and new names. It seems as strong or even stronger than ever in its attacks upon the church. However, these attacks are only the efforts of one who has received his death-stroke. These attacks are signs not of continuing life but of approaching death (17:11). John says that "the whole earth wondered after the beast." World power is always adored where worldliness prevails, and it is always able to command the homage of that worldly spirit to which in so many ways it makes appeal (Smith). World power is very persuasive and threatening. It is convincing and at times very attractive.

v. 4 John saw the people of the world worshiping the dragon because the satanic power of the dragon is incarnate in the beast. Because they worship the dragon, they also worship the beast to whom the dragon gives authority. They pay the homage to Satan which Christ refused to pay (Matt. 4:8-10). They wonder after and worship him who pretends to bestow upon them all the kingdoms of the world and the glory of them. They worship brute force more than moral strength. They are convinced that the dragon will succeed in the war with the Lamb (ch. 14). ***Who is like the beast*** is a parody of the word "Michael," which means, "Who is like God?" This indicates that the worship of world power was a substitute for true worship, belonging to him whom Michael represents. The people of the world are convinced of the futility of resisting the absolute and uncontrollable power and the overwhelming influence of the invincible beast.

vv. 5-6 The verb *was given* is repeated often in these verses. This shows that the true and ultimate source of all power is God, without whose permission the dragon and the beast combined are powerless. It is God who determines the limits within which they operate. They have no power beyond what is given. The power represented by the beast is blasphemous in its claims and pretensions. It is blasphemous because the beast attempts to do or to say things which only God can do or say. The "haughty and blasphemous words" are the promises of superior power and good with which Satan seeks to allure men. This power is given to the beast *for forty-two months.* This is the conventional limit of the time of the power of evil and represents the End time between the two Parousias (Rissi, p. 40). There is to be an end to the sway of evil, and that end is fixed (Calkins). Everything that is held sacred by the church is blasphemed by the beast; God, his name, and his tabernacle, that is, his people.

v. 7 The first part of this verse is lacking in some Greek manuscripts, but it probably should be included. The saints will not escape the wrath of the beast if they fail to worship him. John again stresses the beast's subordinate position. He can function only by divine permission (Morris).

The beast is allowed to defeat the church in the same way he overcame Christ. The beast so far succeeds that the saints must suffer or submit (Carpenter). The beast killed Christ, but out of his death came victory (cf. 2:10). The fourfold enumeration applied to the earth denotes the universal character of the description (cf. 4:6; 5:9; 7:9; 11:9; 14:6). Although the authority of the beast extends to every nation of the earth, yet men are not delivered irrevocably into its power. From every part of mankind, men are also redeemed.

v. 8 All humanity is divided into two groups. The beast wins all except those whose names have been written in the *book of life* of the Lamb slain from the foundation of the world. The phrase "from the foundation of the world" can be taken grammatically with "written" or with "slain." It seems best to take it with slain (John 17:24; 1 Pet. 1:19-20). If this is John's meaning, he is saying that the self-giving of God incarnate on the cross is but an outward expression of what has always been true of his fatherly heart (Eph. 1:4). Self-sacrificing love is not new but is an eternal principle in God. It is in the original scheme of the universe. Charles writes, "The conquest of sin is only to be achieved through self-sacrifice. Nothing but the self-sacrifice of holy love can overcome the principle of selfishness and sin that dominates the world" (*The Revelation of St. John*). In the Old Testament and in apocalyptic literature, the *book* of life is a heavenly book in which the names of the righteous are inscribed (Ps. 139:16; Luke 10:20; Phil. 4:3; Heb. 12:23; 1 Enoch 104:1; 1 Clem. 45:8). It is referred to five times in the Revelation (3:5; 13:8; 17:8; 20:12,15). The beast has no power over those who are true servants of God. Their eternal security is based on the eternal love of God, and their names have been written in God's permanent record.

v. 9 This last solemn appeal to attention so frequent in Revelation (2:7,11,17,29; 3:6,13,22; cf. Matt. 11:15) calls attention to the warning words of the next verse. If God allows the beast to wage war on his people and to conquer them, what must God's people do? (Caird, *The Revelation of St. John the Divine,* p. 169).

v. 10 There are textual problems in this verse. However, the best texts contain a prediction and a warning. The faithful can expect persecution and suffering. In their persecution and suffering the saints are not to defend themselves by the use of the sword. They must accept God's will submissively. The background of this verse seems to be Jeremiah 15:2 and 43:11. There also may be a reference to Jesus' statement recorded in Matthew 26:52. John affirms the principle upon which God's government of the world operates: sin must bring its reward of suffering and ultimate frustration. This is how God's wrath works out. Christian insight into history consists in holding on to this clue. All power belongs to God and he is still in control even when evil seems omnipotent (Preston and Hanson). It is impossible for the church to defeat the forces of world power with violence. The church is not to resist force with force. The killer is killed. Suffering patterned after the example of Jesus constitutes the very heart of the Christian vocation (1 Pet. 1:11; 2:21-23; 4:1,13; 5:1,10). The church is to stake its existence in the imitation of the Lamb. This course of action is proof of the endurance and faith of the saints.

(5) *The Beast Out of the Earth (13:11-18)*

[11] Then I saw another beast which rose out of the earth; it had two horns like a lamb and it spoke like a dragon. [12] It exercises all the authority of the first beast in its presence, and makes the earth and its inhabitants worship the first beast, whose mortal wound was healed. [13] It works great signs, even making fire come down from heaven to earth in the sight of men; [14] and by the signs which it is allowed to work in the presence of the beast, it deceives those who dwell on the earth, bidding them make an image for the beast which was wounded by the sword and yet lived; [15] and it was allowed to give breath to the image of the beast so that the image of the beast should even speak, and to cause those who would not worship the image of the beast to be slain. [16] Also it causes all, both small and great, both rich and poor, both free and slave, to be marked on the right hand or the forehead, [17] so that no one can buy

or sell unless he has the mark, that is, the name of the beast or the number of its name. [18] This calls for wisdom: let him who has understanding reckon the number of the beast, for it is a human number, its number is six hundred and sixty-six.

v. 11 The second beast differs from the first beast to which it is auxiliary and subsidiary. The second arose out of the earth, that is, out of settled human society. As the first beast symbolized world power, the second signifies the more subtle yet more deadly power of false religion.

False religion is the personification of godless authority and the prostrating of man's instinctive religiousness and natural tendency to worship. It is an invention of man with creeds that have been developed out of his own self-consciousness, and it springs from fear without knowledge of God. It has no foundation in truth or in reality and is one way man attempts to escape from his restless conscience. It is in nature eclectic and syncretistic, and it is characterized by luxury and ostentation. It places undue reliance upon externals and blends avarice and superstition. It is supported by diabolical supernaturalism. It makes gods out of God's gift by producing imitations of God's blessings. It has an abundance of rites of worship but is averse to the inward holiness and entire submission of life to God. It demands no strain of energy of spiritual nature and makes no demand upon the will. It gives license to the sensual nature of man. It proclaims an accommodation theology and separates religion from morality. It seeks earthly advantage.

False religion is one of the most inhuman forces in the world. It encourages the wicked in their evil ways. It is hostile to righteousness and seeks to frustrate true religion and to overthrow the foundations of righteousness. It strives to arrest the process of God's reign and endeavors to make the worst things appear the best (Isa. 5:20). It teaches that unrighteous lives can be compensated for by formal acts of religion. Plato says that the Greeks thought that they might commit any number and any kind of sins or crimes, and obtain pardon for them at the hands of the gods, if they offered sufficient sacrifices (Plato, "Republic" 2.7).

The second beast represents false religion which uses force, persuasion, and magic in order to make "the earth and its inhabitants worship the first beast" (13:12). It simulates miracles by satanic magic in order to induce people to worship the first beast. It is the instrument of the revelation of satanic authority as the Holy Spirit is the mediator of God's revelation. The description which John gives of this creature leaves little doubt that this is the meaning of his symbolism. All the actions of this beast suggest religious activities. The symbolism stands for any religious system which allies itself with the hostile forces of world power against Christ and his church. It is that system which persuades humanity to worship evil under the guise of good. The aim of this beast throughout is to assume a plausible exterior so that men may be beguiled by him. The phrase *two horns like a lamb* is a parody of true religion. The church worships the Lamb, and so the symbol of false religion is a beast with two horns like a lamb. The beast has the appearance of gentleness about him, but he speaks as deceitfully as the dragon (Matt. 7:15). While simulating an appearance of Christ, his words betray his devilish nature. "He looks like Christ and is like Satan" (Simcox). This beast was operating in John's day through the priesthood which administered the rites of emperor worship. However, John made a wider application. He saw the beast as a moral state of mind, pervading all places, and running through all End time. This beast is also called "false prophet" (16:13; 19:20; 20:10).

v. 12 The second beast's authority over men, though less directly asserted, is equal to that of the first beast. The second supports and enforces the authority of the first upon men. He has all the authority of the first beast, but he is in no sense a rival, for he makes men worship the first beast. He is ostensibly an advocate of religion but is in reality an anti-religious power. His function is to make all people worship the first beast. "Though differing in form and in origin, the two beasts are in spirit, purpose, and effect, identical" (Smith).

v. 13 The second beast does (present tense) *great signs* to impress and deceive gullible people, like the magicians of Egypt who imitate the signs God gave through Moses (Ex. 7:8-19). An example of these signs is to make *fire come down from heaven to earth in the sight of men.* The background of this sign is the experience of Elijah on Mount Carmel (1 Kings 18). It is also a parody of the work of the two witnesses (11:5). The descent of fire in the Old Testament and apocalyptic writings was a sign of God's approval (cf. Gen. 15:17; Lev. 9:24; Judg. 13:19-20; 2 Chron. 7:1). This is only one of the most impressive of the signs. The allusion is doubtless to pretended signs by which "religious" leaders impose upon the credulity of people. With fraudulent miracles, they contrive to deceive people. The use of such means is only too common in religion. Mere signs are no sure credentials of a true prophet (Deut. 13:1-3; Matt. 24:24; 2 Thess. 2:9; Rev. 16:14). John gives a true test to discover a false prophet (1 John 4:2-3).

v. 14 To deceive mankind is the chief prerogative and power of Satan. The "religious" leaders using satanic authority, deceive people by deifying the spirit of worldliness and by persuading them to believe that the worship of world power is valid and right (Matt. 24:24). With signs they deceive men and establish their position with unregenerate mankind. With these seemingly supernatural signs they deceive people and lead them to believe that the signs come from the divine power of the beast. They persuade men to raise up an image and worship the beast whose deadly wound was healed. All who devote themselves to world power raise up an image to bow down before (13:15; 14:9,11; 15:2; 16:2; 19:20; 20:4). Paul said that covetousness is idolatry (Col. 3:5).

v. 15 In this verse, John continues to relate how false religion aids world power. Another example of the signs attributed to the second beast is that of giving life to the image of the first beast, enabling it to speak. Thus, the image of the first beast is endued with apparent vitality.

As the giver of *breath,* the second beast is the satanic counterpart of the Holy Spirit, who is the "breath of life from God" (11:11; cf. John 6:63). False religion convinces men that they must conform to world power or suffer death; the exact opposite is true.

vv. 16-17 The second beast claims universal jurisdiction. The chief effect of the listing of the various classes of men is to make the expression comprehensive. The *mark* of the beast is a parody of the mark of God that rests on his faithful ones (7:3). It figuratively denotes that everyone gives evidence of loyalty. In symbolic language, John says that the worship of world power transforms one into the world's likeness. The "mark" is imprinted on the faithful ones' *right hand* or *forehead* in imitation of Israel in Egypt (Deut. 6:8). The mark can not be hidden. A person becomes increasingly in the image of his master. Worshipers are forced to show their loyalty to the beast in public ways; and if they refuse, they are publicly ostracized. No man who refuses the dominion of world power may enjoy its privileges. This verse sets forth the ostracisms and boycotts to which the saints are subjected if they persist in refusing homage to world power.

v. 18 *This calls for wisdom.* This is a pause for emphasis. In this point is the trial of wisdom; only the truly wise can understand it (Eph. 1:17). The highest moral wisdom is needed to understand this truth (1 Cor. 1:18-25). In this verse, John makes a further effort to identify the second beast who exercises the dragon's authority. Its mark is at the same time its name or the number of its name (666).

From early Christian history, interpreters have labored with this verse without much success. The variety of interpretations shows how little any one can be trusted. In the Greek, there are letters which if taken as numerals make up the sum of six hundred and sixty-six. (Some manuscripts have letters which make up the sum of six hundred and sixteen.) But interpreters are not agreed that the letters should be taken in this way. Some interpreters think they *should* be taken in this way. Some interpreters think they should be taken as the first letters of words for which they stand.

However, most commentators take the letters as numerals. Since the time of Ireneus, (ca. 130-ca. 202) scholars have computed the numbers and have come up with a variety of names. The possibilities are almost limitless. Using this method, the most favored solution for the past century is "Nero Caesar." If the Greek form of the Latin name is transliterated in Hebrew and the final letter is omitted, the name will yield 666. However, no one has shown why a Hebrew name should be used in a Greek writing. Also, no one has shown why the early interpreters never thought of the "Nero Caesar" solution (Morris).

In accord with John's symbolic method, it seems best to interpret this enigmatical number as a reference in the thrice-repeated 6 to incompleteness as opposed to 7 which was regarded as the number of perfection. The number "6" symbolizes incompleteness, sham, deceit, unrest. It represents the absence of all that is good, perfect, and complete. It represents depravity and evil. The triple use of any number was a completion of it. By the 666, John points to an unholy trinity of evil, a symbol of evil multiplied. It is the perfection of imperfection. The 666 is "a symbolical number, expressing all that is possible for human wisdom, and human power; when directed by an evil spirit, to achieve, and indicating a state of marvellous earthly perfection, when the beast-power has reached its highest development" (Carpenter). The phrase, *the number of the beast,* means that this number would so represent the beast that he could be identified by its proper application. *For it is a human number* is a very doubtful translation of the Greek, which seems rather to mean, "for number is man," that is, "it is man's number," or "a number of man." It describes something which is peculiarly a characteristic of mankind. False religion persuades men to accept world power as a substitute for God, or, at least, as not antagonistic to him.

(6) The Third Interlude; Comfort in the Certainty of Victory (14:1-20)

In the preceding vision, John has seen three terrible enemies which were arrayed against the church; the dragon, the beast out of the sea, and the beast out of the earth. This was a vision of the struggle and conflicts of the church in End time. The truths expressed are of timeless character. After describing these three enemies, with which Christ and his people contend, the vision now shows the blessedness of the faithful Christians and the judgment of the dragon and his followers.

a. The Lamb and His Company (14:1-5)

¹ Then I looked, and lo, on Mount Zion stood the Lamb, and with him a hundred and forty-four thousand who had his name and his Father's name written on their foreheads. ² And I heard a voice from heaven like the sound of many waters and like the sound of loud thunder; the voice I heard was like the sound of harpers playing on their harps, ³ and they sing a new song before the throne and before the four living creatures and before the elders. No one could learn that song except the hundred and forty-four thousand who had been redeemed from the earth. ⁴ It is these who have not defiled themselves with women, for they are chaste; it is these who follow the Lamb wherever he goes; these have been redeemed from mankind as first fruits for God and the Lamb, ⁵ and in their mouth no lie was found, for they are spotless.

v. 1 This company is seen gathered around the Lamb on Mount Zion. *The Lamb* is the same one mentioned in 5:6 whom the second beast (false religion) of 13:11 attempted to personate. *Mount Zion,* the highest part of Jerusalem, is a symbol of the dwelling place of God (Pss. 9:11; 68:16; 76:2; 132:13-18). It is a type of a safe citadel, the spiritual city, whose citizens are true to their king (Pss. 2:6; 74:2; Heb. 12:22-24). This scene symbolizes the security and peace that belongs to the people of God, the redeemed church (Isa. 28:16; 51:11; Heb. 12:22).

The *hundred and forty-four thousand* represents the same group that is described in 5:9-10; 7:1-8, and stands in contrast to those who worship the beast (13:12). It is the church's symbol of twelve reproduced and multiplied. It symbolizes and represents the whole church, the redeemed from the earth (14:3), in its ideal completeness and blessedness. John sees all the faithful Christians standing in the presence of Christ with the name of God inscribed on their foreheads in contrast to those who carry the mark of the beast (Ps. 16). God's name is the security of those who trust in him. This seal, the mark of messianic salvation, has its root in the historical Christ-event. The seal is a sign that the faithful Christians are forever Christ's, and hence, are always under his watchful care. This symbolizes the actuality of the members of Christ's congregation in the End time (Rissi, p. 46). Those who have made the break with world power walk with Christ in perfect security, whatever tribulation or persecution may befall.

v. 2 The *voice from heaven* is that of the whole court of heaven. It simply indicates that the voice is of divine origin (10:4; 14:15; 18:4). It is "the voice of a vast heavenly orchestra swelling in regal beauty like the voice of many waters, the thunderous chant of a mighty host of redeemed" (Torrance).

v. 3 The *new song* of praise is sung especially for the 144,000 standing on Mount Zion. It indicates a special act of thanksgiving for a special deliverance (Pss. 33:3; 40:3; 96:1; 98:1; 144:9; Isa. 42:10). It is a heavenly song and only the redeemed (144,000) can learn it. The *new song* is the result of the experiences through which they have passed victoriously in the battles with the dragon, the beast out of the sea, and the beast out of the earth. The *new song* is sung *before the throne* (4:2 f.) *and before the four living creatures* (4:6 f.) *and before the elders* (4:4). All of the redeemed come from, or out of the earth, but they leave behind them the "earth nature."

vv. 4-5 The character of the 144,000 (church) is described in these verses. First, they are described as *chaste*. Adultery and fornication are widely used in Scripture as a figure of idolatry (Jer. 5:7-8; 7:9; 23:10; Ezek. 23:45; Hos. 4:2). The statement that they are *chaste* is to be taken metaphorically as a symbol of the character of the faithful Christians who have not participated in idolatry. In this symbolism, John is viewing the church (144,000— men and women) as the bride of Christ (21:9; cf. 2 Cor. 11:2). The 144,000 have kept themselves from intercourse with world power. They are free from spiritual impurity and unfaithfulness. They are pure and faithful and loyal in their relations with their God. They have not worshiped the dragon and his two beasts. True virginity is that which belongs to the pure in heart (Matt. 5:8). The 144,000 are ever in the presence of the Lamb and follow (present tense) him wherever he may go (present tense) (Ps. 23:1-2; Matt. 10:38; 13:21; John 21:19). This implies fellowship, loyalty, and obedience. They follow Christ in times of suffering (John 13:36), as well as in times of joy. They follow him through his passion, death, and victory over death. They are as *first fruits for God and the Lamb.* This means that the 144,000 in a special sense belong to God (Ex. 23:19; 34:26; Neh. 10:35; Prov. 3-9). It does not necessarily imply that others will follow; it simply means that they are a holy offering unto the Lord. Their speech, in contrast to the worshipers of the beast, is characterized by complete truthfulness. The clause "they are spotless" means that as worshipers they are in a condition of acceptance with God (Rom. 12:1-2). In this paragraph, the 144,000 are described as the ones who are proving themselves faithful to God and who are separating themselves from the worship of world power, and are consecrating themselves to the service of God.

b. The First Angel Announcing the Triumph of the Gospel (14:6-7)

⁶ Then I saw another angel flying in midheaven, with an eternal gospel to proclaim to those who dwell on earth, to every nation and tribe and tongue and people; ⁷ and he said with a loud voice, "Fear God and give him glory, for the hour of his judgment has come; and worship him who made heaven and earth, the sea and the fountains of water."

vv. 6-7 In this symbolic vision, John saw *another angel.* The word *another* is a link to the former visions. The angel is *flying in midheaven* and, therefore, could be seen and heard by the whole inhabited world. His message is intended for worldwide proclamation. The fourfold enumeration (nation, tribe, tongue, and people) also stresses the universal nature of the proclamation in reference to the world (cf. 13:7). The angel proclaims from heaven the universal *eternal gospel* of God's victory. The way a man responds to the "eternal gospel" is a test or proof of what he is. Jesus said, "For judgment came I into the world" (John 9:39). The proclamation of the *eternal gospel* of God's message issues in a choice of salvation or judgment. Torrence comments, "It is impossible for the Church at any time to come to easy terms with the contemporary order . . . as long as the Cross is in the field and the everlasting Gospel is preached, God's love will strike in judgment at all the defenceworks of evil thrown up in state and society and history by the banding of men together in massive reaction and perverted self-defence against the will and Word of God."

c. The Second Angel Announcing the Fall of Babylon (14:8)

⁸ Another angel, a second, followed, saying, "Fallen, fallen is Babylon the great, she who made all nations drink the wine of her impure passion."

v. 8 In the beginning of this chapter, John has shown the blessedness of those who worship the Lamb; so now he shows, with terrible imagery, the punishment of those who worship the beast. The second angel proclaims the fact that the great city of Babylon is fallen (cf. 1 Pet. 5:13). In the sight of God, Babylon had already fallen. Its deathblow had been given by the life, death, and resurrection of Christ. It fell because this "eternal gospel" (14:6) had undermined world power. This fall is described at greater length in later visions (chaps. 17—18). In its oppression of the Jewish nation, the city of Babylon on the Euphrates had come to be used as a type of godless world power which persecutes the people of God and causes men to be unfaithful to his claims upon their lives (Isa. 13:19; 21:8-9; 47:5,9; 48:14; Jer. 50:2; 51:7-8; Dan. 4:30). Every time John mentions Babylon he uses the adjunct *the great* or "the great city" (14:8; 16:19; 17:5; 18:2,10,21). Morris comments, "Babylon is the great city, the symbol of man in community opposed to the things of God." Tenney comments, "It [Babylon] stands for the entire system of man's rulership, the acme of a prosperous but faithless culture."

d. The Third Angel Announcing the Doom of Those Worshiping the Beast (14:9-12)

⁹ And another angel, a third, followed them, saying with a loud voice "If any one worships the beast and its image, and receives a mark or his forehead or on his hand, ¹⁰ he also shall drink the wine of God's wrath, poured unmixed into the cup of his anger, and he shall be tormented with fire and brimstone in the presence of the holy angels and in the presence of the Lamb. ¹¹ And the smoke of their torment goes up for ever and ever; and they have no rest, day or night, these worshipers of the beast and its image, and whoever receives the mark of its name.'

¹² Here is a call for the endurance of the saints, those who keep the commandments of God and the faith of Jesus.

vv. 9-11 The third angel warns all the people not to identify themselves with world power and describes the retribution upon those who do so. To "worship" the beast simply means submission to it, to affirm its supremacy and worthiness and power. The worshipers of God have his seal upon them (7:1-8), and they also have Christ's name and the Father's name imprinted upon their foreheads (14:1). In like manner, the worshipers of world power and his image have his mark upon them (13:11-18). Those who worship the beast and those who worship his image are regarded as one. No one who worships the beast and his image can escape from bearing the mark of the beast. According to a law of life the object of a man's devotion transforms him into its character. Therefore, no one can escape from bearing either "the mark of the beast" or the name of Christ and the name of the Father (14:1). The penalties for bearing the mark of the beast are great and manifest. The ones who have the beast's mark upon them share in his punishment. The imagery in which these penalties are described is almost wholly derived from the Old Testament. The *cup* is God's "cup of the wine of wrath" which Jeremiah was directed to take from God's hand and to cause all the nations to whom he was sent to drink it (Jer. 25:15; cf. Ps. 75:8; Isa. 51:17). God' "wrath" is the disastrous consequences of sins working themselve out on those who have deliberately incurred them. If men reject the moral structure of God's universe, they must suffer (Preston and Hannon). The "wine of her impure passion" (14:8) and the **wine of God's wrath** (14:10) are treated as one and the same. The latter is the retribution for the former, and the former turns into the latter. The figure *fire and brimstone* is taken from the account of the destruction of Sodom and Gomorrah (Gen. 19:28). This awful scene is used in apocalyptic writings as a fitting symbol of the punishment for sins (Ezek. 38:22). Isaiah (30:33) adopts this figure when he predicted the punishment of the king of Assyria. He also used the symbolism when he described the temporal judgments that were to come upon Edom (Isa. 34:8-14). The punishment is inflicted **in the presence of the holy angels and in the presence of the Lamb.** Wretchedness in the presence of holy blessedness, combined with the knowledge of its inaccessibility, is torment (Luke 16:23). To those with a guilty conscience the sight of holiness is torture (Swete). The punishment for the worshipers of the beast is depicted in dramatic apocalyptic language. In contrast to the **rest** of the saints (14:13), the worshipers of the beast **have no rest, day or night.** Their state is one of ceaseless and intense agony. It is a state of constant restlessness. There is no sight of any end to the suffering.

v. 12 Perhaps the best rendering of this verse is: "Here is the steadfastness of the saints who keep the commandments of God, and the faith of Jesus." The first part of the verse is repeated from 13:10. The word "patience" (*hopomenē*) indicates steadfastness and endurance in trying circumstances. One of the most effective forms of witness-bearing is faithful living (Gal. 6:9; 2 Thess. 3:13). Tenney says, "For the believer who endures persecution it will be a supreme proof of patience." The saint is thereby able to prove the validity of his faith and derive eternal benefits which he would not have known otherwise (13:10). The reason why the saints should be steadfast is that their sufferings are short and their glory long, while the triumph of the idolaters and the persecuters is short and their torment long.

e. The Certainty of Those Who Die in the Lord (14:13)

¹³ And I heard a voice from heaven saying, "Write this: Blessed are the dead who die in the Lord henceforth." "Blessed indeed," says the Spirit, "that they may rest from their labors, for their deeds follow them!"

v. 13 The fourth proclamation stands in closest relation with that which precedes it. In the preceding verse, John mentions the necessity for steadfastness on the part of the saints; in this verse, an encouragement and incentive to the steadfastness are given. The voice which gives this assuring word is *from heaven*, that is, it is a divine message. The alternative to worshiping the beast is in many cases at least, death. But to die for Christ's sake and *in the Lord* has a blessedness attached to it. The historical Christ-event in the course of history is designated as the beginning of the time of redemption, as the turning point of the world's history (John 12:31; 14:7; Rom. 5:11; 1 John 3:2; cf. Matt. 26:64; 1 Cor. 13:12; 1 Pet. 1:6,8). The ones who die in the Lord leave their labors (*kopos*, that is, toil resulting in weariness, laborious toil, trouble) behind them. Their *deeds* will remain before God when all godless works are destroyed. The efficacy of Christ's act even over death is emphasized. Since the first advent of Christ there has been a dying "in the Lord" (Rissi, pp. 30,108).

f. The Harvesting of the Saints (14:14-16)

The figure of the harvest and the vintage is taken from Joel 3:12-13. In these two figures, Joel pictured the deliverance of Judah and the judging of the nations. It seems that John uses the two figures in a similar way. The symbols clearly reflect the parable of the wheat and the tares (Matt. 13:25-30). The harvest and the vintage together represent the all-inclusive act of gathering all mankind before the judgment seat of God (Rom. 14:10-12). The harvest symbolizes the gathering of the redeemed and the vintage symbolizes the judgment of the unredeemed. In 14:14-16 the assurance of victory is demonstrated by the harvesting of God's elect.

¹⁴ Then I looked, and lo, a white cloud, and seated on the cloud one like a son of man, with a golden crown on his head, and a sharp sickle in his hand. ¹⁵ And another angel came out of the temple, calling with a loud voice to him who sat upon the cloud, "Put in your sickle, and reap, for the hour to reap has come, for the harvest of the earth is fully ripe." ¹⁶ So he who sat upon the cloud swung his sickle on the earth, and the earth was reaped.

v. 14 The *white cloud* represents heaven or divinity (Matt. 17:5). In apocalyptic writings, clouds are used as vehicles or clothing of deity (Matt. 24:30; 26:64; Luke 21:27; Acts 1:9; 1 Thess. 4:17). The fact that the one in the vision is *seated* indicates that he is a judge with authority to hear and decide cases. The title *son of man* among other things means that he is human (Dan. 7:13; cf. Robbins, pp. 173 f.). This was Jesus' favorite term of himself, and he is quoted as using it seventy-five times in the Gospels. The incarnation was supreme divinity in full humanity and humanity full of God. The golden crown (*stephanos*) is the emblem of victory which he gained as a man (6:2). The *sickle* is a symbol of reaping of a harvest. The emblem "harvest" is often employed by the writers of the Gospels to describe moral subjects (Matt. 9:37,38; 13:30,39; Mark 4:29; Luke 10:2; John 4:35). There can be no doubt that John uses this figure to symbolize Jesus Christ in his mission of ingathering the redeemed of the earth (Matt. 9:37 f.; Mark 4:29; Luke 10:2; John 4:35-38). The whole New Testament testifies to the fact that the purpose of his coming was to reap the harvest of the earth. In Acts, Luke is especially careful to stress that the work through the Holy Spirit is the continuing work of Jesus (Stagg, *The Book of Acts*, p. 29). In dramatic symbolism, John is saying that Jesus Christ is the harvester of the world.

vv. 15-16 In these verses *another angel* acts as a messenger of the will of God to Christ in his capacity as Son of man. The angel announces that *the hour to reap has come* (let the hour come). Only the Son of man has the divine command to reap the *fully ripe* harvest of the earth (cf. 4:1-8; John 3:16-17; 4:35; 5:19; 10:18;

12:49). The harvest is going on during all End time as the Lord is adding to the church day by day those who are being saved (Acts 2:47b). The Father has committed all judgment unto the Son and calls upon him to exercise it (John 5:22). The angel who announces that the harvest is *fully ripe* comes from the temple, the dwelling place of God (cf. 11:1 f.). The background of this vision seems to be Daniel 7:13-14 and Zechariah 6:13. The Son of man reaps the harvest in obedience to the Father (John 4:34; 5:30; 6:38). He gathers his own unto himself from out of the whole world (Matt. 3:12; 9:37; 13:30; Mark 4:29; 13:27).

g. The Vintage of the Church's Enemies (14:17-20)

In this paragraph, the assurance of victory is demonstrated by the indication of destruction of all the foes of the church. John pictures in a dramatic way the overflowing wrath of God in store for those who deny his sovereignty and refuse his salvation. When one refuses the "eternal gospel," the gracious word turns into a word of divine judgment. The tares are gathered along with the wheat.

> [17] And another angel came out of the temple in heaven, and he too had a sharp sickle. [18] Then another angel came out from the altar, the angel who has power over fire, and he called with a loud voice to him who had the sharp sickle, "Put in your sickle and gather the clusters of the vine of the earth, for its grapes are ripe." [19] So the angel swung his sickle on the earth and gathered the vintage of the earth, and threw it into the great wine press of the wrath of God; [20] and the wine press was trodden outside the city, and blood flowed from the wine press, as high as a horse's bridle, for one thousand six hundred stadia.

v. 17 In this verse, *another angel* comes out of the temple, the dwelling place of God. The sickle-bearing angel is also a messenger of God. The mission of this angel is to gather all the unredeemed of the earth as the Son of man gathers all the saints. Notice that this positive judgment is carried out by an angel.

v. 18 The angel of this verse has power over fire and comes from the altar. He comes from the altar of incense to show that the prayers of the saints are about to be answered. The altar has been associated with the prayers of the saints and with judgment (6:9-10; 8:3-5; cf. Isa. 63:3 f.). Fire is often associated with judgment in Scripture and in apocalyptic writings.

vv. 19-20 The angel of judgment obeyed. The grapes are gathered and thrown into the winepress. The graphic symbolism of the winepress is used to describe the divine wrath (Isa. 63:1-6; Jer. 49:9; Lam. 1:15). The *blood* which *flowed from the wine press* reached *as high as a horse's bridle* for a distance of *one thousand six hundred stadia* (approximately 200 miles). This hyperbole emphasizes the enormity of the punishment and the great number that was slain. The winepress is without the *city*, because the city represents the place where the saints are safely gathered and nothing unclean shall enter it (21:27). Also, Jesus "suffered outside the gate" (Heb. 13:12).

John mixes the metaphor of winepress and battlefield. The combination makes the representation more terrible. In this dual symbolic representation, John pictures an appalling scene of wrath and judgment on the enemies of God. All evil is punished.

The *one thousand six hundred stadia* symbolizes the whole world. Four, the cosmic number, multiplied by itself and then multiplied by a hundred (ten times ten) show that the judgment is universal (Richardson, pp. 127-28). The whole world, of which Satan is the prince (John 12:31; 14:30; 16:11; Eph. 2:2), is judged and condemned and punished. The whole dreadful picture is intended to convey the awesome nature of the judgment and the completeness with which the powers of evil are overthrown. These forces of evil have seemingly achieved universal sway, but their overthrow is certain.

5. The Seven Bowls (15:1 to 20:15)

In this section John sets forth in more detail the divine judgments upon the church's enemies: the dragon, the beast out of the sea, and the false prophet. The bowl symbol seems to have been taken from the shallow bowls which were placed upon the golden altar and in which incense was burned (Ex. 30:1-10).

The vision of the bowls stresses the note of triumph. Each bowl contributes its part to the song of triumph of the redeemed. In the vision of the bowls the writer uses much of the Exodus typology. The fact that all the series deals with the same theme, the victory of Christ and the church over evil, shows that the various series are parallel, and that each gives a different aspect of the same temporal judgments during all End time with a growing intensity. All the series are not to be taken separately but superimposed upon one another. In the vision of the bowls there is a recapitulation of what has already been given in the seals and trumpets visions. This recapitulation, however, is not a mere repetition. The ideas included in the former visions are strengthened in the bowls vision. The severity of the nature of the bowls—judgment is easy to see. Under the seals vision, one fourth is afflicted, and under the trumpets vision one third is afflicted. However, there is no indication that any are exempt from the judgments of the bowls vision. It is, therefore, significant of retribution more dreadful than that symbolized by the trumpets, just as the trumpets indicate greater severity than the seals vision.

(1) Introductory Vision: *The Song of the Redeemed and the Seven Angels (15:1-8)*

In chapter 15 a new series of seven scenes begins. It gives a short summary of the events which are expanded in the next chapter. It is an interlude in which attention is drawn away from judgment to focus upon the victory of the redeemed. It is intended to fortify the saints and encourage those living in the tribulation.

a. The Seven Angels with Seven Plagues (15:1)

[1] Then I saw another portent in heaven, great and wonderful, seven angels with seven plagues, which are the last, for with them the wrath of God is ended.

This introductory verse serves as a superscription for chapters 15 and 16. In this verse John describes what he sees as if all the actors were present at one moment. He sees another great and wonderful *portent* in heaven (12:1,3). The angels and the plagues are seven which stresses the apocalyptic number of completeness. The word "plague" (literally, a stroke or a blow) had become proverbial, since the visitations in Egypt, for God's punishment upon the defiant pride of godlessness. Like the ten plagues in Egypt, these seven plagues show God's righteous power and expose the false pretensions of those who oppose God's sovereignty. The plagues of the bowls are said to be the *last, for with them the wrath of God is ended* (literally, was ended). These plagues are "last," because they culminate what has gone before and include all the expressions of divine indignation toward defiant pride and godlessness. There can be no expression of the wrath of God in degree beyond its direction toward evil which denies the sovereignty of God in Christ (1 John 2:22). These bowl plagues symbolize the ultimate expression of God's wrath against evil. God's wrath is simply the inexorable consequences of breaking his laws. Sin and suffering are linked together. God gives men time to repent; he bears long and warns often, but the last time comes at length. He uses both natural and supernatural forces to bring judgment upon the disobedient.

b. The Conquerors Praise the Justice of God's Judgments (15:2-4)

²And I saw what appeared to be a sea of glass mingled with fire, and those who had conquered the beast and its image and the number of its name, standing beside the sea of glass with harps of God in their hands. ³And they sing the song of Moses, the servant of God, and the song of the Lamb, saying,
"Great and wonderful are thy deeds,
O Lord God the Almighty!
Just and true are thy ways,
O King of the ages!
⁴Who shall not fear and glorify thy name, O Lord?

For thou alone are holy.
All nations shall come and worship thee,
for thy judgments have been revealed."

v. 2 In this verse, John sees those who have come victoriously out of the conflict with the enemies of the church (7:1-8; 14:1-5). The victory has been achieved over the enemies described in chapter 13. They have conquered the beast by not submitting to his agents. This vision emphasizes the faithful love of God assuring his people of their absolute safety whatever may be their fate at the hands of ungodly men (Isa. 26:20). Those who have been victorious stand upon *what appeared to be a sea of glass mingled with fire* (4:6). The allusion seems clearly to be the deliverance of Israel from Egypt (Ex. 15:1). Like the Hebrews, these victorious ones have made their exodus from spiritual Egypt, and they now occupy a position of splendor and safety. They stand in the very presence of God and are therefore beyond the power of the dragon and his agents. Only the redeemed who have been faithful in their struggle against the dragon and his agents can rejoice in the overthrow of evil. This unusual combination of images of sea and fire seems to represent God's holiness and justice or purity and judgment (8:5). "It is a sea of glass mingled with fire: of glass, because the judgments of God are crystal clear and they pierce down to the dark depths of iniquity and nothing is hidden from its searching light: mingled with fire, for our God is a consuming fire in the passion of his holy love, and at last all the sin of humanity that has gone to the making of the anarchy and wickedness that have covered the earth will perish for ever in the heat of the burning" (Torrance, p. 104). The *harps of God* indicate that the victory is due to God. "The splendor of the scene is an apocalyptic representation of the glory of redemptive triumph" (Dana, pp. 138-39). The whole scene is intended as a preparation for what is to come in the outpouring of the bowls.

v. 3 In the same way that the Hebrew people sang a song of thanksgiving after their deliverance from Egyptian bondage (Ex

14:31; 15:1-19), the redeemed celebrate their deliverance from spiritual bondage. The *song of Moses* was sung after the Israelites had crossed the Red Sea to safety. In like manner, in spontaneous ecstasy, the redeemed break forth in chorus as they sing the praises of the Lamb. Apparently they sing to the accompaniment of their own harps. The victory song is being sung (present tense) simultaneously with the struggle. The victory is being won while the tribulation is going on. Their song of victory is a mosaic of Old Testament phrases. It is a perfect blend of salvation and judgment, love and wrath, and mercy and truth. It emphasizes divine attributes, divine government according to moral principles, divine greatness, and righteous acts of God. It is a song of triumphant praise. The title **King of the ages** is found in some manuscripts; however, the true reading is probably "King of nations," that is, "King of the heathen." Some manuscripts have "the King of the saints." The title "King of nations" has great force here, because by the exercise of his power, God has proved himself king of "the nations." The next verse says that because of what God is and does *all nations shall come and worship thee.*

v. 4 The rhetorical question in this verse is an answer to the rhetorical questions of the worshipers of the beast, "Who is like the beast, and who can fight against it" (13:4). The valid reason for the question is given in the three clauses which follow in the verse. A *name* stands for the whole person who hears it. God is holy because he is just and true. His ways are in strict accordance with his nature and purposes. Carpenter says, "It is the remembrance that God will, as Judge of all the earth, do right, and will vindicate the expectations of those who stay themselves upon his character, which generate a holy fear of him." The bowl judgments are intended for the glory of God and for the redemption of man. As a consequence of these judgments, all nations will be brought to acknowledge God as Lord of all the earth. God is now accessible to all in the new covenant relationship which is through the Lamb. The song expresses confidence in the complete overthrow of all that opposes the Lamb and anticipates victory for Christ in the struggle between good and evil.

c. The Seven Are Given Seven Bowls Full of the Wrath of God (15:5-8)

⁵ After this I looked, and the temple of the tent of witness in heaven was opened, ⁶ and out of the temple came the seven angels with the seven plagues, robed in pure bright linen, and their breasts girded with golden girdles. ⁷ And one of the four living creatures gave the seven angels seven golden bowls full of the wrath of God who lives for ever and ever; ⁸ and the temple was filled with smoke from the glory of God and from his power, and no one could enter the temple until the seven plagues of the seven angels were ended.

v. 5 The phrase *temple of the tent of witness* (cf. 3:12; 7:15; 14:15,17) symbolizes the very presence of God among his people (Ex. 40:34; Num. 9:15-23; 10:11; 17:7; cf. Acts 7:44). According to Smith, "The phrase seems to be suggested by the fact that the ark of the covenant and the tables of stone (called, in Ex. 31:18, 'the tables of testimony') were for Israel, during the long period of their history, a 'witness' of that covenant which God had made with them as his chosen people." Rist asks, "could this 'tent of witness' associated with the Exodus be an allusion to the new exodus, in which the new Israel, comprised of witnesses and martyrs who have been liberated from Egypt, is traveling through the wilderness to the eternal promised land, i.e., to God's temple in heaven?" The *tent* had its counterpart in heaven (Heb. 8:5). The *temple* (*naos*) is the innermost part of the building, the holy of holies, the depository of the ark of the testimony, the dwelling place of God. This temple (*naos*) was usually closed, it is now *opened* for a clearer vision into the presence of God. The command to execute the judgments of the bowls full of the wrath of God comes directly from God himself (Ezek. 9:2).

v. 6 It is out of the immediate presence of God that the angels come to serve as God's agents to fulfill his covenant promise to bless his people and judge their enemies (1 Sam. 2:10; Ps. 10:18;

82:8; 96:13; 110:6; Isa. 2:4; 54:5). God's agents perform judgment for him in the world. These judgments of the seven angels have the fullest divine sanction. The sanctity of the covenant is emphasized by the appearance of the angels in the vestments of priesthood (Ezek. 9:2; 44:17-18). The *pure brite linen* (or stone?) symbolizes their purity and holiness. The judgment is pure. It is concern for the vindication of right (6:10). "The wrath which they (angels) are about to pour out upon the earth is a pure and sinless wrath, priestly in its function and golden in its integrity, quite unlike the wrath of man. There is no bestial passion, no spite, no hate, no anger of sin at all in it" (Torrance, p. 106).

v. 7 *The four living creatures,* representing the created world and all life on the earth, are appropriately chosen as the agents for conveying to the seven angels the seven plagues of bowls. These *seven golden bowls,* indicating completeness, are filled with that which represents God's wrath as the bowls of the elders were filled with that which represents the prayers of the saints (5:8). The laws and forces of nature fill the bowls of wrath and place them in the hands of the angels. These plagues are the penalties of broken laws. Carpenter says that these bowls "are given by one of the living creatures who represent creation; it is thus through creation that the wrath of God can visit the rebellious; that wrath of God is simply the operation of God's righteous law against sin. His statutes are eternally righteous. He has given to all things a law which cannot be broken; that law is adverse to evil, and will in the end root it out, for it does the bidding of God." Barnes says that the reason John refers here to the fact that God lives "for ever and ever" is "that though there may seem to be delay in the execution of his purposes, yet they will be certainly accomplished, as he is the ever-living and unchangeable God. He is not under a necessity of abandoning his purposes, like men, if they are not soon accomplished."

v. 8 Isaiah's impressive vision of the manifested presence of God in the temple seems to be the background of this verse (Isa.

6:1 ff.). Cloud and smoke are symbols of God's powerful presence in glory, majesty, and holiness (Ex. 16:10; 19:18; 24:16; 40:34-35; 1 Kings 8:11; Ezek. 10:4; Isa. 6:4). God is a consuming fire against sin (Heb. 12:29). The smoke in the temple (*naos*) indicates that God is in the temple. This is a dramatic picture of judgment. No one can enter the temple to intercede. Retribution must inevitably follow sin, and intercession will not avail to avert impending punishment. It is impossible to break the divine order established in the nature of things. God's arrangements are carried out. There is no possible evasion of the law of causation. The consequences of conduct are natural and are not assigned by an arbitrary decree.

(2) The First Four Bowls in the Sphere of the Physical (16:1-9)

Chapter 16 relates the pouring out of the contents of the seven bowls. As each bowl of God's wrath is emptied, certain actions occur. The results of these actions bear a close resemblance to the opening of the seven seals and the sounding of the seven trumpets. This is John's method of emphasizing the judgments by recapitulation. However, in the previous visions the punishments for sin were localized, and there was hope for repentance. The previous plagues fell on grass, trees, sea, rivers, fountains, sun, moon, and stars. There are clouds of locusts, and armies of horsemen and angels are loosed at the river Euphrates. In the bowls vision, the wrath of God is poured out upon the whole heedless ungodly world.

The plagues fall upon the sea, rivers, fountains, sun, throne of the beast, river Euphrates, and upon the air. The purpose of the pouring out of God's wrath from the bowls is to enlist the natural order in the service of divine retribution. These are the judgments that fall upon the enemies of Christ and the church.

a. A Command from the Temple to the Seven Angels (16:1)

¹ Then I heard a loud voice from the temple telling the seven angels, "Go and pour out on the earth the seven bowls of the wrath of God."

The command to the angels comes from the temple (*naos*), the dwelling place of God mentioned in 15:8, which no one could enter. It must be the voice of God. The metaphor, *pour out* is used in the Old Testament with reference to God's wrath (Ps. 79:6; Zeph. 3:8). This is a good illustration of the manner in which John's vision takes the place of metaphor. These bowls are suggestive of Jeremiah's cup of God's righteous wrath (Jer. 25:15). In this verse, God commands the seven angels to fulfill the task which is assigned to each by emptying the contents of his bowl upon the earth. The bowls vision has many references to the Egyptian plagues and like the other vision is meant to be taken symbolically.

b. The First Bowl: Evil Sores upon Men (16:2)

² So the first angel went and poured his bowl on the earth, and foul and evil sores came upon the men who bore the mark of the beast and worshiped its image.

The first plague which is introduced here is the sixth in order in the Egyptian plagues (Ex. 9:8-12). In Egypt, when the boils appeared, the magicians could not stand before Moses (Ex. 9:11). In Egypt the boils too were a mark, offensive and disgraceful, called "the boil of Egypt" (Deut. 28:27). The first bowl plague is the judgment of God meted out upon the earth so that all *who bore the mark of the beast and worshiped its image* are given over to the consequences of ungodliness. This symbolism probably refers to bodily disease which is the outcome of sin. These *evil sores* afflict those who give themselves to these practices, but they do not affect other people. Carpenter says, "The plague of the evil sore denotes some throbbing and hateful sore, perhaps spiritual or mental, which distracts attention and disturbs the personal serenity and self-complacency of the worshipers of the world-power."

c. The Second Bowl: The Sea Like the Blood of a Dead Man (16:3)

³ The second angel poured his bowl into the sea, and it became like

the blood of a dead man, and every living thing died that was in the sea.

The second bowl vision corresponds generally with the second trumpet vision (8:8), and both are suggested by the first Egyptian plague (Ex. 7:14 ff.). The second angel emptied his ***bowl into the sea, and it became like the blood of a dead man, and every living thing died that was in the sea.*** The *sea* is often used in apocalyptic writings as a symbol of mankind. The metaphor *blood of a dead man* symbolizes decay and corruption. The dying of the creatures in the sea is mentioned both in the book of Exodus (Ex. 7:18) and with the sounding of the second trumpet (8:9). This emphasizes the grievous character of the plagues. This second bowl vision seems to give special force and prominence to the social aspects of sin. Sin not only affects the individual as a sinner but the entire community of persons living together as a group. It causes social life to lose all vital force and life.

Carpenter concludes, "The sea represented the tumultuous impulses and passions of the masses; there is a certain healthy force in these, but under certain conditions, when devoted to selfishness and earthliness, they become corrupt and deadly. Ruled by God and by right, the voice of multitudes is melodious as the voice of the sea . . . but swayed by impulse, or directed by worldliness they become an element of corruption killing every token of a better life."

d. The Third Bowl: Rivers and Fountains Become Blood (16:4-7)

⁴ The third angel poured his bowl into the rivers and the fountains of water, and they became blood.
⁵ And I heard the angel of water say,
"Just art thou in these thy judgments,
thou who art and wast, O Holy One.
⁶ For men have shed the blood of saints and prophets,
and thou hast given them blood to drink.
It is their due!"
⁷ And I heard the altar cry,
"Yea, Lord God the Almighty,

true and just are thy judgments!"

v. 4 The pouring out of the third bowl echoes the first Egyptian plague, which turned water into blood (Ex. 7:19-25). It also coincides in part with the sounding of the third trumpet (8:10-11). In this plague, the rivers and fountains, the natural sources of life and health for the sea, become blood. Not only is the sea (symbol of human society) turned to the "blood of a dead man" (symbol of slaughter, decay, and corruption), but the sources of life for society are turned into instruments of judgment when used in God's wrath. The wrath of God falls upon the tributaries of corrupt society.

vv. 5-6 In apocalyptic writings, angels are assigned jurisdiction over certain areas of creation. The *angel of water* is charged with the guardianship of the rivers and fountains. This *angel of water* recognizes the justice of these judgments. He speaks of God as *just,* and regards the action of turning the water into blood as one of judging. The judgments may seem harsh and arbitrary, but the angel sees in all this the acts of a righteous God bringing retribution on the ungodly. He also sees these judgments of the God of history and the present as unfailing. God proves himself to be the *Holy One* because he always judges righteous judgment. The ones who *have shed the blood of saints and prophets* have been given blood to drink. This was a recompense for persecuting the godly. God's judgments are ever at work, and in them there is nothing contrary to perfect equity. God's judgment is the operation of his self-acting law. His judgments have the power of ensuring their own vindication. The Incarnation has placed man into the inevitable position that he must either accept or reject God's salvation.

v. 7 In the vision, the voice proceeding from the altar is the voice of the altar itself. It expresses the utterance of those who in 6:10 are represented as crying beneath the altar. The altar is represented as rejoicing in the vindication of God's honor by the execution of his judgments on those who have slain his servants (cf. Gen. 4:10; 1 Kings 13:2; Luke 19:40; Heb. 12:24). Carpenter says, "The altar beneath which the souls of the martyrs cried, and on which the prayers of the saints were offered, is represented as confirming the testimony to the just dealings of God."

e. The Fourth Bowl: The Sun's Scorching Heat (16:8-9)

⁸ The fourth angel poured his bowl on the sun, and it was allowed to scorch men with fire; ⁹ men were scorched by the fierce heat, and they cursed the name of God who had power over these plagues, and they did not repent and give him glory.

v. 8 When the sixth seal was opened (6:12), and when the fourth trumpet was sounded (8:12), the sun was darkened like the Egyptian plague (Ex. 10:21-23). Under the symbolism of the pouring out of the contents of the fourth bowl, the sun is employed as an instrument of scorching heat (cf. Ps. 121:6; Isa. 4:6). The symbolism conveys the idea that the sun sends forth such intense and consuming heat that men would be "scorched." The reference here is to some calamity that could be represented by such an increase of the sun. The sun, which is such a blessing, becomes a curse. In apocalyptic and many other writings, God is often spoken of as the "Light" of the world (1 Tim. 6:16; Jas. 1:17; 1 John 1:5).

Philo, a contemporary of John, speaks of God as the "spiritual sun" before whom the darkness of passion and evil is dispersed (Strachan, p. 207). Jesus told the Jews that he was the "light" of the world (John 8:12; 9:5; 12:46). John here seems to be using a common metaphor by referring to the revelation of God as *sun.* Like the sun, God's revelation of himself can be an instrument of blessing or an instrument of suffering. The revelation of the love of God for sinful man which brings salvation to the responsive does not form a contradiction to the revelation of his wrath which brings judgment upon the unresponsive. The spiritual state of every person is determined by his relationship to the light which has appeared. The light either blesses or it curses (John 3:17-21). The one who accepts the light is not judged (John 3:18) and does not come into judgment (John 5:24), while the one who rejects the light has been judged already (John 3:18; 16:11; 12:31). Judgment is not an arbitrary sentence, but the working out of the justice of God. The very offer of salvation involves judgment and condemnation. The essence of judgment is not the sentence but the verdict, the discrimination between the approved and the condemned.

v. 9 The moral effect of God's revelation of himself to the worshipers of the beast is not remedial. Instead of repenting and giving God the glory, they blaspheme the name of God and blame him for their suffering. Their wickedness is intensified by the judgment, and their rebellion finds expression in words of blasphemy. The unrepenting heart is hardened in sin and more set in enmity against God because of his righteous judgments. He perverts God's revelation and makes it a means of his own hardening in sin (Ex. 7:13-14,22; 8:15,19,32; 9:7,12,34,35; 10:1,20,27; 11:10; 14:8; Deut. 2:30; 1 Sam. 6:6; 2 Chron. 36:13; Isa. 63:17; Dan. 5:20; Mark 6:52; 8:17; John 12:40; Heb. 3:13).

(3) The Last Three Bowls in the Spiritual Realm (16:10-21)

As in the opening of the seals (6:9) and in the blowing of the trumpets (9:1), there is a break between the pouring out of the fourth and fifth bowls.

a. The Fifth Bowl: The Beast's Kingdom Darkened (16:10-11)

¹⁰ The fifth angel poured his bowl on the throne of the beast, and its kingdom was in darkness; men gnawed their tongues in anguish ¹¹ and cursed the God of heaven for their pain and sores, and did not repent of their deeds.

v. 10 The pouring out of the contents of the fifth bowl upon the *throne* of world power indicates that his power at its center is threatened. The very center of his authority is menaced. The very seat of world power's dominion is assailed.

The basis of the darkness symbolism in the pouring out of the fifth bowl is the ninth plague in Egypt (Ex. 10:21 ff.) which John accentuated. The symbolical use of darkness is very common in Jewish and Christian literature. This darkness symbolizes internal strife, confusion, calamity, disorder, distress, and division. It is a condition of gloom, its inhabitants are helpless. When men refuse the light which is granted them at some particular point, they shall not have the illumination which they need for life and conduct. The darkness here is the result of the worshipers of the beast turning away from the light (John 3:19-20). Men should be ashamed of this darkness (Eph. 5:12; cf. John 3:20). This self-inflicted darkness renders people spiritually blind (John 9:39-40; Acts 26:18; 1 John 2:9-11). In figurative language, darkness often appears as a symbol of moral evil or sin (Isa. 5:20; Matt. 4:16; John 3:19) and of ignorance (Ps. 82:5; Isa. 42:7). To be in a state of sin and ignorance is to be in darkness (Ex. 20:21; Deut. 4:11; 5:23; 1 Kings 8:12; Pss. 18:9,11; 97:2; Amos 5:18; Zeph. 1:15; Luke 1:79; John 8:12; Rom. 2:19; Col. 1:13; 1 Thess. 5:4 f.; 1 John 1:6,8; 2:9). The metaphor also is found frequently in Johannine writings.

The statement *men gnawed their tongues in anguish* symbolizes great spiritual pain, suffering, remorse, and torment. Darkness is punishment. It is a cause-and-effect relationship. Paul says that "God gave them up" to the evils which they had chosen with all the disastrous results which naturally followed (Rom. 1:18-32).

v. 11 Instead of the worshipers of the beast repenting because of the righteous judgments, they are more set in enmity against the God of heaven (16:9; cf. Dan. 2:19). There is a hardening of their hearts, as with Pharaoh in Egypt, so that they refuse to repent as God demands. They attribute their pain to God instead of their own sins, and this increases the blasphemy of the name of God (cf. Isa. 52:5; Rom. 2:24; 1 Tim. 6:1; Jas. 2:7).

b. The Sixth Bowl: Drying Up the Euphrates and the Gathering of the Kings of the World (16:12-16)

[12] The sixth angel poured his bowl on the great river Euphrates, and its water was dried up, to prepare the way for the kings of the east. [13] And I saw, issuing from the mouth of the dragon and from the mouth

of the beast and from the mouth of the false prophet, three foul spirits like frogs; ¹⁴ for they are devil spirits, performing signs, who go abroad to the kings of the whole world, to assemble them for battle on the great day of God the Almighty. ¹⁵ ("Lo, I am coming like a thief! Blessed is he who is awake, keeping his garments that he may not go naked and be seen exposed!") ¹⁶ And they assembled them at the place which is called in Hebrew Armageddon.

v. 12 When the sixth trumpet was blown four angels were released from the Euphrates, and a large army of men gathered together from that river (9:13-21). In this vision, an army comes from the same river which is dried up to give them free passage. The drying up of the Euphrates was suggested by the drying up of the Red Sea (Ex. 14:21) and the Jordan (Josh. 3:17; cf. Isa. 11:11-16; Jer. 51:36; Zech. 10:11), and possibly by the account of the capture of Babylon by Cyrus when he changed the course of the river (Her. 1:191).

vv. 13-14 John now pictures the hosts of evil against which the kings from the sunrising, the agents of God, enter into conflict. Three *foul spirits* are seen that are out of the mouths of the dragon (12:3; i.e., Satan), the beast (13:1; i.e., world power), and the false prophet (13:11; 19:20; 20:10; i.e., false religion). The fact that the foul spirits came out of their mouths indicates that they are false teachings. The number "three" is a parody on the holy number. These spirits are the foes of Christ and his church. "Christ expelled unclean spirits, but his enemies send them forth" (Swete). These spirits are the combination of all that is evil in the world against all that is good. They represent the messages and influence of the dragon, the beast, and the false prophet. They are like frogs in their common quality of uncleanness (Ex. 8:2; Lev. 11:10). They are the enticing speech of evil which intrigues people to unite with Satan against God in the struggle between good and evil. The task of these foul and demonic spirits is to gather all men for the war (not battle) which is being waged against God by all the forces of evil all through the history of the world. This is not a war between nations but a war against God (Ps. 2:2). The **great**

day of God the Almighty is any day when God executes judgment in decisive conflict between the worship of Satan and the worship of Christ.

v. 15 Many commentators have concluded that this verse is an interpolation or out of place here. However, these conclusions are not necessary. Rist says, "in order to warn his followers to be on their guard, and at the same time to give them fresh assurance concerning the outcome, the heavenly Christ dramatically interjects himself into the scene . . . there is no need to suppose either a displacement or an interpolation." The verse begins with the same metaphor that is used in 3:3. When the forces of evil are all combining against God, Christ calls the church back to the realities of the situation. Christ comes in every struggle with evil to help. Christ is present with his people (Matt. 18:5,20; 25:45; 28:20; Luke 10:16; John 14:3,18,21,23,28; 17:11,21,23-24; 20:21-22; Acts 18:10), and yet his *coming* is an oft-repeated promise in the New Testament (Matt. 24:43; 1 Thess. 5:23; 2 Pet. 3:10; Rev. 3:3).

In this verse his *coming* is his continuous coming in judgment that evil shall be destroyed in the world and also in the individual. He comes as a thief, unheralded and totally unexpected (3:3; cf. Matt. 24:43-44; Luke 12:39-40; 1 Thess. 5:2,4; 2 Pet. 3:10). The *garments* are the deeds of righteousness without which the believers are not the church. The church must maintain its watchfulness and personal holiness during the conflict, and in this way it can recognize the coming of the Lord in the victory over evil.

v. 16 The three foul and demonic spirits, like frogs, assemble the kings of the whole world ***at the place which is called in Hebrew Armageddon.*** By stressing the Hebrew word attention is called to the symbolical use of the name. The word *Armageddon* means literally "mountain (hill) of Megiddo." It probably refers to Mount Carmel, at the foot of which lies the plain of Megiddo in the valley of Esdraelon. Carmel was the scene of Elijah's struggle with the prophets of Baal (1 Kings 18:20 ff.). This level piece of land at the entrance of the hill country from the north was the gathering place for hostile forces and the scene of many battles. It was here that the Canaanitish kings were defeated by Deborah and Barak (Judg. 5:19). This was the place where Ahaziah, king of Judah, was defeated and slain (2 Kings 9:27). It is referred to in Zechariah 12:11 as a type of great mourning and sorrow because of the overthrow and death of Josiah having occurred there (2 Kings 23:29; 2 Chron. 35:22-24). It was used symbolically in a way similar to the way Waterloo is used today. John uses the name as a symbol of decisive struggle, conflict, strife, and battle. It is a figure to describe the struggle of the forces of good against the forces of evil. John says nothing here about the time of Armageddon. It will occur at no particular time; it is occurring all the time. The truth which he is seeking to express is timeless and universal. Armageddon has no location on any map of the world (Barclay). It is nowhere, and it is everywhere. It is not a place but an occasion. It is the world, and it is within the soul of man. The struggle is moral and spiritual.

c. The Seventh Bowl: Contents Poured into the Air (16:17-21)

[17] The seventh angel poured his bowl into the air, and a great voice came out of the temple, from the throne, saying, "It is done!" [18] And there were flashes of lightning, loud noises, peals of thunder, and a great earthquake such as had never been since men were on the earth, so great was that earthquake. [19] The great city was split into three parts, and the cities of the nations fell, and God remembered great Babylon, to make her drain the cup of the fury of his wrath. [20] And every island fled away, and no mountains were to be found; [21] and great hailstones, heavy as a hundredweight, dropped on men from heaven, till men cursed God the plague of the hail, so fearful was that plague.

v. 17 The seventh angel poured out the contents of his bowl into the air. In apocalyptic writings the *air* was the special sphere and abode of Satan, who is "the prince of the power of the air" (Eph. 2:2). Evil spirits have their abode in the atmosphere, or at least haunt it, being invisible like the air. In the *air,* Satan is a prince with other evil spirits under him. Another symbolic meaning of "air" in apocalyptic writings was the unlimited i.e., everywhere, in every place or part. John seems to use this symbol with both of these ideas. Evil is now being attacked in its own sphere and in all places. The purpose of the pouring out the contents of the seventh bowl into the air was not to pollute the air but to produce convulsions of earthquakes, lightning, and peals of thunder as means of judgment. These catastrophes are omens, and are similar to the ones brought on by the trumpets (8:5; 9:15). "The last bowl of wrath set the whole of nature at war with man" (Barclay). The **great voice** which came out of the temple from the throne was the voice of God. God himself says the bowl plagues are finished. This is the final visitation of the wrath of God. God's purpose is accomplished.

v. 18 The convulsions and upheavals of nature mentioned in this verse are the usual accompaniments of any special manifestation of God's presence in judgment (4:5; 6:12-17; 11:19).

v. 19 The **great city** is Babylon, the symbol of all concentrated godless world power. Any nation or political power in history that sets itself against the kingdom of God is Babylon. She is the earthly source of the evils that challenge the forces of righteousness.

The idea in the symbols of this verse is that of total destruction of world power. God's wrathful judgment will destroy it (cf. Ezek. 5:2; Heb. 12:26-29). The calamities came because God caused world power to **drain the cup of the fury of his wrath** (cf. Jer. 25:15). Babylon (world power) receives the most wholehearted opposition from God. Not only will the **great city** fall but also every lesser form of evil. (The word "great" is used eleven times in this chapter.) The same judgment of God is at work on a large scale in the history of nations that is at work on a smaller scale of individual life and experience.

v. 20 The two figures in this verse continue the description of the effects of the earthquake given in 16:18. Such convulsions of the earth generally indicate judgment. The meaning of these two symbols is that God's judgment changes conditions when world power seems to be fixed and permanent.

v. 21   The bowls judgments concludes with a reference to another of the plagues of Egypt (Ex. 9:24). The *great hailstones* (about one hundred pounds) are added here to heighten the general effect of the judgment and give vividness to the imagery. Hail is often mentioned as a means of the judgment of God (Ex. 9:22-26; Josh. 10:11; Pss. 78:47; 105:32; Isa. 28:2; 30:30; Ezek. 13:11; 38:22; Hag. 2:17). The design of the whole symbolism is to show that the judgment of God is complete. It is a frightful image to denote the terrible and certain destruction which comes (present tense) upon world power (Babylon). There is no escape from God's judgments. Instead of the judgments bringing repentance, ungodly men blasphemed God because of the judgments.

(4) The Overthrow of Satan and His Subordinates (17:1 to 20:15)

The vision of the seven bowls lead naturally up to the present series of visions. In fact, the events referred to under the seventh bowl are elaborated and particularized in 17:1 to 20:15. In these visions, John is making use of symbols which had acquired a certain well-defined significance for the Hebrews in the course of their history. The meaning of many of these symbols had been stamped upon their consciousness by the prophets of Israel.

a. The Nature and History of the Great Harlot Babylon (17:1-18)

¹ Then one of the seven angels who had the seven bowls came and said to me, "Come, I will show you the judgment of the great harlot who is seated upon many waters, ² with whom the kings of the earth have committed fornication, and with the wine of whose fornication the dwellers on earth have become drunk." ³ And he carried me away in the Spirit into a wilderness, and I saw a woman sitting on a scarlet beast which was full of blasphemous names, and it had seven heads and ten horns. ⁴ The woman was arrayed in purple and scarlet, and bedecked with gold and jewels and pearls, holding in her hand a golden cup full of abominations and the impurities of her fornication; ⁵ and on her forehead was written a name of mystery: "Babylon the great, mother of harlots and of earth's abominations." ⁶ And I saw the woman, drunk with the blood of the saints and the blood of the martyrs of Jesus.

When I saw her I marveled greatly. ⁷ But the angel said to me, "Why marvel? I will tell you the mystery of the woman, and of the beast with seven heads and ten horns that carries her. ⁸ The beast that you saw was, and is not, and is to ascend from the bottomless pit and go to perdition; and the dwellers on earth whose names have not been written in the book of life from the foundation of the world, will marvel to behold the beast, because it was and is not and is to come. ⁹ This calls for a mind with wisdom: the seven heads are seven hills on which the woman is seated: ¹⁰ they are also seven kings, five of whom have fallen, one is, the other has not yet come, and when he comes he must remain only a little while. ¹¹ As for the beast that was and is not, it is an eighth but it belongs to the seven, and it goes to perdition. ¹² And the ten horns that you saw are ten kings who have not yet received royal power, but they are to receive authority as kings for one hour, together with the beast. ¹³ These are of one mind and give over their power and authority to the beast; ¹⁴ they will make war on the Lamb, and the Lamb will conquer them, for he is Lord of lords and King of kings, and those with him are called and chosen and faithful."

¹⁵ And he said to me, "The waters that you saw, where the harlot is seated, are peoples and multitudes and nations and tongues. ¹⁶ And the ten horns that you saw, they and the beast will hate the harlot; they will make her desolate and naked, and devour her flesh and burn her up with fire, ¹⁷ for God has put it into their hearts to carry out his purpose by being of one mind and giving over their royal power to the beast, until the words of God shall be fulfilled. ¹⁸ And the woman that you saw is the great city which has dominion over the kings of the earth."

v. 1 One of the seven angels mentioned in 17:1 tells John that he will show him the judgment of the ***great harlot*** (Jer. 51:9). This statement connects the following vision with the bowl judgments. This ***great harlot*** is a parody of the church. Just as the majestic, glorious, pure, sunclothed, and star-crowned woman in chapter 12 symbolizes the church, the ***great harlot*** symbolizes human society without God (Isa. 23:15-17; Nah. 3:4). She epitomizes irresponsible power, inhumanity, and hatred of all that the church stands for. She is a harlot because she turns people away from their true loyalty to God and causes them to practice idolatry. She is not said to be adulterous (Isa. 1:21; Jer. 2:2; Ezek. 16:36 ff.; 23:2 f.; Hos. 2:5), for she is not God's people, his bride. The prophets sometime speak of Jerusalem as a harlot (Isa. 1:21; Jer. 2:20; 3:1,6; Ezek.

16:25; Hos. 1:2; 4:15; Mic. 1:7). This *great harlot* is a reincarnation of godless, idolatrous, ancient Babylon (14:8; 16:19). Babylon was situated on the Euphrates and had many artificial streams throughout the city, so the "great harlot" is *seated upon many waters.* The Old Testament uses streams to refer to people (Isa. 8:7-8; 23:10; Jer. 46:7; 47:2; Ezek. 29:10). The *many waters* upon which she sits are symbolical of the people over which she reigns. She is afterwards shown to be a city, and the many waters are "peoples and multitudes and nations and tongues," as 17:15 shows (cf. Jer. 51:12-13). This illustrates the wide influence of the great harlot. Her sway is as wide as world power. She represents evil human society, human collectivity, as it stands in antithesis to the church. She never dies, until Satan himself is destroyed. "As long as evil remains, it will be incorporated on earth in some visible embodiment of its power. The conscience of the Christian church will always confront some Babylon" (Calkins).

v. 2 This verse declares that idolatrous and corrupt human society had seduced the rulers of the earth and that the people have joined in her sins against God (Jer. 3:8-9; 5:7; 13:27; 23:14; Ezek. 16:32; 23:37; Hos. 2:2; 4:2). As fornication is a form of false affection, so human society without God is a leaguing of people in a false alliance. The language of profligacy is used in the Old Testament to describe sin, especially the sin of disobedience to God's will. The intercourse of Israel with foreign nations is described as fornication, because it was mixed up with idolatry and false pretences of friendship, when self-interest was the real motive (cf. Ezek. 16:25-26,28; Nah. 3:4). The symbol here represents all that which seduces, allures, tempts, and draws people away from God.

The *kings of the earth* and the *dwellers on earth* have joined in the sin of disobedience to God's will. The expression *wine of . . . fornication* is a repetition of 14:8 and is derived from Jeremiah 51:7. The people follow the great harlot with a fanaticism like intoxication.

v. 3 John is again a participant in the ecstatic vision (1:10; 4:2; 21:10). He is carried away *in the Spirit into a wilderness* where he sees a woman sitting upon a beast (cf. Isa. 21; Ezek. 3:14 f.; 8:3; 11:24). This is the same *wilderness* in which the persecuted woman (church) finds safety and refuge (12:6,14). The church and the people of the world live together in the same place (John 17:14-17). The woman described in this verse is the great harlot (people of the world) of 17:1. She symbolizes a form of evil that is continually supported by the beast. The scarlet beast upon which the woman is sitting is world power, as described in 13:1 f., which rose out of the sea. The scarlet color expresses sin, violence, and cruelty (Isa. 1:18), and also worldly preeminence and power. The woman exercises control and guidance over the beast and relies upon it for support and safety. The beast is *full of blasphemous names* (blasphemy in its fullest measure), because it assumes divine authority and prerogatives. In 13:1, this beast had a "blasphemous name" on its head; now, however, its body is full of blasphemous names. The seven heads symbolize universal dominion (17:9 ff.), and the ten horns symbolize complete human power (17:12 ff.).

v. 4 The description of the woman given in this verse is a weak imitation of the description of the church (12:1 ff.). It also suggests the woman's splendor and luxury and her material wealth and magnificence (Jer. 51:7; Ezek. 28:13). She is one with the beast upon which she rides, even seeming to rise out of its own being, since its scarlet coloring is seen upon her own rich garments. The *gold, jewels, and pearls* are simply her trappings to intensify her pretensions to sovereignty. They are characteristic of the world's attractions. The splendid and attractive *golden cup,* which she holds in her hand, which leads naturally to the expectation of a satisfying drink, is full of all things that are displeasing to God and robs men's senses and degrades them.

v. 5 In 7:3; 9:4; 14:1; and 22:4 the people of God, the church, have God's name written on their foreheads. In 13:1,16; 14:9; and 20:4, the worshipers of world power have "a blasphemous name" or "a mark" written upon their heads or on their right hand. In each case, the owner's prominent and unmistakable identification is clear. In this verse, the woman, representing the worshipers of world power, has **Babylon the great, mother of harlots and of earth's abominations** written on her forehead. This inscription on her head marks the worshipers of world power as belonging to the world. The last part of the verse asserts that the harlot (17:1) is Babylon, that is, world power, which is openly antagonistic to God. John has now combined the harlot (worshipers of world power) and the beast or Babylon (world power), for in fact they are one. Babylon is symbolic of all that which allures, tempts, seduces, and draws people away from God. *Mystery* means that it is symbolic and is subject to be made known. Its explanation is given in 17:7 f.

v. 6 In his vision, John *saw the woman, drunk with the blood of the saints and the blood of the martyrs of Jesus.* This metaphor suggests not only that vast extent of her slaughter but also the crazed effect that her murderous acts produced (Jer. 2:33-34; 7:6-7; 19:4). The woman is (present participle) intoxicated with a fanatical zeal to exterminate the saints and martyrs (people of God), and she enjoys her performance (Jer. 51:7). Caird says, "She makes others *drunk on the wine of her fornication* and herself *drunk on the blood of God's people.*" John **marveled greatly** because of the *mystery* of the seeming defeat of good and the seeming victory of evil. He had been invited to look at the judgment of the great harlot (17:1); instead he sees her destroying the people of God. The picture he sees is shocking, unbelievable. How long would God allow it to continue? The angel proceeds to show John her fate.

vv. 7-8 John's angel-interpreter told him that he would explain the meaning of the mystery. The woman and the beast that carries her form one mystery. To know the one is to know the other. The explanation of the symbolism of the beast is a parody of the title given to God in 1:4. The enigmatic phrase, **was, and is not, and is to ascend** is an intentional imitation of God described as "who is and who was and who is to come" (1:4). In contrast with the never-dying life of God, world power is constantly passing away to be reborn in new forms which in their turn perish. Three stages are marked out in the existence of world power: it was, it is not now, it ascends from the bottomless pit to go into perdition. The ascending from the bottomless pit and the going into perdition indicate permanent attributes of the beast rather than single episodes in his career (11:7). This existence, nonexistence with existence, and subsequent reappearance describes the same truth as expressed by the mortal wound that was healed (13:3). Evil seems to disappear, but it only seems to do so. It does not need to have a Nero *redivivus* myth to make it reappear. Before the Christian's conversion, the beast was in power. Since his conversion, there is a sense in which the beast has no existence, it exists only in the bottomless pit (i.e., the natural abiding place of evil) and the dwelling place of Satan while working in the world (9:11; 11:7; 20:1,3). As the Christian overcomes evil, Satan goes to the bottomless pit. Unregenerate man will not understand the meaning of this language, but the people of God will understand.

v. 9 John begins this verse with a call for the mind with true wisdom to interpret his symbolism (cf. 13:18). Only the truly wise can understand and interpret this truth (1 Cor. 1:25-31; 2:6-8) He has used language and numbers symbolically. A mountain symbolizes strength (Pss. 30:7; 121:1-2; 125:2; Isa. 41:15; Jer 51:25). Seven is the number signifying universality (1:4; etc.). The meaning of this verse then is that the woman relies upon a universa power (17:3). The most prominent form of world power in John': day was Rome. However, Rome was only a partial fulfillment of this truth. It has its embodiment in every age.

v. 10 The *seven kings* represent the same world power as the woman on the beast. It is here viewed in its successive exhibition: by different nations, though here again the seven must not be interpreted literally. The "seven" symbolizes universality. The *sever kings* means that world power is exhibited by successive nations as many as have existed or shall exist. The number *five* was used in apocalyptic writings to symbolize supernatural power and control over the fate and destiny of man. John seems to be saying that God is in control no matter what nation is ruling at any particular time. This interpretation is in harmony with many of the prophets of Israel. The statement *one is* indicates that world power always has a manifestation of its opposition to the people of God. The concluding statement in this verse *the other has not yet come, and when he comes he must remain only a little while* refers to the seventh king. The seven again symbolizes universality. World power is passing away (1 John 2:8,17). The "little time" refers to the remainder of the time of the world existence, End time (1:1,3; 2:5,16; 6:11; 12:12; 22:12).

v. 11 This verse sums up what is intimated in the preceding verse: that is, that the beast is the sum total of what has been described under the form of five kings, then one king, and then one king again. The beast which is described in this verse is the same beast with the seven heads, and ten horns (17:7-8). It consists of and is formed by what has been denoted by the seven kings. The seven kings describe world power as it exists throughout all ages. The phrase, *belongs to the seven,* means made up of seven, including and containing within itself all the seven already spoken of. The number eight was looked upon in apocalyptic circles as an all-inclusive number for the totality of all supernatural powers. The beast, the basic source of evil, finds a kind of incarnation in each of the seven kings. "In a way he is each of them" (Morris, p. 211). John says in this enigmatic statement that one after another the kingdoms of the world fall; then, last of all, that apparent supernatural power which sustains them shall go to destruction. Its overthrow is reasserted.

v. 12 The ten horns are all on the seventh head (Dan. 7:24). They express widespread complete human power and indicate that world power expresses itself in many and various forms. The ten kings symbolize the completeness of all nations subservient to world power. In apocalyptic writings, ten was the number adopted when a whole was to be divided into parts. In the furniture of the Temple, Solomon had Hiram of Tyre to make ten bases, ten lavers, and ten lampstands (1 Kings 7). In marriage ceremonies and in funeral processions ten attendants were required (cf. Matt. 25:1). No synagogue could be organized unless there were ten adult males present. John says in this verse that the fullness of world power has not been reached. He thus points to coming power hostile to God, such as he described in that part of the account of the seven kings which states, "the other has not yet come" (17:10). The conflict will continue. The *one hour* corresponds to the "little time" in 17:10 (cf. Rom. 16:20; 1 Cor. 7:29).

v. 13 This verse states that the ten kings act by and for the beast on whose side they range themselves. They are not independent thinkers but are willing collaborators. Their one fixed purpose, in which all alike join, is to oppose the kingdom of God in Christ (17:14).

v. 14 This war between the Lamb and all the powers of evil extends throughout the history of the world (cf. 17:10,12). The beast may exercise dominion and power in the world as "prince of this world," yet the Lamb is still greater. The Lamb is not just another king; he is *King* of kings (Deut. 10:17; Ps. 136:3; Dan. 2:47; 11:36). He has supreme power over all the earth (19:16). The beast will be overcome by the unconquerable and invincible Lamb. Not only will the Lamb (***Lord of lords and King of kings***) war and overcome, but those associates with him (***called and chosen and faithful***) are permitted to share in the battles and in the victory. John pictures the Lamb as engaging in the struggle because the victory is won in a gentle, quiet, and spiritual method of warfare (2 Cor. 10:3-6).

v. 15 Having explained the mystery of the beast, to which the woman looks for support, the angel proceeds to unfold the mystery of the harlot herself. In 17:7 the beast carries the woman and in this verse she sits upon ***waters***, that is, the confused and sinful human race (Isa. 8:7; Jer. 47:2). These statements say the same thing in different ways. The beast is world power which is found among the *peoples and multitudes and nations and tongues.* These four terms form a description of the human race (5:9) which serves the beast (13:3,8,12,16), and out of which are selected the redeemed (5:9; 7:7; 19:9).

v. 16 This verse describes the fate of false religion. By its very nature, false religion develops the elements of its own destruction. The world power (the beast with the ten horns), in which she trusts, rises in rebellion and destroys her (Ezek. 16:35-43; 23:22). The statements *devour her flesh* and *burn her up with fire* describe similar results. The first is thought of in connection with the symbol of *harlot* and the other with the symbol of "city." Both of these statements indicate absolute and total destruction and also the feelings of those who destroy the *harlot* and the "city." False religion is completely destroyed by those whom she seduces and makes drunk with the wine of her fornication (17:2).

vv. 17-18 The "peoples and multitudes and nations and tongues" are performing the will of the beast, and yet God is working above all. God utilizes them as his agents in bringing about his designs (Hab. 1:5-10). He gives them life, capacity, and opportunities; but he does not inspire or coerce them. He so disposes their hearts that they have God's mind, though they little realize whose will they are performing. In destroying false religion, they think they are accomplishing their own purposes, as did the Assyrians (Isa. 10:5 ff.), but in fact they are carrying out God's purposes. This is a vivid statement of the self-destroying power of evil. Both world power and false religion in opposition to the plan and purpose of God goes down in ruins. Antichristian forces are doomed, and God is victorious. The harlot and Babylon are again said to be identical (17:5).

b. The Fall of Babylon Depicted in Old Testament Doom Songs (18:1-24)

¹ After this I saw another angel coming down from heaven, having great

authority; and the earth was made bright with his splendor. ² And he called out with a mighty voice,
"Fallen, fallen is Babylon the great!
It has become a dwelling place of demons,
a haunt of every foul spirit,
a haunt of every foul and hateful bird;
³ for all nations have drunk the wine of her impure passion,
and the kings of the earth have committed fornication with her,
and the merchants of the earth have grown rich with the wealth of her wantonness."
⁴ Then I heard another voice from heaven saying,
"Come out of her, my people,
lest you take part in her sins,
lest you share in her plagues;
⁵ for her sins are heaped high as heaven,
and God has remembered her iniquities.
⁶ Render to her as she herself has rendered,
and repay her double for her deeds;
mix a double draught for her in the cup she mixed.
⁷ As she glorified herself and played the wanton,
so give her a like measure of torment and mourning.
Since in her heart she says, 'A queen I sit,
I am no widow, mourning I shall never see,'
⁸ so shall her plagues come in a single day,
pestilence and mourning and famine,
and she shall be burned with fire;
for mighty is the Lord God who judges her."
⁹ And the kings of the earth, who committed fornication and were wanton with her, will weep and wail over her when they see the smoke of her burning; ¹⁰ they will stand far off, in fear of her torment, and say,
"Alas! alas! thou great city,
thou mighty city, Babylon!
In one hour has thy judgment come."
¹¹ And the merchants of the earth weep and mourn for her, since no one buys their cargo any more, ¹² cargo of gold, silver, jewels and pearls, fine linen, purple, silk and scarlet, all kinds of scented wood, all articles of ivory, all articles of costly wood, bronze, iron and marble, ¹³ cinnamon, spice, incense, myrrh, frankincense, wine, oil, fine flour and wheat, cattle and sheep, horses and chariots, and slaves, that is, human souls.
¹⁴ "The fruit for which thy soul longed has gone from thee,
and all thy dainties and thy splendor are lost to thee, never to be found again!"
¹⁵ The merchants of these wares, who gained wealth from her, will stand

far off, in fear of her torment, weeping and mourning aloud,
  ¹⁶ "Alas, alas, for the great city
  that was clothed in fine linen, in purple and scarlet,
  bedecked with gold, with jewels, and with pearls!"
  ¹⁷ In one hour all this wealth has been laid waste."
And all shipmasters and seafaring men, sailors and all whose trade is on the sea, stood far off ¹⁸ and cried out as they saw the smoke of her burning,
  "What city was like the great city?"
¹⁹ And they threw dust on their heads, as they wept and mourned, crying out,
  "Alas, alas, for the great city
  where all who had ships at sea grew rich by her wealth!
  In one hour she has been laid waste.
  ²⁰ Rejoice over her, O heaven,
  O saints and apostles and prophets,
  for God has given judgment for you against her!"
²¹ Then a mighty angel took up a stone like a great millstone and threw it into the sea, saying,
  "So shall Babylon the great city be thrown down with violence,
  and shall be found no more;
  ²² and the sound of harpers and minstrels, of flute players and trumpeters,
    shall be heard in thee no more;
  and a craftsman of any craft
    shall be found in thee no more;
  and the sound of the millstone
    shall be heard in thee no more;
  ²³ and the light of a lamp
    shall shine in thee no more;
  and the voice of bridegroom and bride
    shall be heard in thee no more;
  for thy merchants were the great men of the earth,
    and all nations were deceived by thy sorcery.
  ²⁴ And in her was found the blood of prophets and of saints,
    and of all who have been slain on earth."

v. 1 After one of the seven angels (17:1) had shown the "mystery" of the beast and the harlot, another powerful and magnificent angel declared the judgment from heaven upon Babylon (10:1). The authority and splendor of the angel is conveyed by the description (Ex. 24:16; Ezek. 43:1-2; Matt. 17:2; Luke 2:9; Acts 9:3).

His description indicates that he is particularly important. He comes *down from heaven*, that is, from the presence of God. "So recently has he come from the Presence that in passing he flings a broad belt of light across the earth" (Swete). He is symbolic of and represents God's authority and purpose. As the dragon gave authority to the beast (13:2), so God gives authority to his messenger. God's messenger announces the triumph of the gospel and the liberation of the people of God from false religion.

v. 2 In this verse the angel announces *with a mighty voice* the utter destruction of Babylon. The announcement is made with the emphasis of repetition (Isa. 21:9). Babylon is to be identified with the harlot in the preceding chapter. It symbolizes false religion which deceives the whole world and for whom a supra-historical judgment waits. It is here graphically symbolized as a pretentious, worldly, corrupt, and domineering city. The three phrases which John uses to describe fallen Babylon express the loathsome and hateful state to which she is reduced. He draws a picture of utter destruction, emptiness, and desolation (Beckwith). The very words of Isaiah and Jeremiah are employed in this description of Babylon's wretched state (Isa. 13:19-22; 21:8-9; 34:11,14; Jer. 50:39; 51:8,37). Her fall symbolizes the destruction of false religion, which opposes the people of God. The outward desolation of the city is only a symbol of the downfall of false religion when brought into conflict with God in Christ. John pictures the complete ruin which overtakes false religion.

v. 3 In this verse John tells why antichristian forces are doomed (Isa. 23:17). False religion is obliterated because it beguiles and corrupts the people of the earth and leads them into estrangement from God and into pollution and sin. The figure *all nations have drunk the wine of her impure passion* implies a drunken insanity which brings inevitable doom to those who participate in it. Like the people of Tyre (Ezek. 27:9-27), people are persuaded by false religion to put their trust in self-indulgence and arrogance which destroy character.

v. 4 John hears an unidentified voice from heaven which calls the people of God to separate themselves from Babylon in order to escape her punishments (Gen. 12:1; 19:12,22; Num. 16:23 f.; Isa. 48:20; 52:11; Jer. 50:8; 51:6,45; Zech. 2:6-7; Matt. 24:16; 2 Cor. 6:14).

The fact that it comes from *heaven* indicates that it is God's message. The command to *come out of her* is not to be understood as a separation from society, but a warning to the church not to share in the principles of false religion (John 17:15-16). God's undiscriminating judgment comes upon false religion no matter where it is found. It is the operation of the principle of cause and effect. If Christians are to escape the woes of false religion, they must escape from the unreal. Compromise with the artificial in religion is fatal. This is a direct warning to the church. The mark which the people of God carry on their foreheads must be the mark of a godly heart and a holy life.

v. 5 John depicts in a vivid hyperbole the accumulation of the sins of Babylon and states that God does not forget the iniquities of false religion. He remembers them in judgment. There may be an allusion here to the tower of Babel, whose top its builders proposed should reach unto heaven (Gen. 11:4). A similar description is given of the heaped-up sins of Babylon in Jeremiah 51:9.

v. 6 This description of God's judgment is founded on the denunciations against Babylon (Isa. 40:2; 61:7; Jer. 1:15-19; 16:18; 51:21; Zech. 9:12). The command is addressed to the angelic agent of judgment to render in like kind and in proportion to her sin. *Double* is used in apocalyptic writings to express abundance. The double recompense was also according to the Levitical law (Ex. 22:4,7,9). When judgment is *double,* it is because the sin is *double,* that is, very great (Jer. 16:18; 17:18). John asserts the extremity of Babylon's guilt, which calls for punishment in full measure. The iniquities with which she filled her cup (17:4) have now turned into the wine of the wrath of God. The seeds of judgment lie in every evil principle, and these seeds must germinate and produce fruit when they are planted.

v. 7 This verse continues the address to the angelic agent of judgment. The extremity of Babylon's guilt calls for extremity of retribution. She is pictured as a wealthy, magnificent, and arrogant queen who has unquestioning faith in her own inexhaustible resources but who will soon become a mourning widow (Isa. 47:7-9; Lam. 1:1). The cause of her fall is her self-glorification. She has a high estimate of herself. She envisions herself supreme over all and looks for the same state to continue. She fulfills the proverb, "Whom the gods would destroy, they first make mad with power." The allusion to harlotry is an echo of the prophets who used the term to describe man's unbelief in God, especially in connection with idolatry. False religion is condemned to failure and ruin.

v. 8 In spite of Babylon's pride, presumption, and power, her destruction will be absolute and complete. The proud powerful queen forgot *the Lord God who judges her.* He is able to carry out his will, to defeat all the forces of evil. None can frustrate or defeat him, not even false religion with all her pomp and glory. He directs to the purposed end the agencies necessary for her destruction (17:17). He directs the invincible and unalterable law of moral retribution. "Her plagues are four-fold, as though from every quarter her trouble came" (Carpenter).

This verse emphasizes with a great variety of emphatic images the total destruction of false religion *in a single day,* that is, with a fearsome brevity. This judgment of God is not arbitrary but is according to her sins.

vv. 9-10 The picture in these verses is intended to make more vivid and intense the complete destruction of Babylon. The kings (the embodiment of all political power of the world; 16:14; 19:19) are the first of three groups who have been associated with Babylon and have been benefited by her to lament her destruction (Isa 23; Jer. 50:46; Ezek. 26–27). All three groups *stand far off* with no thought of comforting or helping her, but taking heed not to be involved in her ruin. Each one was interested in the city for what he could get out of her. The kings are distressed at her fate, for they have been closely associated with her in the sins that brought about her destruction (17:2; 18:3). "The grief described is the result of fear mingled with selfishness" (Carpenter). They mourn more for themselves than for the fallen city. Their ally is destroyed and much of the source of their power is taken away, because false religion contributes to and sustains oppressive and arbitrary government. "The secular spirit rebels against the corruption of even a decadent religious authority, while it mourns the loss of commercial and social advantages" (Tenney). The *one hour* denotes a period whose shortness should be emphasized.

v. 11 The merchants lament (present tense) the fall of the doomed city because *no one buys their cargo any more.* This lamentation of the *merchants of the earth* is based on Ezekiel 27:28-36. These lamenting merchants symbolize those who have been accustomed to doing business with the leaders of false religion and who have been enriched by this trade. False religion provides abundant wealth, extensive commerce, and diffused luxury to those who engage in her traffic. When false religion is destroyed, those who engage in her commerce lose their hope of profit. They lose their market, and there is no one to purchase their wares. This principle was vividly illustrated when Paul's preaching threatened the sales of the images of Artemis in Ephesus (Acts 19:23-41).

vv. 12-13 In these verses are listed 29 articles of commerce which false religion fashions into items of extravagant luxury. Many of these articles are worn by the harlot (17:4). Ezekiel 27:1-24 supplies the imagery for these verses. To create such commerce, the merchants have entered into an unholy alliance with false religion. With the destruction of Babylon, the market for this unrighteous wealth will be destroyed.

These articles seem naturally to fall into six classes (13:18). They are all valuable and seem to be arranged in a progressive order of importance. The following scheme may be noted: articles of personal adornment—gold, silver, jewels, pearls, fine linen, purple, silk, and scarlet; articles used for furniture, and the like—scented wood, ivory, costly wood, bronze, iron, and marble; objects of sensual gratification—cinnamon, spice, incense, myrrh, and frankincense; articles of food—wine, oil, fine flour, and wheat; animate possessions—cattle, sheep, and horses and chariots; slaves—human souls.

v. 14 In this verse John speaks directly to the city under the image of harlot. The identity of description of the harlot and the city is another proof of the fact that they symbolize the same thing (17:1,4-5; 18:2-3,7-8,10).

He tells her that the harvest of the desire of her soul is departed once for all from her. Men will no longer find exotic foodstuff and decorative clothing in Babylon. With the complete destruction of the city, her wares that made her attractive are gone. She has nothing to allure.

vv. 15-17a After the digression in which John addresses the city as the harlot, he resumed the description of the wailing and lamentations of the merchants. Their wailing does not express sorrow for the doomed city, but their grief at the loss of their wealth and the opportunities for commerce. They have vested interest in false religion, and they bewail the passing of their profits. The great city is depicted in terms which almost exactly reproduce the description of the harlot (17:4). The items of her clothing are supplied by the merchants. In a very brief period, ***one hour***, her destruction is sudden and complete.

vv. 17b-19 In these verses John shows in a dramatic way the effects of the destruction of the great city upon merchants who travel by sea, shipmasters, and sailors (Ezek. 27:27-32). The extravagance, splendor, and luxury of the rituals of false religion draws materials from all parts of the world. These seafarers express grief and despair. They lament, but they do not offer help. Their loss of profit excites their distress. They mourn because they also have vested interest in the maintenance of false religion. Their lamentation is just as selfish as their commerce had been. They *threw dust on their heads,* a common sign of deep mourning and grief among Orientals. The graphic details of their lamentations emphasize the complete destruction of the incomparable city. The substance of each lamentation is that in one hour judgment has come (18:10,17,19). False religion will be destroyed!

v. 20 This is an unidentified summons to heaven and the whole church to rejoice over the victory of Christ and the destruction of false religion (Isa. 44:23; Jer. 51:48; Luke 15:7,10). The voice (possibly John's) orders celebration, because justice has been done, and Christian faith has been vindicated. Right has triumphed, righteousness and truth have prevailed, and God is glorified. The service of God is established, and there is no more resistance to his will. God has confirmed the judgment of the church.

v. 21 This verse pictures an enacted parable of the utter ruin of Babylon (Neh. 9:11; Jer. 51:60-64; Acts 21:11). As a large millstone sinks to the bottom of the sea, never to be recovered, so false religion is to be destroyed and will never appear again. It is not to exist forever. Because Babylon is evil, all voices are silenced and all crafts terminated. "In the short day of Babylon's downfall is telescoped the downfall of evil systems throughout the centuries" (Blaney). The symbolism describes the complete and final destruction of false religion. The total nature of this destruction is indicated by the frequency of the words, *no more* (18:21-23). Six times this expression occurs, and always concerning the same fact.

vv. 22-24 In these verses John gives a graphic and dramatic picture of the desolation of Babylon. The destruction of the city is complete. The list of the things which will not be heard, seen, or done include: music, crafts, sound of the millstone grinding grain, the light of a lamp, and the voice of the bridegroom and bride. These five items emphasize the utter desolation and ruin of the once busy and populous city. In intense symbolism, John assures the church that false religion is to be destroyed. Christ is in his church (1:12-20), and he will not forget his promises; nor will his faithfulness fail. God in Christ is pledged to the overthrow of false religion. The destruction of Babylon is the overthrow by God of all that is false and passing, in order that the true and eternal may take its proper place (Wernecke).

The causes of the destruction are the result of deceiving the nations and the slaying of God's saints.

c. The Judgment of Heaven upon Babylon (19:1-10)

¹ After this I heard what seemed to be the mighty voice of a great multitude in heaven, crying,
"Hallelujah! Salvation and glory and power belong to our God,
² for his judgments are true and just;
he has judged the great harlot who corrupted the earth with her fornication,
and he has avenged on her the blood of his servants."
³ Once more they cried,
"Hallelujah! The smoke of her goes up for ever and ever."
⁴ And the twenty-four elders and the four living creatures fell down and worshiped God who is seated on the throne, saying, "Amen, Hallelujah!"
⁵ And from the throne came a voice crying,
"Praise our God, all you his servants,
you who fear him, small and great."
⁶ Then I heard what seemed to be the voice of a great multitude, like the sound of many waters and like the sound of mighty thunderpeals, crying,
"Hallelujah! For the Lord our God the Almighty reigns.
⁷ Let us rejoice and exult and give him the glory,
for the marriage of the Lamb has come,
and his Bride has made herself ready;
⁸ it was granted her to be clothed with fine linen, bright and pure"—
for the fine linen is the righteous deeds of the saints.
⁹ And the angel said to me, "Write this: Blessed are those who are invited to the marriage supper of the Lamb." And he said to me, "These are true words of God." ¹⁰ Then I fell down at his feet to worship him, but he said to me, "You must not do that! I am a fellow servant with you and your brethren who hold the testimony of Jesus. Worship God." For the testimony of Jesus is the spirit of prophecy.

v. 1 The final pronouncement of doom upon the harlot issues from heaven. Judgment is followed by a hymn of praise (4:8-11;

5:9-14; 7:10-12; 11:15-18; 15:3; 16:5). The *great multitude in heaven* refers to the redeemed in heaven (7:9-10). There is no separation in interest between the church militant on earth and the church triumphant in heaven. The great multitude ascribes united praises to God, because he is responsible for the defeat of false religion and the victory of the gospel. Their paeans of praises also form a response to the exultant cry to rejoice over the victory of Christ in 18:20. The word *Hallelujah* occurs four times in this chapter (vv. 1,3-4,6) but nowhere else in the New Testament. It is a transliteration of a Hebrew word which means, "Praise ye Jah" (Vine, p. 190). The victorious church affirms the fact that all of their salvation, glory, and power belong to God. These three words express God's redemption on behalf of man (7:10; 12:10). He is the author of all salvation. The victory of God is the victory won by the redeemed, and their victory is the victory of the cross (Caird). As false religion claims to give salvation, glory, and power, her fall is a threefold vindication of God's supremacy. Not only does God possess unlimited power, but he uses that power to effect his sovereignty. This "Hallelujah Chorus" is also the triumphant rejoicing over the downfall of false principles and deceitful practices at the hand of God.

v. 2 In this verse John gives a twofold reason for the united praises of the victorious church for the overthrow of the city (16:7). The harlot *corrupted the earth with her fornication,* that is, brought moral ruin upon the earth, and persecuted God's servants. God's judgment upon the harlot are *true and just,* that is, the destruction which has come upon her is deserved. The moral law can no more be broken than the law of gravitation, it can only be illustrated! (Kepler). A godless and guilty religion feels the terror of God's avenging and destroying wrath (Deut. 32:43; 2 Kings 9:7). God's judgments against falsehood are the guards of truth. He has passed judgment upon the harlot because the martyred saints have given in their sacrificial lives the evidence which secured her condemnation (Caird). The destruction of Babylon was preliminary to the new Jerusalem coming down out of heaven.

v. 3 In this verse, the complete destruction of false religion is again pictured as a burning city (18:9,18). The statement that her smoke *goes up for ever and ever* means that her destruction is eternal, since false religion will never recover. This image is derived from the description of the smoke ascending from Sodom and Gomorrah (Gen. 19:28; cf. Isa. 34:10). The great multitude is in reality expressing the victory of the gospel over all forms of counterfeit religion, because the destruction of false religion is but the prelude to the victory of the church.

v. 4 The church on earth and creation are represented as uniting with the redeemed in heaven in the song of triumph and thanksgiving. God is represented as sitting on the throne to emphasize the fact that he is exercising power and dominion. He has all-controlling authority. The word *Amen* indicates their assent to God's righteous judgment upon false religion. The church and creation worship and praise God for what he has done in causing righteousness and truth to triumph in the world.

vv. 5-6 An unidentified voice from God's throne (14:2) calls on the whole company of God's servants to join in universal praise of God for what he has done. In response to the invitation, powerful and musical voices seem mingled in praise. The reason for the strong and sustained praise is that **the Lord our God the Almighty reigns** (1:8; 4:8; 11:17; 15:3; 16:7,14; 19:15; 21:22). World power and false religion have fallen in order that the spiritual and eternal may take their place. "The day that sees the end of a false statecraft will see also that of a false priestcraft" (Swete). Smith says this praise "is a thankful and joyful recognition of his sovereignty called forth by recent events, in which the fact [God's reign] has found signal illustrations." It is easy to catch the practical encouragement found in these verses, both as it affected the churches addressed and the churches in all times.

The devil may rage, the beast may fight, and the false prophet may join hands with both, but all of them together are impotent

THE SEVENFOLD VISION OF CONFLICT

in conflict because God is on the throne of the universe and one like a son of man walks among the seven golden lampstands (1:13). The pledge of victory is sure!

vv. 7-8 The unidentified voice calls for universal praise to God because of the prospect of the nearer union of joyous fellowship between the Lamb and his Bride. The figure *marriage of the Lamb* is a representation of the union and fellowship between Christ and his church (Isa. 54:1-8; 60:4-5; Jer. 3:14; 31:32; Ezek. 16:7; Hos. 2:16,19-20; 2 Cor. 11:2; Eph. 5:23-33). This figure expresses the meaning of eternal life in its widest embrace (John 17:3,21-22; 1 John 1:3). This union stands in marked contrast with the fornication of the harlot, the union of those who worship world power with that power. The glory is given to God because it is by his power alone that counterfeit and compromise are purged out of the church. The *Bride has made herself ready* by putting on her bridal garments; however, her wedding garments were *granted her,* that is, they were bestowed upon her by Christ (Eph. 5:25; Phil. 3:8-10). The church makes herself ready for Christ, and Christ makes her ready (Phil. 2:12b-13). Without him, she cannot make herself ready, and without her consent, he will not make her ready. Cooperation on her part is needed to make effective his restoring work. There is a manifest contrast between the dress of the harlot (17:4; 18:16) and the wedding garment of the bride.

The emphasis in these verses is upon the clothing of the bride. No nuptial scene is shown or described. The white garments are emblematic of purity and righteousness. It is the purpose of God and the care of the church to produce a holy people, fitted by God's grace to be the bride of the Lamb. The church must make herself ready by putting on the pure spirit and faithful service which God provides.

v. 9 John is again commanded to write (1:11,19; 2:1,8,12,18; 3:1,7,14; 14:13; 21:5), one of the seven beatitudes of the Revelation (1:3; 14:13; 16:15; 19:9; 20:6; 22:7; 22:14). This beatitude is pronounced upon those who have received the call to the *marriage* *supper of the Lamb.* This is a supper of fellowship based on love. Jesus compared the kingdom of heaven with a marriage feast (Matt. 22:1-14; 25:1-13; cf. Luke 12:35-38). The actual wedding supper is not described. John changes his imagery in this verse, and those who constitute the bride (19:7-8) become guest at the great and joyful marriage feast. He is stressing here the close relationship between Christ and his followers. In fact, this metaphor expresses the most intimate and personal contact between Christ and his church (Isa. 61:10; Ezek. 16; Hos. 2; Mark 2:19). There is an indissoluble union between Christ and the people of God.

Jesus said, "As you did it to one of the least of these my brethren, you did it to me" (Matt. 25:40). Jesus also said, "I in them and thou in me, that they may become perfectly one" (John 17:23). Paul, in his Damascas road encounter, learned of the personal and intimate character of the relation between Christ and his people (Acts 9:1,4-5; cf. Rom. 12:5; 1 Cor. 8:12; 12:20,27; Eph. 4:12,25). The Christians are "in Christ," and therefore, anything done to them is done to him (Matt. 10:40; Luke 10:16; John 13:20). The verse concludes with a solemn confirmation of the truth and certainty of the message. The truth that God in Christ does triumph helps the church in every persecution, trial, and temptation.

v. 10 John was so overwhelmed by the messenger and the tremendous character of the truth which the angel disclosed to him that he fell upon the earth in a posture of adoration and worship. The angel reproved him and informed him that only God is worthy of worship. The angel also told him that he was his fellow servant along with his brethren who were engaged in the same worship and service. This statement is directed against angel worship, a practice which Paul warned against in Colossae (Col. 2:18).

The gnostic cults emphasized the distance between God and man and attempted to fill the gap with a hierarchy of angelic and superhuman mediators. The angel places himself on a par with John as a servant of the same God, charged with the same testimony (Heb. 1:4-14). The angel, John, and all other fellow servants are engaged in the service of bearing testimony to Jesus. The angel's protest was a salutary warning to John not to mistake the cause he was championing for the one true God. John is told that only God is to be worshiped (Matt. 4:10). The paragraph concludes with the statement, *For the testimony of Jesus is the spirit of prophecy.* This is probably an explanation added by John. The witness of testifying to Christ is the spirit of Jesus at work in the redeemed. This is the same spirit of those who prophesy for Christ (1 Cor. 12:10; 1 Pet. 1:11; 2 Pet. 1:21). The witness of the prophet and that of the Christian are essentially the same. The true spirit of prophecy was the testimony which Jesus bore and also the testimony borne to Jesus (Morris). "It is the word spoken by God and attested by Jesus that the Spirit takes and puts into the mouth of the Christian prophet" (Caird). It is to understand and proclaim the truths concerning God as revealed by Jesus.

d. The Vision of the Conquering Christ (19:11 to 20:15)

In this section the overthrow of the enemies of Christ and the church is viewed under various symbols. This vision shows that back of all history is the supreme will and work of the conquering Christ. His conquests are portrayed to the end of time. He is ever engaged in the war of triumph so long as there is evil to be overcome by good. The victory which he wins is absolute, not negotiated as between equals, but dictated by the supreme power of righteousness. The struggle does not end until the very principle and source of evil has been discovered and conquered. This means ultimate moral victory.

(a) Christ the Captain and His Armies (19:11-16)

[11] Then I saw heaven opened, and behold, a white horse! He who sat upon it is called Faithful and True, and in righteousness he judges and makes war. [12] His eyes are like a flame of fire, and on his head are many diadems; and he has a name inscribed which no one knows but himself. [13] He is clad in a robe dipped in blood, and the name by which he is called is The Word of God. [14] And the armies of heaven, arrayed in fine

linen, white and pure, followed him on white horses. ⁱ⁵ From his mouth issues a sharp sword with which to smite the nations, and he will rule them with a rod of iron; he will tread the wine press of the fury of the wrath of God the Almighty. ¹⁶ On his robe and on his thigh he has a name inscribed, King of kings and Lord of lords.

v. 11 John introduced this vision by saying that he saw *heaven opened.* This means that he had insights which were beyond earthly reasoning, events, and circumstances (4:1; 11:19; 15:5). In the vision John saw a mysterious warrior on a white horse. The white warhorse is emblematic of victory. The rider is Christ. The attributes and traits of the rider are elsewhere applied to him. He is called *Faithful* (1:5; 3:14) and *True* (3:7,14). His word shall not fail. He is worthy of the confidence of the church in delivering it from all its enemies and true to all the promises that he has made to it (Wernecke). Because he is faithful, he cannot allow his people to struggle alone; and because he is true, he must bring truth to victory.

The purpose of his expedition is to judge and make war (Isa. 11:1-5; Joel 3:1-16). He is both Judge and Warrior, but he does both in righteousness (15:3; 16:5,7; 19:2; cf. John 17:25). *Judges* denotes the part played in the lawcourt by the witness to secure a conviction (Matt. 12:41-42; Luke 11:31-32; Rom. 2:27). Jesus *judges* because it is on his evidence that the victory turns (Caird). The war that he makes is against evil in its various guises. This warfare is not with flesh and blood but with "principalities," "powers," "world-rulers of this darkness," and with all spiritual forces which give support and authority to the forces of evil upon earth (Rom. 8:38-39; Eph. 1:21; 3:10; 6:12; Col. 2:15).

This picturesque military imagery represents the victorious Christ as coming from heaven to fight the battles of earth. "This is not some supernatural figure from the fantasies of Jewish apocalyptic, but the Jesus of history, whose final victory in the battle to come serves only to make plain to the world the victory seen by faith from the beginning of the cross" (Caird).

vv. 12-13 The attributes and traits of the victorious Christ are continued in these verses. *His eyes are like a flame of fire,* penetrating and piercing so that nothing can escape his vision (1:14; 2:18). He knows the true meaning of all events and actions. The beast out of the sea (world power) had a diadem on each of his ten horns (13:1); Christ wears many diadems to show that all power is united and concentrated in him. He is king of all nations, and universal reign truly belongs to him (Zech. 6:11-12; Phil. 2:9). He has many names which may be understood, but he has one name which is incommunicable to men, and into which no one penetrates to the full but the Father and Christ himself (Matt. 11:27). The name expresses the person. To know a name is to know the person and also to possess power over him whose name is known (Gen. 32:29; Judg. 13:18; Isa. 9:6). There is in Christ's nature hidden depths which are beyond the capacity of man to comprehend, and no one has power over Christ. "Only the Son can understand the mystery of His own Being" (Swete).

It is not so much the name, as the full import of the name, which no one knows (Matt. 11:27). The bloodstains upon his robe are symbolic of that self-sacrifice in the power of which he goes forth to conquer (Isa. 63:1-4). He is the personified *Word of God* (John 1:1-14; Col. 1:15-17). This means that he is the agent through whom the thought of God is expressed to men (Eph. 6:17; Heb. 4:12). He is the final and perfect revelation of God and the full expression of his whole being (John 1:18; 10:30; 14:9). He is close to God and he gets his power directly from God—"In him the whole fulness of deity dwells bodily" (Col. 2:9).

v. 14 The victorious Christ is not by himself. He is followed by celestial troops mounted on white horses *arrayed in fine linen, white and pure.* These *armies of heaven* symbolize the redeemed, the church. Their garments are the usual attire of the righteous (3:4-5; 4:4; 6:11; 7:9,13-14; 15:6), and they resemble the dress worn by the bride (19:8). They have put on the "whole armor of God" (Eph. 6:13).

They are clad with purity and power, for they "follow the Lamb wherever he goes" (14:4). The blood of their leader "has made their robes white, and theirs has made his red" (Caird). These celestial troops are the "called and chosen and faithful" (17:14). This picturesque symbol represents the victorious Christ leading forth his faithful followers to do battle against evil in all its guises. It declares the conquering power and effect of the gospel. There is no mention of weapons; neither are the troops depicted as taking any hostile action. This is a spiritual rather than a military conflict. The redeemed do not overcome evil with evil, but they overcome evil with good (Rom. 12:21). Christ and his people are united in his purpose and plan of redemption. As the first beast (world power; cf. 13:1) makes use of his helper, the false prophet (13:11 ff.; 16:13), who belongs inseparably to the first beast and dragon, so Christ makes use of his followers in the struggle with evil.

vv. 15-16 In these verses John concludes his list of the attributes and traits of the victorious Christ. Most of these features, found earlier in Revelation (1:16; 2:27; 12:5; 14:19-20), are associated in Jewish writings with Messiah. He fights, not with carnal weapons, but with the sharp sword of his word, with which he conquers the nations (1:16; cf. Isa. 11:4). This sharp sword is the truth of God as it is in Christ. The only weapon which the rider uses to conquer the nations is the proclamation of the gospel (Isa. 49:2). He leads the forces of righteousness to victory by his penetrating word. The war he wages and the victories he achieves are moral. The "rod of iron" (Ps. 2:9, ASV) which Christ uses to overcome opposition is the inflexible rod of God's truth and the testimony of the saints (2:27; 12:5,17; 13:10). The symbolism ***he will tread the wine press of the fury of the wrath of God the Almighty*** is descriptive of warfare, victory, and judgment (Isa. 11:4; 63:3; Joel 3:13). One of his names, ***King of kings and Lord of lords,*** is conspicuously written on his robe or on his thigh or on both (17:14; 1 Tim. 6:15). This name means that he is sovereign over all rulers of the earth (Deut. 10:17). The dominating idea in these symbols

THE SEVENFOLD VISION OF CONFLICT

is that of complete victory (John 8:32).

(b) The Defeat of the Beast and His Allies (19:17-21)

¹⁷ Then I saw an angel standing in the sun, and with a loud voice he called to all the birds that fly in midheaven, "Come, gather for the great supper of God, ¹⁸ to eat the flesh of kings, the flesh of captains, the flesh of mighty men, the flesh of horses and their riders, and the flesh of all men, both free and slave, both small and great." ¹⁹ And I saw the beast and the kings of the earth with their armies gathered to make war against him who sits upon the horse and against his army. ²⁰ And the beast was captured, and with it the false prophet who in its presence had worked the signs by which he deceived those who had received the mark of the beast and those who worshiped its image. These two were thrown alive into the lake of fire that burns with brimstone. ²¹ And the rest were slain by the sword of him who sits upon the horse, the sword that issues from his mouth; and all the birds were gorged with their flesh.

vv. 17-18 An unidentified angel *standing in the sun,* that is, *in midheaven,* where his voice could be clearly heard, summons the birds of prey to assemble together to feast upon the carcasses of the slain (Ezek. 39:17-20; Matt. 24:28). It must be remembered that the battle is a symbol. The struggle between good and evil is symbolized under the figure of a battle. The complete overthrow of evil is represented by the total defeat of an army, the bodies of the slain being left unburied upon the battlefield. It is a graphic figurative representation of the utter defeat of all enemies of Christ and the church.

The **great supper of God** is in grim contrast with the marriage supper of the Lamb (19:9). This feast is made from all classes of men. It is universal. None can escape. The victory of Christ's cause over evil is certain. The account indicates the widespread and complete nature of God's judgment, which none shall be able to escape. To John the triumph is so certain that he speaks of it as already accomplished. Caird says that "divine retribution is not less reliable than the birds."

v. 19 This is a picture of the assembling of all the antichristian forces for the conclusive war (16:13-14). The beast (13:1) and the kings of the earth (16:13-14,16) with their armies gather for "the" war. The war is being waged by the antichristian forces against Christ and his church and will not be terminated until the end of time.

v. 20 The vision contains no description of the battle but passes directly to the outcome. "Victory happens infallibly, inevitably, automatically" (Calkins). The beast (13:1) and the false prophet (13:11; 16:13; 17:1,18) were captured and thrown alive into the *lake of fire* (Dan. 7:11). The *lake of fire* is a familiar apocalyptic term which represents eternal torment (20:10,14-15). The beast and false prophet are abstractions or personifications of hostility to Christ. They describe the earthly manifestations of Satan's power and are the true spiritual leaders of all antichristian forces in the world. In like manner, the *lake of fire* is an image of utter destruction. This symbol is used in other apocalyptic literature. It was borrowed from the Dead Sea, the *brimstone* lake which covers the cities of Sodom and Gomorrah (Gen. 19:24-29). John means that the destruction of these powers is as complete as if they were thrown into a burning lake. The victory of Christ's cause and his people over evil is certain. Evil itself, and not merely the temporary manifestations of it, is destined to be destroyed. Richardson says, "Rebellion against God ends in death of the deepest kind."

v. 21 In this verse John completes the picture of the destruction of the armies who were opposed to Christ. The *rest* includes all the antichristian forces described as those following the beast and the false prophet (19:18-19). These were slain with the sword that issues from the mouth of *him who sits upon the white horse* (1:16 19:15). His truth is a spiritual weapon of resistless power (Isa. 11:4 Dan. 7:11). No rebellion against the King of kings and Lord o lords can prevail. The nature of the disaster is emphasized by th reference to the indignity offered to their bodies after death. Unde this graphic symbolism, John represents the triumph of the gospel The victory is complete. Evil is defeated when the church goe

THE SEVENFOLD VISION OF CONFLICT 221

forth into combat with Christ leading them.

(c) The Abridgment of Satan's Power (20:1-6)

¹ Then I saw an angel coming down from heaven, holding in his hand the key of the bottomless pit and a great chain. ² And he seized the dragon, that ancient serpent, who is the Devil and Satan, and bound him for a thousand years, ³ and threw him into the pit, and shut it and sealed it over him, that he should deceive the nations no more, till the thousand years were ended. After that he must be loosed for a little while. ⁴ Then I saw thrones, and seated on them were those to whom judgment was committed. Also I saw the souls of those who had been beheaded for their testimony to Jesus and for the word of God, and who had not worshiped the beast or its image and had not received its mark on their foreheads or their hands. They came to life, and reigned with Christ a thousand years. ⁵ The rest of the dead did not come to life until the thousand years were ended. This is the first resurrection. ⁶ Blessed and holy is he who shares in the first resurrection! Over such the second death has no power, but they shall be priests of God and of Christ, and they shall reign with him a thousand years.

v. 1 Chapter 20 is a continuation of the victory events related in chapter 19, forming the concluding part of the vision. In the dramatic symbolism of the previous section, the battle has been fought, the two leaders captured and hurled to utter destruction, and the vast army of evil destroyed. This vast army of evil, led by the beast and the false prophet, is really under the direction of the dragon. The dragon alone is left, like a great general left behind on a battlefield. He is baffled, deserted, and helpless, awaiting the sentence of the foes by whom he is surrounded. An unidentified angel comes **down from heaven** with a **key** and **chain** (1:18). Both the key and the chain are clearly symbolical, for there cannot be a key to the bottomless pit, nor can a spirit be shackled with a chain (Morris). The word meaning **bottomless pit** is connected with ideas which were held concerning the shape of the earth. The earth was thought to be a flat disc floating on water. The "bottomless pit" stood for the immeasurable depths beneath the earth to which there was thought to be a shaft capable of being sealed (Scott).

The fact that the angel comes from heaven means that what transpires is not what man does but what God does. The symbols of key and chain express the reduction in the scope of the dragon's power. This curtailment is described by Jesus under the figure of a strong man bound by a stronger one (Matt. 12:26,29; Mark 3:27).

v. 2 The dragon is seized by the angel and bound for a thousand years. The ***dragon*** is now identified as the ***ancient serpent, the Devil and Satan*** (12:3,9). The dragon personifies the very principle and essence of evil. The one-thousand-year period is symbolical. It expresses no period of time. It expresses an idea. In apocalyptic writings numbers have symbolical rather than numerical significance. The number ten was the number of a complete man. One thousand is the cube of ten, which symbolizes a period of time encompassing all humanity. It symbolizes all people between the incarnation and the second coming. "We have no more right to take the thousand years literally than we have to take the ten-headed and seven-horned monster literally" (Torrance).

The Jews divided history into "the present age" and "the age to come." They expected their Messiah to usher in the age to come or the messianic age. They sometimes spoke of his reign as lasting forty years, four hundred years, and one thousand years. The early Christians accepted Jesus as the Messiah; therefore, they believed that he ushered in the age to come and settled the doom of the old. They were absolutely certain he inaugurated the new age, so that the two ages overlap. They were convinced that they had been delivered out of the present evil age and had already begun to taste the powers of the age to come (Gal. 1:4; Heb. 6:5). They knew themselves to be living "in the end of the ages" (1 Cor 10:11). The incarnation ushered in the "age to come" breaking into the present evil age (Gal. 4:4; Eph. 1:10; 1 Tim. 2:6; Titus 1:3). The New Testament writers never describe the chronology of the age to come, but they did not anticipate that it would last forever. They used many terms to refer to End time (Acts 2:17

1 Cor. 10:11; 1 Tim. 4:1; 2 Tim. 3:1 ff.; Heb. 1:1-2; Jas. 5:3; 1 Pet. 1:5,20; 2 Pet. 3:3; Jude 18). The actual historical realization of what the completion of End time would be was never described, but it was apodictic that a beginning was made when Jesus began his preaching in Galilee (Mark 1:15).

In the incarnation, God's reign was already on the way, already in the process of arrival, or realization, or establishment on the earth. It was this great conviction of the triumph of God's reign through Christ, not only in his earthly ministry but also in his triumph over the forces of evil in this present age, which supported the early Christians in their darkest hours.

Therefore, the messianic kingdom (40, 400, or 1,000 years) that the Jews hoped for had been fulfilled in Christ. In symbolism, the effectual restraint of evil is pictured as a single act. The binding of Satan and the reign of the church represent the victory of Christ in the world. The figure of the binding of Satan is compatible with the expression in Ephesians which names him as the "prince of the power of the air, the spirit that is now at work in the sons of disobedience." He is restrained but not destroyed. Within his restrained sphere, he rages furiously (1 Pet. 5:8). For the Christians, Satan has been completely bound, and they need not fear his deception or his power. He is deprived of his power over the saints of God. For them he is rendered powerless, and his rule is suspended. Satan does not act autonomously, but is subject to the permissive will of God (1 Cor. 10:13). The Christian's true life is beyond Satan's reach, and he cannot prevent the establishment of Christ's kingdom (Matt. 28:19-20). However, so long as evil is restrained but not destroyed, the freedom from struggle will be temporary, and not eternal. Not Satan bound, but Satan destroyed, is the promise and purpose of God (Calkins).

v. 3 This verse gives more details concerning the complete binding of Satan in his character as deceiver (12:9; cf. Isa. 24:22; 53:12; Luke 11:21-22; Col. 2:15). The verbs *shut* and *sealed* are natural symbols of imprisonment. He is imprisoned in order to curtail his activities so that he will not be able to deceive the nations during the time from the incarnation to the second coming. The **nations** are the ungodly, the people among whom Christians live, and from whom they themselves have been redeemed (5:9; 7:9). They are the ones who are made drunk and seduced by the harlot (14:8; 17:15; 18:3,23). They are also the ones to whom John was sent to speak his prophetic message (10:11). They are the ones to whom the angel with the eternal gospel was sent (14:6) and whose conversion the church celebrates (15:4). During this period of Satan's restraint the nations are free from his deceptions (Caird). His power to deceive has been destroyed by the incarnation. If any man remains in Satan's bondage, it is because that man chooses bondage rather than Christ's freedom (John 8:32-36; Rom. 5:15-18; 6:18-23; 8:2; 1 Cor. 7:22; Gal. 4:26; 1 Pet. 2:16). Lenski says, "Those who are deceived are deceived willingly by scorning the heralded eternal gospel." The statement *after that* is literally "after these things" that is, the thousand years. After the thousand years are started, Satan is loosed "for a little time." During the thousand years when Satan is bound in regard to the redeemed, he is also loosed in regard to the unredeemed. The binding and the loosing describe two events that occur contemporaneously. The statement *a little while* is the exact phrase used in 6:11 where it means that period of time from the incarnation to the second coming. The *little while* and the *thousand years* are concurrent and refer to the same period of time whose end is appointed by God and is bound by a special condition (Rissi, p. 24).

v. 4 This verse has a vision of the victorious Christians and martyrs enthroned with Christ. This reign with Christ is simply the positive side of the binding of Satan. The reign is located upon the earth (5:10). The conduct of the redeemed judge and condemn the world (Dan. 7:21-22; Matt. 12:41-42; 19:28; 1 Cor. 6:2). The last part of this verse is a special reference to faithful saints during the thousand years. John promises the same benefits to the martyrs as he does to all those who have refused to worship the beast or his image. The object of these promises is to encourage Christians in their warfare to be true to Christ. These faithful saints, no matter how they suffer, live and reign with Christ during the thousand years. The Greek word translated "lived" does not mean "lived again," but *came to life.* There is no mention of a resurrection in this verse (Smith). When anyone passes from death to life, he "comes to life" or is "risen with Christ" from the death of sin to a life of holiness (John 5:24-25; Rom. 6:4-5; 2 Cor. 5:15; Eph. 2:5-6; Col. 2:12; 1 John 3:14).

v. 5 All the redeemed were once dead in "trespasses and sins" (Eph. 2:1), but in Christ they have "come to life." The phrase "rest of the dead" refers to the unredeemed who do not "come to life."

The spiritually dead who are not spiritually resurrected do not live during the whole Christian age. Richardson says, "They are dead in the deepest sense of the word, suffering now the penalty of sin and rebellion against God; and in the end they shall be plunged into the terrible second death of the lake of fire." The redeemed rise twice, and die but once, while the unredeemed rise but once, and die twice.

The word translated *until* is a particle marking a limit. By usage it gets the force of an adverb which is translated "as long as," "as far as," and "even to" (Thayer, p. 268). The *first resurrection* is the rising of a person from sin and spiritual death to a higher life in Christ. The redeemed, living and reigning with Christ, are partakers of *the first resurrection.*

v. 6 John does not use the phrase "second resurrection," but he does use the words *second death.* Both the *first resurrection* and the *second death* are spiritual operations. In the first part of this verse, John describes the blessedness of those who have part in the spiritual resurrection with Christ. In the second part, he gives to oppressed Christians the reason for patience and perseverance. No one who shares in the *first resurrection* is subject to the power of the *second death* (21:8). The *second death* is the eternal separation from God which the unredeemed experience after physical death. The ones who share in the *first resurrection* are *priests of God and of Christ,* and they reign with Christ during all the End time (1:6; 5:10; Matt. 19:28).

(d) Satan's Final Defeat and Punishment (20:7-10)

⁷ And when the thousand years are ended, Satan will be loosed from his prison ⁸ and will come out to deceive the nations which are at the four corners of the earth, that is, Gog and Magog, to gather them for battle; their number is like the sand of the sea. ⁹ And they marched up over the broad earth and surrounded the camp of the saints and the beloved city; but fire came down from heaven and consumed them, ¹⁰ and the devil who had deceived them was thrown into the lake of fire and brimstone where the beast and the false prophet were, and they will be tormented day and night for ever and ever.

v. 7 The power of Satan has in principle been completely overthrown by Christ; and yet, he is still permitted to exercise sway and wage war on the earth. Just when he appears to be restrained, he breaks out in new effort at deceiving the nations by seducing them with worship opposed to the worship of Christ (Wernecke). However, the concurrent "binding and loosing" of Satan will not last forever. Satan's final and complete elimination from the scene and the termination of this evil and corrupt age is certain (Rist).

Whenever the End time has been brought to its maximum completeness, there is a resurgence of Satan and his complete overthrow. In order to picture the complete defeat of Satan, John renews the battle imagery (16:12-16; 17:14-18; 19:11-21). This verse reflects the tenacity of evil and also the final victory of Christ over it.

v. 8 In Ezekiel 38—39, *Gog* is the name for a chief prince and *Magog* is the name for the land over which he ruled (Gen. 10:2). In Ezekiel 38:17, the names are symbolical of all the foes of the people of God. In apocalyptic writings they symbolize rulers and their peoples who are enemies of the Messiah and who obey the behests of Satan. They always stand for the heathen and God opposing nations of the earth. John, in like manner, uses the terms to denote the ungodly people of the world among whom Satan still exercises power. Among these people "the powers of evil have a defense in depth, which enables them constantly to summon reinforcement from beyond the frontiers of man's knowledge and control" (Caird). Gog and Magog are in number "like the sand of the sea." This statement is an Oriental hyperbole to exaggerate the great size of the multitude (Gen. 22:17; 32:12; Josh. 11:4; Judg. 7:12).

v. 9 The image in this verse is that of a large army that spreads *over the broad earth* (Hab. 1:6). This army surrounds *the camp of the saints and the beloved city* but is consumed by fire from heaven. This is a moral and spiritual destruction, as was that of Babylon (18:1-24). The defeat comes by God's action. The *camp of the saints* and *the beloved city* both refer symbolically to the church under the protecting care and love of God (Swete). The protective power of God is so overwhelming that there is not even the appearance of a battle when God wills to destroy the forces of evil. The symbolism of this verse shows that by divine intervention the hostile army of evil is destroyed (Gen. 19:24; 2 Kings 19:35).

v. 10 This verse pictures the judgment and punishment of the devil. His fate is set forth as that of utter, hopeless, final defeat. The *fire and brimstone* is most likely an allusion to the fate of Sodom and Gomorrah (Gen. 19:24-28). Fire is a symbol of suffering (Ezek. 38:22; Zech. 13:9; 1 Cor. 3:13-15; 1 Pet. 1:7). Brimstone is a symbol of desolation (Job 18:15). In this symbolism John says that the church will be freed from the devil, the beast, the false prophet, and Gog and Magog forever. Wernecke says, "Like a dragon consigned to a lake of fire and brimstone from which there is no escape, the spirit of evil shall be cut off forever from the life of redeemed humanity.... The universe which God has created and rules cannot tolerate evil as a permanent fact in the world of reality." Every vestige of evil will be obliterated and every enemy of the church will be destroyed. The triumph of the kingdom of

God is complete. John has been building up to this climax.

(e) The Judgment of All Enemies of Christ and His Church (20:11-15)

The enemies of Christ and his church have one by one passed from view and have been thrown into the lake of fire and brimstone. Only people remain to be dealt with, both redeemed and unredeemed. In this paragraph, John makes known the fate of all people who rebel against the will of God.

> [11] Then I saw a great white throne and him who sat upon it; from his presence earth and sky fled away, and no place was found for them. [12] And I saw the dead, great and small, standing before the throne, and books were opened. Also another book was opened, which is the book of life. And the dead were judged by what was written in the books, by what they had done. [13] And the sea gave up the dead in it, Death and Hades gave up the dead in them, and all were judged by what they had done. [14] Then Death and Hades were thrown into the lake of fire. This is the second death, the lake of fire, [15] and if anyone's name was not found written in the book of life, he was thrown into the lake of fire.

v. 11 In this verse John saw a great white throne with an unidentified judge upon it from whose presence earth and sky fled away. The *throne* is the focal point of this vision and represents the supreme authority for the judgment of the universe. This scene of infinite majesty emphasizes the fact that everything has vanished except God's authority (Isa. 24:19; 51:6; Matt. 24:35). The Greek word translated *white* implies not so much whiteness as pure brightness. Throughout Revelation it belongs especially to heavenly persons and things (1:14; 2:17; 3:4; 7:9; cf. 1 Kings 10:18-20; Mark 9:3). The *white throne* symbolizes perfect judgment according to absolute and unswerving equity (Isa. 6:1; Dan. 7:9). It denotes the judge's power and the absolute purity of the justice he administers. The judge on the white throne is not identified, but apparently he is God (4:2,9; 5:1,7,13; 6:10,16; 7:10,15; 16:7; 19:2,4; 21:5), but the Father has given all judgment to the Son (John

5:21-22; Acts 17:31; Rom. 14:10; 2 Cor. 5:10; 2 Tim. 4:1). "But a reconciliation of the two views may be found in the oneness of the Father and the Son" (Swete). There was something about the one on the throne that caused the *earth and sky* to flee away from him. The old order vanishes from human view and entirely disappears because it is unfit for the moral grandeur of the Judge. The old earth and sky are dissolved to make way for a "new heaven and a new earth" (2 Pet. 3:10-13). Wernecke interprets, "The old creation has run its course and must die, that it may be renewed into a more permanent form. But in this new creation there is no place for evil in all its varied forms."

vv. 12-13 In these verses the destinies of men are represented under the image of a solemn judicial procedure. The real significance of the scene is the fact that none will elude the judgment of God (John 5:28-29; Rom. 2:3; 14:10,12; 2 Cor. 5:10). His judgment is universal and all inclusive. The separate mention of the sea and Death and Hades as giving up the dead in them is John's way of indicating that all the dead are included (Morris). The redeemed, however, have in one sense already been judged (John 3:18; 5:24; Rom. 8:1). The works, their whole spiritual being and activity, by which the redeemed will be judged are their trust and faithfulness to Christ. The *books* preserve an account of the deeds of men (Dan. 7:10). The *book of life* records the names of the redeemed (3:5; 13:8; 17:8; cf. Ps. 69:28; Dan. 12:1; Luke 10:20; Phil. 4:3; Heb. 12:23). The *books* show why certain names are inscribed in the *book of life.* McCan says, "This is a picturesque way of saying that the all-wise God keeps in his understanding all that has been done." The representation is that all that people have done is recorded and will constitute the basis of judgment. "In a significant sense judgment is always in progress, but this does not cancel the necessity or the fact of a final judgment" (Blaney). The judgment simply confirms character into destiny.

vv. 14-15 In this passage John continues the discussion of the judgment. He wants to assure the church of the certain overthrow and destruction of all their enemies, who are also enemies of Christ. **Death** and **Hades,** though in reality abstractions, are here personified (6:8). Death is the common foe of all men, and Hades is their common destination (the abode of the dead). They have long been the dread enemies of man, but their power is only temporary (1:18). The beast, the false prophet, and the devil were thrown into the lake of fire and brimstone (19:20; 20:10), so now Death and Hades are thrown into the same lake. This signifies the complete victory over these agents of evil (1 Cor. 15:26,50-57). They will never be able to kill or receive the dead any more (Isa. 25:8; 1 Cor. 15:26,54-55). Death, or the general place of the dead, no longer has power over the redeemed who await the new Jerusalem from heaven. All evil of every kind has been destroyed and only God's power remains. This leaves no further obstacle to the establishment of the reign of God. John has not used the phrase "first death," but he has alluded to the fact. The "first death" is physical death. The "first resurrection" is the risen spiritual life of conversion (John 11:25). The *second death* (2:11; 20:6; 21:8; cf. Matt. 25:41), which is the same as the lake of fire, is the continuation of the punishment of the unredeemed. Everyone whose name is not **written in the book of life** is **thrown into the lake of fire** (20:12-13). There is in the universe of God a judgment where all receive their retribution.

6. The Blessedness of the New Jerusalem (21:1 to 22:5)

In the preceding vision John saw the "earth and the sky" which "fled away" (20:11). Not only is God's judgment active upon all who oppose Christ and his church, but his grace is generous toward all who accept and follow him. In this vision, John turns from the judgment of the evil to the reward of the good.

It is an idealistic picture of the glorious reality of the church as it will be, and an idealistic portrayal of the earth when the church shall have accomplished its mission. The central thought in this passage is the complete and eternal triumph of the cause of Christ. It is a pictorial representation of the ideal life toward which God through Christ in the church is moving forward, to be progressively realized in this world, yet consummated only in the next (Allen).

(1) Fellowship with God in the Holy City (21:1-8)

¹ Then I saw a new heaven and a new earth; for the first heaven and the first earth had passed away, and the sea was no more. ² And I saw the holy city, new Jerusalem, coming down out of heaven from God, prepared as a bride adorned for her husband; ³ and I heard a great voice from the throne saying, "Behold, the dwelling of God is with men. He will dwell with them, and they shall be his people, and God himself will be with them; ⁴ he will wipe away every tear from their eyes, and death shall be no more, neither shall there be mourning nor crying nor pain any more, for the former things have passed away."
⁵ And he who sat upon the throne said, "Behold, I make all things new." Also he said, "Write this, for these words are trustworthy and true." ⁶ And he said to me, "It is done! I am the Alpha and the Omega, the beginning and the end. To the thirsty I will give water without price from the fountain of the water of life. ⁷ He who conquers shall have this heritage, and I will be his God and he shall be my son. ⁸ But as for the cowardly, the faithless, the polluted, as for murderers, fornicators, sorcerers, idolaters, and all liars, their lot shall be in the lake that burns with fire and brimstone, which is the second death."

v. 1 In this verse John pictures a re-creation of the world. The expectation of a "new birth" of the world is found in the Old Testament and in many apocalyptic writings (Isa. 65:17 ff.; 66:22). Josephus uses the same idea to refer to the restoration of Judah (Ant. XI, 3.9). Sometimes it was thought that the new world would be a renovation of the present world order in a changed earth, and sometimes it was thought that a new world order would replace the present world after its destruction. This is John's picturesque symbol of a new sphere and a new order to show the renovating, renewing, and regenerating power of Christ through the church in the world (Matt. 19:28; 26:29; John 3:3; Acts 3:20-21; 2 Cor. 4:16; 5:17; Gal. 6:15; Eph. 4:20-24; Col. 3:10; Titus 3:5; 2 Pet. 3:10-13).

It is the spiritual reformation which Christ came into the world to promote among men and which has been proceeding ever since, and will continue from age to age "until the time for establishing all that God spoke by the mouth of his holy prophets" (Acts 3:21).

The Greek word *new* designates something which already exists but now appears in a new or fresh aspect. It is an already existent heaven and earth which is completely transformed. It is the same world but gloriously rejuvenated. God in Christ through the church provides the means of re-creation by which the old is transformed into the new. The world comes into its own (Rom. 8:18-22). The *sea*, which is a symbol of separation, isolation, unrest, and rebellious power set against God (Pss. 65:7; 93:3), has disappeared from the new world.

v. 2 The new Jerusalem, antithetic to Babylon, is described in all her radiance and glory (Rowley, *The Relevance of Apocalyptic*, p. 132). The notion of a renewed Jerusalem is prevalent in apocalyptic and prophetic thought (Isa. 54-55,60; Ezek. 40—48; Hag. 2:7-9). In Galatians 4:26, Paul personified the Jerusalem from above as the mother of true Israel (cf. Heb. 12:22). The new Jerusalem is pictured here not as a city of foundations, walls, and streets, but as a city of people. The city symbolizes redeemed humanity, the church. The figure *coming down out of heaven from God* emphasizes its origin and source (3:12). The church is not something man builds; it is something given man by God (Preston and Hanson). There is no idea in the Revelation of a natural and inevitable progress of society upward and onward toward perfection. The likeness of *a bride adorned for her husband* stresses the sacred bond between God and his people (14:3-4; 19:7,9; 21:9) The church enjoys the most intimate relationships with God and finds their real blessedness in perfect union with him. The essence of the blessedness of the people of God consists in its close unior with Christ (Eph. 5:25-32). The figures of the city and the bride suggest unhindered and uninterrupted fellowship.

v. 3 An unidentified voice directly from the throne (16:1; 19:5 20:11) says, **Behold, the dwelling of God is with men.** The tabernacle a portable sanctuary, was the place at which God revealed himself to and dwelt among his people. The holy of holies was the peculiar shrine of God's presence. Ezekiel, who described the restored temple, promised that God would "dwell in the midst of the people of Israel for ever" (43:7; cf. 37:27). God himself makes his abode with the faithful who constitute the holy city (Lev. 26:11-12; Jer. 31:33; Ezek. 37:12). Jesus was Emmanuel, "which means, God with us" (Matt. 1:23). He became flesh and dwelt (literally, "tabernacled") among us (John 1:14). God dwells with his church, they are his people, he is with them, and he is their God. In the church, man is fully and forever reconciled to God. God's immediate and eternal purpose and plan in creation of dwelling with his people are fulfilled in the church. The church finds its real blessedness in union with God and in the realization of God's presence with his people.

v. 4 So real and so perfect is the fellowship between God and his people that God eliminates sorrow, pain, and death from their lives (Isa. 25:8; 35:10; 65:19). These things are part of the old order which has passed away (2 Cor. 5:17). The things pertaining to the first heaven and earth have been completely done away (Morris). In this vision John is giving content and fuller meaning to the reality of the new order. Pain, sorrow, and tears are absent from the new order (7:17; cf. Isa. 25:8; 65:19). The experience of *death shall be no more* (John 6:47,50-51; 8:51; 11:26). This is a description of the original creation fully restored in redemption.

v. 5 With the possible exception of 1:8, this is the only time in the Revelation that God himself speaks (Swete). God has a message for his church. He says emphatically that his message is **trustworthy and true.** He is faithful to his church and true to his word. The creator God declares that he is making (present tense) all things new (Ps. 102:25-26; Isa. 45:18-19; 65:17; 66:22; Jer. 31:22; 2 Cor. 3:18; 4:16-18; 5:17; Col. 3:1-4).

This symbolism emphasizes the fact that it is God who is transforming the old into the new. He is on the throne; that is, he has the sovereign power to carry on and complete the new creation (4:2). As in the creative process from chaos to order (Gen. 1), so God by his redemptive power is producing a new moral and spiritual order out of moral chaos. It is probable that it is also God who commands John to write because the truth of the revelation is accurate. What he has revealed about making a new creation has been done, is being done, and eventually will be completed. The convulsive struggles of the old order are but the birth pangs of the new creation (Rom. 8:22-25).

vv. 6-7 Apparently God continues to speak as he says, *It is done!* He literally says, "they have come to pass"; that is, the promises and purposes of God are accomplished. The long process of redemption will be brought to culmination. He is **the Alpha and the Omega.** These two letters of the Greek alphabet, the first and the last, were used to express the timeless being and eternity of God. His character guarantees the truth of this revelation. He is the source and origin of all things, and he is the goal and consummation of all things (Isa. 44:6). All things begin and end in him (Rom. 11:36; Eph. 4:6). From start to finish the work of renovation is the work of God. He is in control and he works out things according to his will. He is often challenged, but never successfully. Carpenter says, "He finishes as well as begins" (Phil 1:6; Col. 1:20). All of God's transcendence and greatness, however are used to help his creatures (John 3:16). He is the bountiful giver (Jas. 1:5,17). The word "thirst" represents the worthy desires and aspirations of man that cannot be satisfied apart from God (Pss. 42:1 f.; 63:1; Isa. 44:3; 55:1 f.; Matt. 5:6; John 4:13; 7:37). The thirsty are given **water without price from the fountain of the water of life.** Each victor is assured that he will receive the blessing enumerated. The primary purpose of the revelation is to encourage each person to gain the victory (2:7,11,17,26; 3:5,12,21). The unhindered and uninterrupted fellowship between God and a man is suggested by the filial relationship (Gen. 17:7-8; Lev. 26:12; Sam. 7:14; Jer. 24:7; John 1:12; Rom. 8:17; Gal. 4:7; 1 John 3:1-2

5:2). To be a son of God is to belong to the family of God, the church.

v. 8 This verse stands in sharp contrast to the first seven verses in this chapter (Charles). The ones mentioned in this verse are the followers of the dragon, the beast, and the false prophet and they share their fate (19:20; 20:10). Eight epithets are used to describe those who preclude themselves from the kingdom of God. Their names are not written in the "book of life" (20:15). They have no part in the "first resurrection" (20:6); therefore, they have a part in the *second death* (20:14). Wernecke says, "They are consigned to the lake of fire and brimstone—the second death—that they may no longer threaten the close union and communion between God and his redeemed." These have no place in the "holy city," the church (21:2).

(2) *A Description of the Holy City (21:9-27)*

John is not picturing a scene in some distant heaven somewhere in space. He is recording a vision of the church on earth. He is not concerned with a place but a people. He is employing physical objects to represent spiritual realities. The church he describes is an ideal church. It is not to be separated from the final abode of the redeemed. It now exists, but its perfected splendor will appear only in the age to come. The heavenly begins on earth, and this is a vision of the heavenly on earth (Eph. 1:3,20; 2:6; 3:10; Phil. 3:20). This is a vision of the redeemed of God of all time in the life of the spirit that lives beyond the limitations of time and place. This life begins when one "faiths" Christ, and it continues while he is in time and place and into the eternal state (John 11:25-26). The only title for Christ in this section is "Lamb," which occurs seven times (21:9,14,22-23,27; 22:1,3). This title emphasizes Christ's giving of himself to the uttermost and the boundless love that prompted this self-giving (Allen, p. 161). This title points to the character in which salvation is accomplished.

[9] Then came one of the seven angels who had the seven bowls full

of the seven last plagues, and spoke to me, saying, "Come, I will show you the Bride, the wife of the Lamb." ¹⁰ And in the Spirit he carried me away to a great, high mountain, and showed me the holy city Jerusalem coming down out of heaven from God, ¹¹ having the glory of God, its radiance like a most rare jewel, like a jasper, clear as crystal. ¹² It had a great, high wall, with twelve gates, and at the gates twelve angels, and on the gates the names of the twelve tribes of the sons of Israel were inscribed; ¹³ on the east three gates, on the north three gates, on the south three gates, and on the west three gates. ¹⁴ And the wall of the city had twelve foundations, and on them the twelve names of the twelve apostles of the Lamb.

¹⁵ And he who talked to me had a measuring rod of gold to measure the city and its gates and walls. ¹⁶ The city lies foursquare, its length the same as its breadth; and he measured the city with his rod, twelve thousand stadia; its length and breadth and height are equal. ¹⁷ He also measured its wall, a hundred and forty-four cubits by a man's measure, that is, an angel's, ¹⁸ The wall was built of jasper, while the city was pure gold, clear as glass. ¹⁹ The foundations of the wall of the city were adorned with every jewel; the first was jasper, the second sapphire, the third agate, the fourth emerald, ²⁰ the fifth onyx, the sixth carnelian, the seventh chrysolite, the eighth beryl, the ninth topaz, the tenth chrysoprase, the eleventh jacinth, the twelfth amethyst. ²¹ And the twelve gates were twelve pearls, each of the gates made of a single pearl, and the street of the city was pure gold, transparent as glass.

²² And I saw no temple in the city, for its temple is the Lord God the Almighty and the Lamb. ²³ And the city has no need of sun or moon to shine upon it, for the glory of God is its light, and its lamp is the Lamb. ²⁴ By its light shall the nations walk; and the kings of the earth shall bring their glory into it, ²⁵ and its gates shall never be shut by day—and there shall be no night there; ²⁶ they shall bring into it the glory and the honor of the nations. ²⁷ But nothing unclean shall enter it, nor any one who practices abomination or falsehood, but only those who are written in the Lamb's book of life.

v. 9 Observe that it is **one of the seven angels who had the seven bowls full of the seven last plagues** who showed John the judgment of the great harlot (17:1-3). These angels had carried out God's judgments upon the unredeemed, and one of them had shown the bliss of the redeemed, the "bride adorned for her husband" (21:2). The same angel brings the message of judgment and the message of salvation. Every person must make his choice: Babylon the harlot, or Jerusalem, the bride. The response which a person makes to God's message determines for him whether it will be salvation or judgment. The symbolism of the bride-wife continues to emphasize the close, harmonious, mutual affectionate relationship that exists between Christ and the congregation of the redeemed that was stressed in the previous paragraph.

v. 10 John was again *in the Spirit* when this vision was given (1:10; 4:2; 17:3). It was given to him while he was on *a great, high mountain* (see Ezek. 40:2), from which he could gain a wide and lofty view and see things in the right perspective (Richardson). Morris comments, "John was in a 'wilderness' when he saw great Babylon (xviii. 3); it was from *a great and high mountain* that he saw the new Jerusalem. The heavenly city is to be discerned only from an exalted standpoint, perhaps the high point of faith."

John was told by the angel that he would be shown "the Bride, the wife of the Lamb" and instead he was shown *the holy city Jerusalem coming down out of heaven from God.* This indicates that these two symbols refer to the same reality, the congregation of the redeemed. Just as the harlot, signifying the faithless ones, is identified with Babylon, the worldly city (chap. 18), so the bride, signifying the faithful ones, is merged with Jerusalem, the heavenly city. These two cities are thrown into intentional contrast. The *holy city* comes down from heaven as God's new creation of grace (Heb. 11:10).

v. 11 John does not describe the marriage of the Lamb and his bride, but he proceeds to describe the city. The most important feature of the holy city is that God's glory fills it. It has the *glory of God,* that is, the abiding presence of God (Ex. 40:34; 1 Kings 8:11; Isa. 60:1,19; 2 Cor. 3:18). Aided by the brilliance of precious stones, John attempts to describe the source of the beauty of the holy city. The word *radiance* denotes something in which light is concentrated, and on that account radiates (Dan. 12:3; John 1:8; Phil. 2:15-16). Barclay thinks that it describes the "sheen and the radiance which were over the city." The dazzling brilliance of the divine presence in the church is symbolized by these very costly stones (4:3; 21:23). As the Shekinah lit up the holy of holies in the tabernacle, God's presence radiates through the church. This symbolism shows the divine nature of the congregation of the redeemed, which is a fitting residence of God and Christ (Rom. 8:9; 1 Cor. 3:16; 6:19; Eph. 2:21-22). When the church is in fellowship with God (21:1-8), it reflects his glory or divine presence (15:8). "The 'luminary' of the Holy City is her witness to Christ" (Swete).

vv. 12-14 In this passage Jerusalem is described as a beautiful, strong, and ideal city. Much of the symbolism comes from the last chapter of Ezekiel. The holy city has a **great, high wall** which is emblematic of its security and peace (Isa. 26:1; Zech. 2:5). It is impregnable. The redeemed are a people apart. The **twelve gates** indicate complete and perfect admittance. The city is accessible to all the world (Isa. 45:22; Luke 13:29; 1 Tim. 2:3-5). Richardson says, "From every direction and every part of the world citizens may come and find an easy admission into the city." The **twelve angels** who guard the gates signify that nothing improper or evil can find an entrance into the life of the redeemed community (2 Chron. 8:14; Isa. 62:6). The inscription of the names of the twelve tribes of Israel serves as a symbol to represent the church as the true Israel (Ex. 28:9; 39:14). This is in marked contrast to the names of blasphemy on the beast and the harlot (13:1; 17:3). The **twelve foundations** stand for the completeness and perfection of the supporting part of the wall (Isa. 28:16; Heb. 11:10). The inscription of the **names of the twelve apostles of the Lamb** on the substructure of faithful stones stamps the signature of Israel after the spirit upon the church (Matt. 16:18; Rom. 15:20; 1 Cor. 3:10; Eph. 2:19-22; 1 Pet. 2:5). The church is the true fulfillment of Israel's high calling.

vv. 15-17 The symbolism of the measuring of the holy city comes from Ezekiel 40—43. By this symbolism John intends to show that the whole city, like the holy of holies, is the dwelling place of God. Previously John himself had been told to "measure the temple of God and the altar and those who worship there" (11:1); here the skill of an angel is needed for the task. Although an angel does the measuring, he uses the same unit of measurement as employed by man (21:17). John's instrument of measurement was a reed, but the angel used one which is more suited to his personage and the occasion, *a measuring rod of gold.* The act of measuring is intended to give the greatness, symmetry, solidity, and splendor of the city (Caird). *The city lies foursquare,* that is, it is a perfect cube (Ezek. 45:2; 48:15-20). The cube symbolizes permanence and perfection (Ex. 39:9). The holy of holies in Solomon's temple was a perfect cube (1 Kings 6:20).

The city when measured is *twelve thousand stadia* each way, that is, a cube of about fifteen hundred miles (2,250,000 square miles!). This vast perfect cube, patterned after the holy of holies, symbolizes the perfect symmetry, harmony, completeness, and vastness of the church, the dwelling place of God (Eph. 3:4). The presence of God had been symbolized by the holy of holies, but now the church, the God-inhabited society, manifests his presence. In this vast holy city there is sufficient room for men from every nation, and race, and people, and tongue, and it is high enough to unite earth and heaven. The wall which surrounds the holy city is *a hundred and forty-four cubits,* which is the square of twelve. This symbolizes complete and perfect measurement of the city. The 144 cubits are only 216 feet. High defense walls are not needed and therefore, the wall does not obscure the city. The wall is sufficient for security, but not for obscurity (Matt. 5:14).

vv. 18-21 In this passage, by the splendor of precious stones, by pure transparent gold, and by magnificent pearls, the glory of the holy city is portrayed. Among the Hebrews, precious stones symbolized the divine presence (Ex. 24:10; 28:15-21; 39:10 f.; Ezek. 1:22,26; 28:13). Much of the symbolism of these verses comes from Isaiah 54:11-12. John is attempting in this brilliant assemblage of colors to portray the majesty of God exhibiting itself in his various attributes of wisdom, power, justice, and mercy (4:3). The twelve jewels of which the foundations of the city are built are the same stones which adorn the breastplate of the high priest (Ex. 28:17-20). It is doubtful if the jewels named in the English translations are the same stones as are represented by the Hebrew and Greek names. "The writer is simply trying to convey the impression of a radiant and superb structure" (Moffatt). Whatever gems John had in mind, this wealth of symbolical extravagance is intended to express the radiance of the divine presence (4:3). The communion which every believer has with God is so real that the whole city is a sanctuary (Allen).

vv. 22-23 The description of the holy city is still more wonderful as it proceeds. In Ezekiel's vision the temple is measured and described, because the temple ordinances were still to be maintained. The temple was the symbol of the presence of God in the midst of the people and his claim on the secular world. It was a place where people could specially meet God. In John's vision the temple has no part, because the whole new Jerusalem (21:2) is the dwelling place of God. All the inhabitants of the holy city are conscious of his presence and serve him as priest (7:15; 20:6; 21:3). The Shekinah glory of God and Christ in the holy city makes the church one vast sanctuary where people can specially meet God. The sphere of the holy is expanded to include the whole area of experience and activity. The faithful have attained the longed-for full fellowship with God, and they worship him in spirit and in truth everywhere (John 4:20-24). Jeremiah's prophecy of the new covenant is fulfilled in the holy city (Jer. 3:16; 31:33). This holy city has no need of the light of the sun or moon because the immediate presence of God irradiates it (Isa. 60:19,20; John 8:12; 1 John 1:5). God is himself light (1 John 1:5). Werneck says, "As the holy of holies had no light but the Shekinah of the divine glory, so the light of the Holy City is the glory of God (Isa. 60:20; Zech. 2:5). John emphasizes glory rather than physical brightness. The glory of God is God himself in all his attributes. God's glory through the Lamb fills the entire city with uncreated light. As it is the property of light to shine, it is his nature to reveal himself. The city is flooded with light, and therefore darkness of every kind is banished forever (1 John 1:5). With God and the Lamb at the heart of the church, no other illumination is needed.

vv. 24-27 Isaiah predicted that the nations would be gathered together in Jerusalem under the ensign of the Messiah (Isa. 60:3,5,11; 66:12). John says that these predictions have been fulfilled in the gathering together of all nations into the holy city. It lends its protection to all who inhabit it. John sees the lonely, depressed, despised, and persecuted church as enlarged and honored. The *kings of the earth,* human authority, that are "ordained of God" find their true purpose in ministering to the needs of humanity (Rom. 13:1-7). The church is "the light of the world" (Matt. 5:14). Ezekiel described people dwelling in fancied security as living in "the land of unwalled villages," where they "are at rest, that dwell securely, all of them dwelling without walls, and having neither bars nor gates" (Ezek. 38:11). In John's vision the holy city has its walls to express safety, but its gates are open to show that there is no danger of hostile attack. Carpenter says, "In peace by day, the city gates will be open; nor can there be night when God the Almighty is the sun" (cf. Isa. 60:2; Ezek. 33:2). Those who are admitted into the church are safe forever. The Jews were most careful to exclude from the temple anything that was common or unclean. In Leviticus many provisions whereby men were excluded from the holy precincts by legal defilement are enumerated. In the holy city "coming down out of heaven" the unclean and false may never enter, but the redeemed enter the holy place.

(3) *Life and Light in the Holy City (22:1-5)*

This paragraph, which should have been included in chapter 21, concludes John's description of the holy city. He is picturing verbally the interior of the city (Ps. 46:4). It is a picture of perfect peace; of a garden within the city where all is in order, where a river runs, where flowers and fruits of refreshment and healing abound. The water of the river is sufficient for all needs. In this picturesque symbolism, John means that the redeemed have entered upon a full, meaningful, and abundant life which shall be theirs forever. Their spiritual life here is but the first imperfect stage of the life hereafter (John 5:24; 6:47). The gift of the Spirit is an earnest of their inheritance (2 Cor. 1:23; 5:5; Eph. 1:14; 4:30). In the holy city they have been translated from the death-state into the life-state, which is the "eternal now."

[1] Then he showed me the river of the water of life, bright as crystal, flowing from the throne of God and of the Lamb [2] through the middle of the street of the city; also, on either side of the river, the tree of life with its twelve kinds of fruit, yielding its fruit each month; and the leaves of the tree were for the healing of the nations. [3] There shall no more be anything accursed, but the throne of God and of the Lamb shall be in it, and his servants shall worship him; [4] they shall see his face, and his name shall be on their foreheads. [5] And night shall be no more; they need no light of lamp or sun, for the Lord God will be their light, and they shall reign for ever and ever.

v. 1 The angel (21:9-10,15-17) now shows John the bountiful provision which God has made for the church. There was a river in Eden (Gen. 2:10). Streams gushed forth from the rocks in the wilderness (Ex. 17:6; Num. 20:11; Ps. 78:15; 1 Cor. 10:4). The psalmist, in describing the blessedness of those who trust in God, says, "Thou wilt make them drink of the river of thy pleasures" (Ps. 36:8). Joel, speaking of the End time, says, "A fountain shall come forth from the house of Jehovah" (Joel 3:18). In Ezekiel's vision, he saw healing water issuing out from under the threshold of the temple (Ezek. 47:1 f.). Zechariah foretells that "it shall come to pass in that day, that living waters shall go out from Jerusalem" (Zech. 14:8). Jesus announced in Jerusalem, "If any one thirst, let him come to me and drink. He who believes in me, as the scripture has said, 'Out of his heart shall flow rivers of living water' " (John 7:37-38). Jesus also said to the woman at the well in Samaria "Whoever drinks of the water that I shall give him will never thirst;

the water that I shall give him will become in him a spring of water welling up to eternal life" (John 4:14). The fountainhead of the life-giving river in the holy city is in the throne of God and the crucified Savior. The water of life is available to quench every thirst (Isa. 55:1-2; Matt. 5:6).

v. 2 It seems that John pictures the river in the midst of the only street of the city. The river of the water of life was lined on both sides with the *tree of life.* This phrase refers to the whole class of trees. It symbolizes the restoration to man of the life which was forfeited in Eden (Gen. 3:22-24). It bears fruit continuously: twelve kinds, twelve times a year. Twelve denotes completeness and perfection in religion (church), hence it is especially appropriate that the tree of life by the river of life in the holy city should bear "twelve kinds of fruits" *each month.* The tree not only produces fruit, but its leaves are salutary to all the nations of the earth. Its leaves are used for the *healing of the nations.* The tree of life provides the remedy for hunger and disease. The whole symbolism is an emblem of life which is a heritage of the redeemed. The three basic needs to sustain life are provided: water, food, and health. This is an image of the abundance of grace and life in store for the redeemed. With the church, there comes to fulfillment the historical destiny in which Israel had so often failed, that of being the mediator of the covenant and the promising sign of hope for all nations (Rissi, p. 133).

vv. 3-5 In these concluding verses John repeats with emphasis the condition of blessedness of the inhabitants of the holy city (21:2). There is the absence of anything accursed (Gen. 3:17-19; Josh. 7:12-13; Zech. 14:11); the presence of God and the Lamb (4:2 f.; 20:11; 21:3,5,22-23); the perpetual ministry of his servants (7:15; 19:1-7); his servants' admission into his presence (21:3; cf. Pss. 17:15; 42:2; Matt. 5:8; 1 Cor. 13:12; 1 John 3:2); God's acknowledgment of their sonship (7:3; 14:1; 21:7); his servants' perpetual illumination by his presence with them (21:23,25); and the reign of his servants for ever and ever (11:15; 20:4,6; cf. Dan.

7:18,27; Matt. 19:28; Rom. 5:17).

In this paragraph John reiterates his description of the church. The curse, the element of disorder in the moral sphere, is removed. God and the Lamb rule jointly; that is, they use one double throne. What was formerly the special privilege of the high priest alone (Ex. 28:36-38) to enter the holy of holies, and that but one day in a year, is now the continuous privilege of the whole redeemed community. There is an intimacy to be constantly enjoyed between God and man which was previously impossible. The barriers that separate God and man have been removed. God's authority is everywhere recognized, and his servants serve him. Everything is seen through him, and everything is done for him. Life is flooded with light, darkness of every kind is banished forever. The church shares in the reign of Christ. The goal and essence of true life is realized.

IV. Conclusion
(22:6-21)

The epilogue confirms and reassures the visions that have been seen by John. It is personal and direct. It contains short sayings, practical exhortations, promises, assurances, blessings, and warnings. It consists of short sentences, not very closely related to each other, each of them repeating some phrase which has gone before, showing how the purpose set forth at the beginning has been carried out. The sentences are so written that it is not always easy to distinguish the speakers, or to trace the connection of thought. Charles and others have attempted to rearrange the verses, without too much success, in order to provide a better connection of thought. It contains three prominent themes: the authenticity of the visions (22:6-7,16,18-19), the imminence of Christ's "coming" (22:6-7,10-12,20), and the necessity for choosing Christ soon (22:10-15).

[6] And he said to me, "These words are trustworthy and true. And the Lord, the God of the spirits of the prophets, has sent his angel to show his servants what must soon take place. [7] And behold, I am coming soon." Blessed is he who keeps the words of the prophecy of this book.

[8] I John am he who heard and saw these things. And when I heard and saw them, I fell down to worship at the feet of the angel who showed them to me; [9] but he said to me, "You must not do that! I am a fellow servant with you and your brethren the prophets, and with those who keep the words of this book. Worship God."

[10] And he said to me, "Do not seal up the words of the prophecy of this book, for the time is near. [11] Let the evildoer still do evil, and the filthy still be filthy, and the righteous still do right, and the holy still be holy."

[12] "Behold, I am coming soon, bringing my recompense, to repay every one for what he has done. [13] I am the Alpha and the Omega, the first and the last, the beginning and the end."

¹⁴ Blessed are those who wash their robes, that they may have the right to the tree of life and that they may enter the city by the gates. ¹⁵ Outside are the dogs and sorcerers and fornicators and murderers and idolaters, and every one who loves and practices falsehood.

¹⁶ "I Jesus have sent my angel to you with this testimony for the churches. I am the root and the offspring of David, the bright morning star."

¹⁷ The Spirit and the Bride say, "Come." And let him who hears say, "Come." And let him who is thirsty come, let him who desires take the water of life without price.

¹⁸ I warn every one who hears the words of the prophecy of this book; if any one adds to them, God will add to him the plagues described in this book, ¹⁹ and if any one takes away from the words of the book of this prophecy, God will take away his share in the tree of life and in the holy city, which are described in this book.

²⁰ He who testifies to these things says, "Surely I am coming soon." Amen. Come, Lord Jesus!

²¹ The grace of the Lord Jesus be with all the saints. Amen.

vv. 6-7 These verses are almost a duplicate and a summary of the first paragraph of the book (1:1-3). In them Jesus, through his angel, speaks and attests the divine authority and veracity of the message of the whole book (3:14; 19:11; 21:5). The description of God as the God of the *spirits of the prophets* shows that John was in the same line as the Old Testament prophets. God through his angel was making known to him his will and message for his people (1:1). This is a message of unchangeable principles and unalterable facts. These truths have been, are, and will be. The events that are just beginning to occur are not outside of God's control. Divine intervention by the unveiling of Christ's presence in the struggle is imminent. These things must shortly be done (1:1). He came, he comes, and he is to come. God's truth are practical and must take their actual embodiment and form in human life, and any man is blessed who reads and obeys the message of this book.

vv. 8-9 John begins these verses with another one of his own personal testimonies and experiences. He vouches for what he has heard and seen. He was so overwhelmed with the extraordinary visions and their meaning that he *fell down to worship* the angel who had showed them to him (19:10; cf. 1 Kings 18:7; Dan. 2:46; Acts 10:25-26). The angel assures John that he is in the same class with him and his brother prophets and those *who keep the words of this book.* This experience, as well as the one in 19:10, was probably recorded to correct the overexaltation of all instruments of revelation. It was also possibly written to emphasize the prophetic rank of John and to correct the tendency to venerate angels by the incipient gnostic sects in the churches (Col. 1:15-20; 2:8-13). The gnostics were teaching that angels were emanations from the supreme God (Newman, pp. 107-108). John wants to make it clear that angel worship is forbidden. Only God is to be worshiped (19:10; cf. Ex. 20:3-5; 34:14; Deut. 4:24; 10:20; Luke 4:8).

vv. 10-11 John was told not to write what the seven thunders said (10:4), but he is told not to *seal up the words of the prophecy of this book.* He is to communicate this message to the world for the End time has arrived (1:3; 3:11; 22:7,12,20). If the unredeemed will not respond to the message of the End time (1 John 2:18), there is nothing more that can be done for them. If they will not listen to warning, the time comes when they will be unable, as they were before unwilling, to regard it. They become more habituated to sin, and see less of its seriousness, and of their own danger. This is but a prelude of future punishment.

An element of judgment consists in the fact that the sinner can no longer part from his sins. The sins which he has encouraged cling to him forever. He that is righteous and holy will increase in his practice of godliness. The principles of judgment and reward are already operating in absolute and unswerving equity. The unredeemed do not have to wait for judgment nor do the faithful have to wait for vindication. Moral principles and habits become character. Moral growth or moral decline is inevitable. John is laying upon each person the full responsibility for his character. Smith says, "What he chooses, while the opportunity of choice remains to him, will become destiny, and be changeless forever."

"In this there is nothing arbitrary. It is but the corollary of the love that endowed man with moral freedom to choose for himself the kind of self he would be" (Rowley, p. 176).

vv. 12-13 Christ alone judges the character of each person (John 5:22). The *coming* of Christ for salvation or judgment is the main point here. The purpose of these words is to encourage and exhort the Christians to persevere for the time of recompense is at hand, and at the same time to warn the unredeemed that judgment will overtake them soon. The reward for each is according to *what he has done* (2:23; cf. Job 34:11; Isa. 62:11; Matt. 25:31-46; Rom. 2:5-6). The description *Alpha and Omega, the first and the last, the beginning and the end* is apparently applied to Jesus (1:8,17; cf. Isa. 41:4; 43:10; 44:6; 48:12). This description emphasizes his eternal existence and also the fact that all persons, conditions, and events are encompassed by his changeless being.

vv. 14-15 In these two verses John gives another benediction to the redeemed and a contrast to the unredeemed. These are the results of Christ's coming. The special blessings promised to those who habitually wash (present tense) their robes are: First, they are entitled to approach the tree of life (Gen. 3:24); that is, they are nurtured by the fruit and healed by the leaves of the tree of life (2:7; 22:2,19). Second, they enter as in a triumphal procession through the gates into the city (21:12,15,21,25). John is saying that there is a refuge from Christ's judgment available to those *who wash their robes* (7:14; 12:11; cf. Zech. 3:3-5; Heb. 9:14; 1 John 1:7). Outside of the holy city are the ones who have not been washing their robes.

These seven sins that are listed characterize the unredeemed (21:8; cf. Matt. 8:12; 1 Cor. 6:9-10; Gal. 5:19-21; Phil. 3:2). It is from such sins that God offers to men a way of escape by providing the means by which they may be delivered from sin in all its form. These sins and others make a hell for the man who practices them. Dana says that those outside of the city have "companionship with godless paganism, scheming magic, sordid lust, blood-thirsty crime, dismal idolatry, and delusive fraud."

v. 16 Jesus (Matt. 1:21; Luke 1:31) now authenticates himself as the One who sent the angel with the message and attests and confirms the "testimony for the churches" (1:1; chaps. 2—3). The revelation places obligation on the churches. They are to maintain and proclaim its message (1:20). Jesus identifies himself as *the offspring of David.* Lineally and officially he is the Son of David (5:5; 12:5; cf. Isa. 11:1,10; Jer. 23:5; 33:15-17; (Ezek. 34:23; 37:24 f.; Hos. 3:5; Amos 9:11; Zech. 3:8; 6:12; Robbins, pp. 181 f.). He came from the same ancestral line, and he became king by God's permission. Jesus is also *the bright morning star.* He is a royal king who heralds a new day of hope and promise (2:28; cf. Num. 24:17; Luke 1:78; 1 Pet. 1:19). He has inaugurated the new spiritual day in history (Mal. 4:2).

v. 17 This whole verse is an invitation for all the unredeemed to drink of the water of life. The invitation is extended through the Spirit-guided church, each redeemed person, and the inherent thirst of the human heart for God (John 6:35; 7:37). The Spirit and the Bride utter the same voice, so the Spirit speaks through the church. The members of the churches who listen to the reading of the book invite the unredeemed to *come.* The invitation is repeated to all those who have not yet drunk of the living water, yet who thirst for it (21:6). The "water of life" is freely given without money and without price. The invitation is so broad that everyone is included. It is an invitation to all the unredeemed to come and receive God's mercy and drink of the water of life.

vv. 18-19 A blessing was assured to the one reading and the ones hearing and keeping the words of this prophecy (1:3). Now a solemn warning is issued to anyone deliberately falsifying it by addition or subtraction. This kind of warning was a very common practice in apocalyptic and other writings. It was intended to protect the book and to keep later readers from perverting its message by any interpolation or change. John says the teachings of this book are not to be evaded or modified (Deut. 4:2; 12:32; Prov.

30:6; Jer. 26:2; 2 Pet. 3:16). Any person who adds to, takes from, or in any way modifies the teaching of this book is among the enemies of Christ and the church. The rejection of the teaching of this book indicates the reader's lack of faith. Any addition to the message of this book brings the judgments of God.

vv. 20-21 For the third time in the last chapter Jesus gives his promise and assurance that he is coming soon to the aid of his church (22:7,12). The coming of Jesus for salvation or judgment is certainly the main point here. Dana says, "The living, triumphant Christ of the Apocalypse did indeed 'come quickly' to begin his irresistible (sic) march toward that universal conquest, which shall be the triumphant realization of the vision of hope." To Jesus' promise to come, John replies with the Greek form of the Aramaic word *Maranatha* (1 Cor. 16:22). Caird says, "Week after week that prayer was spoken and answered as the risen Christ made himself known to his disciples in the breaking of the bread." The book closes with a brief apostolic benediction (cf. 1:4). No conclusion to this effort of interpretation could be more suitable than to quote it: ***The grace of the Lord Jesus be with all the saints. Amen.***

Selected Bibliography

ALLEN, CADY H. *The Message of the Book of Revelation.* Nashville: Cokesbury Press, 1939.
ARNDT, WILLIAM F. AND GINGRICH, F. WILBUR. (Translators and Editors). *A Greek-English Lexicon of the New Testament and Other Early Christian Literature.* Chicago: The University of Chicago Press, 1957.
ATKINSON. B. F. *The Revelation of Jesus Christ.* Louisville. Kentucky: Herald Press. 1939.
AUBERLEN, CARL AUGUST. *The Prophecies of Daniel and the Revelation of St. John, Viewed in Their Mutual Relationship.* London: T. & T. Clark, 1857.
BAILLIE, JOHN. *The Idea of Revelation in Recent Thought.* New York: Columbia University Press, 1956.
BARCLAY, WILLIAM. *Letters to Seven Churches.* New York: Abingdon Press, 1957.
———. *The Revelation of St. John.* (2 vols.) Philadelphia: Westminster, 1960.
BARNES, ALBERT. *Notes on the New Testament—Revelation.* Edited by Robert Frew. Grand Rapids: Baker Book House, 1951.
BARRETT, JOHN O. *The Book of the Revelation.* London: The Carey Press, 1947.
BEASLEY-MURRAY, GEORGE R. *Jesus and the Future: The Eschatological Discourse, Mark 13 With Special Reference to the Little Apocalypse Theory.* London: The Macmillan Company, 1954.
BECKWITH, ISBON T. *The Apocalypse of St. John.* New York: The Macmillan Company, 1919.
BEET, J. AGAR. *The Last Things.* New York: Eaton & Mains (3rd ed.), 1898.
BENSON, EDWARD W. *The Apocalypse.* London: Macmillan and Company, Ltd. 1900.
BERDYAEV, NICHOLAS. *The End of Our Time.* Translated by Donald Attwater. London: Shed & Ward, 1933.
———. *The Beginning and the End.* Translated by R. M. French. New York: Hillary House Publishers, n.d.
BLAIR, EDWARD P. *The Acts and Apocalyptic Literature.* Nashville: Abingdon, 1946.

BLAIKLOCK, E. M. *The Seven Churches.* London: Marshall, Morgan and Scott Ltd., n.d.
BLANEY, HARVEY J. S. *Hebrews-Revelation,* "Revelation" ("The Wesleyan Bible Commentary," ed. Charles W. Carter, Vol. VI). Grand Rapids: Wm. B. Eerdmans Publishing Company, 1966.
BOETTNER, LORAINE. *The Millennium.* Philadelphia: The Presbyterian and Reformed Publishing Company, 1958.
BONHOEFFER, DIETRICH. *The Cost of Discipleship.* Translated by R. H. Fuller. New York: The Macmillan Company, 1949.
BOWMAN, JOHN WICK. *The Drama of the Book of Revelation.* Philadelphia: The Westminster Press, 1955.
―――. "Book of Revelation" in *The Interpreter's Dictionary of the Bible.* New York: Abingdon Press, 1962.
BRIGHT, JOHN. *The Kingdom of God.* Nashville: Abingdon Press, 1953.
BRUNNER, EMIL. *The Misunderstanding of the Church.* Translated by Harold Knight. Philadelphia: The Westminster Press, 1953.
BRUNSON, ALFRED. *A Key to the Apocalypse.* Cincinnati: Walden and Stowe, 1881.
BUIS, HARRY. *The Book of Revelation.* Philadelphia: Presbyterian and Reformed Publishing Company, 1960.
BULLINGER, E. W. *The Apocalypse.* (2nd ed.). London: Eyre and Spattiswoode, 1909.
BULTMANN, RUDOLF KARL. *Theology of the New Testament.* Translated by Kendrick Grabel. (2 vols.) New York: Charles Scribner's Sons, 1951.
―――. *The Presence of Eternity.* New York: Harper & Brothers, 1957.
BURGH, WILLIAM. *An Exposition of the Book of Revelation.* Dublin: Richard Moore Tims, 1839.
BUTTRICK, GEORGE ARTHUR (ed.). *Interpreter's Bible.* (12 vols.) New York: Abingdon Press, 1957.
―――. *The Interpreter's Dictionary of the Bible.* (4 vols.) New York: Abingdon Press, 1962.
CAIRD, G. B. *Principalities and Powers.* Oxford: Clarendon Press, 1956.
―――. *The Revelation of St. John the Divine* ("Harper's New Testament Commentaries," ed. Henry Chadwick). New York: Harper & Row, Publishers, 1966.
CALKINS, RAYMOND. *The Social Message of the Book of Revelation.* New York: The Woman's Press, 1920.
CAMPBELL, JOHN M. *Thoughts on Revelation.* Philadelphia: Claxton, Remsen and Haffelfinger, 1874.
CARPENTER, W. BOYD. *The Revelation of St. John* ("Ellicott's Commentary on the Whole Bible," ed. Charles John Ellicott, Vol. VIII). Grand Rapids: Zondervan Publishing House, n.d.
CARROLL, B. H. *The Book of Revelation.* New York: Revell, 1913.

SELECTED BIBLIOGRAPHY

CASE, SHIRLEY J. *The Revelation of John.* Chicago: University of Chicago Press, 1919.
CHARLES, R. H. *The Apocrypha and Pseudepigrapha of the Old Testament.* (2 vols.) Oxford: Clarendon Press, 1913.
_____. *A Critical and Exegetical Commentary on the Revelation of St. John.* ("The International Critical Commentary.") (2 vols.) New York: Charles Scribner's Sons, 1920.
_____. *Lectures on the Apocalypse.* London: Oxford University Press, 1923.
CLARK, FRANCIS E. *The Holy Land of Asia Minor.* New York: Charles Scribner's Sons, 1914.
CLAY, EDMUND, *The Book of Revelation.* London: James Nesbet and Company, 1864.
COCHRAN, JOHN. *The Revelation of John.* New York: D. Appleton and Company, 1860.
COHN, NORMAN. *The Pursuit of the Millennium.* New York: Harper, 1961.
CRISWELL, W. A. *Expository Sermons on Revelation.* (5 vols.) Grand Rapids: Zondervan Publishing House, 1966.
CROSS, FRANK M. *The Ancient Library of Qumran and Modern Bible Studies.* New York: Doubleday, 1952.
CROW, G. R. *The Lamb and the Book.* Bombay: Gospel Literature Service, 1964.
CULLMANN, OSCAR. *Christ and Time.* Translated by Floyd V. Filson. Philadelphia: The Westminster Press, 1950.
_____. *The State in the New Testament.* New York: Charles Scribner's Sons, 1956.
_____. *Immortality of the Soul or Resurrection of the Dead.* New York: The Macmillan Company, 1958.
CULVER, ROBERT D. *Daniel and the Latter Days.* New York: Fleming H. Revell Company, 1954.
CURREY, G. *The Book of Revelation.* ("Commentary on the New Testament.") London: Society for Promoting Christian Knowledge, 1916).
DANA, H. E. *The Epistles and Apocalypse of John.* Dallas: Baptist Book Store, 1937.
DANA, H. E., and J. R. MANTY. *A Manual Grammar of the Greek New Testament.* New York: Macmillan, 1927.
DAVIDSON, A. B. *The Theology of the Old Testament.* Edinburgh: T. & T. Clark, 1904.
_____. *Old Testament Prophecy.* Edinburgh: Morrison and Gibb, 1912.
DAVIDSON, F. (ed.) *The New Bible Commentary.* Grand Rapids: Wm. B. Eerdmans, 1953.
DEAN, JOHN T. *Visions and Revelations.* Edinburgh: T. & T. Clark, 1911.
_____. *The Book of Revelation.* Edinburgh: T. & T. Clark (second impression), 1930.

DeHaan, M. R. *Revelation.* Grand Rapids: Zondervan, 1946.
Deissman, Adolf. *Light From the Ancient East.* Trans. L. R. M. Strachan. London: Hodder & Stoughton, 1911.
DeSanto, Charles. *The Book of Revelation.* ("Shield Bible Study Outlines.") Grand Rapids: Baker Book House, 1967.
Dodd, C. H. *The Authority of the Bible.* New York: Harper, 1929.
_____. *The Apostolic Preaching.* New York: Harper, 1951.
_____. *The Interpretation of the Fourth Gospel.* Cambridge: Cambridge University Press, 1954.
Dodge, Esther. *The Apocalypse and the Twentieth Century.* Washington, D.C.: Caslon Press, 1961.
Eaton, Robert. *The Apocalypse of St. John.* London: Sands and Company, 1930.
Elliott, E. B. *Horae Apocalyptical or A Commentary on the Apocalypse.* (3 vols.) (5th edition) London: Seeley, Jackson, and Halliday, 1862.
Enslin, M. S. *Christian Beginnings.* New York: Harper, 1938.
Epp, Theodore H. *Practical Studies in Revelation.* (2 vols.) Lincoln, Nebraska: Back to the Bible Broadcast, 1969.
Erdman, Charles R. *The Revelation of John.* Philadelphia: The Westminster Press, 1936.
Evans, William. *Christ's Last Message to His Church.* New York: Fleming H. Revell Company, MCMXXVI.
Farrar, F. W. *The Early Days of Christianity.* Boston: DeWolfe, Fiske, 1882
_____. *The Messages of the Books.* New York: Dutton, 1888.
_____. *Texts Explained.* Ohio: Barton, 1899.
Farrer, Austin M. *A Rebirth of Images.* Boston: Beacon Press, 1963.
_____. *The Revelation of St. John the Divine.* Oxford: Clarendon Press, 1964
Flew, R. N. *Jesus and His Church.* London: The Epworth Press, 1938.
Ford, W. Herschel. *Simple Sermons on the Seven Churches of Revelation* Grand Rapids: Zondervan Publishing House, 1959.
Foulquie, Paul. *Existentialism.* Translated by Kathleen Raine. London Dennis Dobson, 1950.
Froom, L. E. *The Prophetic Faith of Our Fathers.* (4 vols.) Washington D.C.: Review and Herald Publishing Association. 1950.
Gaebelein, Arno C. *The Revelation.* New York: Publication Office "Ou Hope," 1915.
Gettys, Joseph M. *How to Study the Revelation.* Richmond: John Knox Press 1946.
Glasson, T. F. *The Revelation of John* ("The Cambridge Bible Commentar on the New English Bible,") Cambridge: Cambridge University Press, 196!
Glover, T. R. *The World of the New Testament.* New York: The Macmilla Company, 1931.
Grant, F. W. *The Prophetic History of the Church.* New York: Loizeau

SELECTED BIBLIOGRAPHY

Brothers, 1955.
GRANT, ROBERT M. *A Short History of the Interpretation of the Bible.* New York: Macmillan, 1963.
GUTHRIE, DONALD. *New Testament Introduction*, "Hebrews to Revelation." Chicago: Inter-Varsity, 1962.
GUY, H. A. *The New Testament Doctrine of Last Things.* New York: Oxford University Press, 1948.
HANSON, A. T. *The Wrath of the Lamb.* London: S.P.C.K., 1957.
HASTINGS, JAMES. ed. *Dictionary of the Bible.* (5 vols.) New York: Charles Scribner's Sons, 1919.
HAYES, D. A. *John and His Writings.* New York: Methodist Book Concern, 1917.
HENDRIKSEN, W. *More than Conquerors.* Grand Rapids: Baker's Book Store, 1940.
HENNECKE, EDGAR. *New Testament Apocrypha.* (2 vols.) ed. Wilhelm Schneemercher. English translation edited by R. McL. Wilson. Pheladelphia: The Westminster Press, 1964.
HODJIANTONIOU, G. A. *The Postman of Patmos.* Grand Rapids: Zondervan Publishing House, 1961.
HOLDEN, GEORGE F. *Lectures on the Revelation of St. John the Divine.* London: Hugh Rees, Ltd., 1903.
HORT, F. J. A. *The Christian Ecclesia.* London: Macmillan & Company, Ltd., 1897.
HOSKIER, H. C. *Concerning the Text of the Apocalypse.* London: Bernard Quaritch, 1929 (2 vols.).
HOYT, EDYTH ARMSTRONG. *Studies in the Apocalypse of John on Patmos.* Ann Arbor, Michigan: Edwards Brothers, Inc. 1949.
HUNTER, A. M. *Interpreting the New Testament.* London: S.C.M. Press, 1961.
IRVING, EDWARD. (Ed. by Garvin Carlyle). *Exposition of the Book of Revelation.* (2 vols.) London: Strahan and Company, 1870.
IRONSIDE, H. A. *Lectures on the Revelation.* New York: Loizeaux Brothers, 1930.
JACOBUS, M. W., LANE, E. C., and COOK, E. J. *A New Standard Bible Dictionary.* New York: Funk & Wagnalls, 1936.
JAMES, MONTAGUE RHODES (trans.). *The Apocryphal New Testament.* Oxford: At the Clarendon Press, 1963.
JONES, BISSELL B. *The Things Which Shall Be Hereafter.* Nashville: Broadman Press, 1947.
KEE, H. C. and YOUNG, F. W. *Understanding the New Testament.* Englewood Cliffs, N.J.: Prentice-Hall, 1957.
KENNEDY, H.A.A. *St. Paul's Conceptions of the Last Things.* London: Hodder & Stoughton, Ltd., 1904.
KEPLER, THOMAS S. *The Book of Revelation.* New York: Oxford University

Press, 1957.

———. *Dreams of the Future.* New York: Abingdon Press, 1963.

KIDDLE, M. *The Revelation of St. John* ("The Moffatt New Testament Commentary"). London: Hodder & Stoughton, 1940.

KIK, J. MARCELLUS. *Revelation Twenty.* Philadelphia: The Presbyterian and Reformed Publishing Company, 1955.

KITTEL, GERHARD (ed.). *Theological Dictionary of the New Testament.* Translated by Geoffrey W. Bromiley. Grand Rapids: Wm. B. Eerdmans Publishing Company, 1964 ff.

KLASSEN, W., and SNYDER, G. F. *Current Issues in New Testament Interpretation.* New York: Harper, 1962.

KNUDSON, A. C. *The Religious Teaching of the Old Testament.* New York: Abingdon Press, 1918.

KROMMINGA, D. H. *The Millennium in the Church.* Grand Rapids: Wm. B. Eerdmans, 1945.

KÜMMEL, W. G. *Promise and Fulfillment: The Eschatological Message of Jesus.* Translated by Dorothea M. Barton. Naperville, Ill.: Alec R. Allenson, Inc., 1957.

KUNKEL, FRITZ. *Creation Continues.* New York: Charles Scribner's Sons, 1947.

KUYPER, ABRAHAM. *The Revelation of St. John.* Grand Rapids: Wm. B. Eerdmans Publishing Company (trans. by John Hendrik de Vries), 1963.

LANGE, JOHN PETER. *Commentary on the Holy Scriptures,* "Revelation." Grand Rapids: Zondervan, n.d.

———. *The Gospel According to Matthew.* (trans. Philip Schaff). New York: Scribner, 1865.

LAWRENCE, J. B. *A New Heaven and a New Earth.* New York: American Press Publications, Inc. 1960.

LAYMON, CHARLES M. *The Book of Revelation.* New York: Abingdon, 1960.

LENSKI, R. C. H. *The Interpretation of St. John's Revelation.* Minneapolis: Augsburg Publishing House, 1961.

L'HATE, J. B. *The Book of Revelation.* Philadelphia: Lippincott, Grambo and Company, 1854.

LIDDELL, HENRY GEORGE, AND ROBERT SCOTT. *A Greek-English Lexicon.* (2 vols.) New (ninth) edition. Oxford: Clarendon Press, 1951.

LIGHTFOOT, J. B. *Saint Paul's Epistles to the Colossians and to Philemon.* London: Macmillan, 1900.

LILJE, HANNS. *The Last Book of the Bible.* Trans. Olive Wyon. Philadelphia: Muhlenberg Press, 1957.

LINCOLN, W. *Lectures on the Book of Revelation.* New York: Fleming H. Revell Company, n.d.

LIPSEY, P. I. *Revelation: An Interpretation.* Jackson, Mississippi: Pursei Brothers, Printers, n.d.

LITTLE, C. H. *Explanation of the Book of Revelation.* Saint Louis: Concordia

Publishing House, 1950.
LOENERTZ, R. J. *The Apocalypse of Saint John.* London: Sheed and Ward, 1947.
MAKRAKIS, APOSTOLOS. *Interpretation of the Book of Revelation.* Chicago: Hellenic Christian Educational Society, 1948.
MANSON, WILLIAM. "Eschatology in the New Testament," *Scottish Journal of Theology Occasional Papers.* Edinburgh: Oliver & Boyd, 1952.
MARSH, JOHN. *The Fulness of Time.* London: James Nisbet & Company, Ltd. 1952.
MARTIN, HUGH. *The Seven Letters.* Philadelphia: The Westminster Press, 1956.
MARTINDALE, C. C. *St. John and the Apocalypse.* London: Sheed and Ward (reprint), 1958.
MCCAN, ROBERT L. *A Vision of Victory.* Nashville: Broadman Press, 1959.
MCDOWELL, EDWARD A. *The Meaning and Message of the Book of Revelation.* Nashville: Broadman Press, 1951.
MILLER, MADELINE S., AND J. LANE. *Harper's Dictionary of the Bible.* New York: Harper, 1954.
MILLIGAN, W. *The Book of Revelation.* ("Expositor's Bible Series") New York: Armstrong, 1889.
MINEAR, P. S. "The Cosmology of the Apocalypse" in *Current Issues in New Testament Interpretation.* Ed. W. Klassen and G. F. Snyder. London: S.C.M. Press, 1962.
MOFFATT, JAMES. *The Revelation of St. John the Divine.* ("The Expositor's Greek Testament," Vol. V) Grand Rapids: Wm. B. Eerdman's Publishing Company, n.d.
MORRIS, LEON. *The Revelation of St. John.* ("Tyndale Bible Commentaries." ed. R.V.G. Tasker, Vol. 20) Grand Rapids: Wm. B. Eerdman's Publishing Company, 1969.
NEILL, J. *The Interpretation of the New Testament.* London: Oxford, 1964.
NEWBOLT, M. R. *The Book of Unveiling.* London: S.P.C.K., 1952.
NEWELL, WILLIAM R. *The Book of Revelation.* Chicago: Moody Press, 1935.
NEWMAN, BARCLAY M. *Rediscovering the Book of Revelation.* Valley Forge: The Judson Press, 1968.
NICOLL, W. ROBERTSON, ed. *The Expositor's Greek Testament.* (vol. V). London: Hodder & Stoughton, n.d.
NIEBUHR, H. RICHARD. *The Meaning of Revelation.* New York: The Macmillan Company, 1946.
NILES, D. T. *As Seeing the Invisible.* New York: Harper, 1961.
OEHLER, G. F. *Theology of the Old Testament.* New York: Funk & Wagnalls, 1883.
OLMSTEAD, C. E. *Religion in America—Past and Present.* Englewood Cliffs, N.J.: Prentice-Hall, 1961.
OMAN, JOHN. *The Book of Revelation.* Cambridge: University Press, 1923.

ORR, JAMES, ed. *The International Standard Bible Encyclopaedia.* (5 vols.). Grand Rapids: Eerdmans, 1943.
PATERSON, JOHN. *The Goodly Fellowship of the Prophets.* New York: Charles Scribner's Sons, 1948.
PEAKE, ARTHUR S. *The Problem of Suffering in the Old Testament.* London: Epworth, 1947.
———. *The Revelation of John.* London: Holborn Press, 1920.
PENTECOST, J. W. *Prophecy for Today.* Grand Rapids: Zondervan Publishing Company, 1961.
PHILLIPS, J. B. *The Book of Revelation.* New York: The Macmillan Company, 1957.
PORTER, FRANK C. *The Messages of the Apocalyptic Writers.* New York: Charles Scribner, 1909.
PRESTON, R. H., AND HANSON, A. T. *The Revelation of Saint John the Divine.* ("The Torch Bible Commentaries") London: S.C.M. Press, 1957.
PRICE, JAMES L. *Interpreting the New Testament.* New York: Holt, Rinehart & Winston, 1961.
RALL, H. F. *Modern Premillennialism and the Christian Hope.* New York: Abingdon Press, 1920.
RAMSEY, WM. M. *The Church in the Roman Empire—Before A.D. 170.* London: G. P. Putnam's Sons, 1893.
———. *The Letters to the Seven Churches.* London: Hodder and Stoughton, fourth edition, 1904.
RATTON, JAMES J. L. *Essays on the Apocalypse.* London: Burns and Oats, 1908.
———. *The Apocalypse of St. John.* London: R. and T. Washbourne, Ltd., 1912.
RICHARDS, HUBERT J. *What the Spirit Says to the Churches.* New York: P. J. Kenedy and Sons, 1967.
RICHARDSON, DONALD W. *The Revelation of Jesus Christ.* Richmond, Va.: John Knox Press, 1964 (late edition).
RIDDLE, MARTIN. *Moffatt New Testament Commentary,* "The Revelation of St. John." London: Hodder & Stoughton, 1952.
RISSI, MATHIAS. *Time and History: A Study on the Revelation.* Translated by Gordon C. Winsor. Richmond: John Knox Press, 1966.
RIST, MARTIN. *Daniel and Revelation.* Nashville: Abingdon Press, 1947.
RIST, MARTIN, AND HOUGH, LYNN HAROLD. *The Revelation of St. John the Divine.* ("The Interpreter's Bible," vol. 12) Nashville: Abingdon Press, 1957
ROBBINS, RAY F. *The Life and Ministry of Our Lord.* Nashville: Convention Press, 1970.
ROBERTSON, A. T. *Syllabus for New Testament Study.* Nashville: Sunday School Board of the Southern Baptist Convention, 1923.
ROBINSON, JOHN A. *Jesus and His Coming.* New York: Abingdon Press, 1957
ROLLS, CHARLES J. *The King's Own Honors Roll.* New York: Fleming H. Revel

Company, MCMXXXIII.
Ross, J. J. *Pearls from Patmos.* New York: Fleming H. Revell Company, 1923.
ROWLEY, H. H. *The Relevance of the Bible.* New York: The Macmillan Company, 1944.
_____. *The Relevance of Apocalyptic.* New York: Harper, 1946.
_____. *Darius the Mede and the Four World Empires in the Book of Daniel.* University of Wales Press, 1959.
RUSSELL, DANIEL. *Preaching the Apocalypse.* Nashville: Abingdon Press, 1935.
SCHMEIDEL, PAUL W. *The Johannine Writings.* (Trans. M. A. Canney.) London: Adam and Charles Black, 1908.
SCOFIELD, C. I. *The Scofield Reference Bible.* New York: Oxford University Press, 1917.
SCOTT, C. ANDERSON. *The Book of the Revelation.* London: Hodder & Stoughton, 1905.
SCOTT, E. F. *The Book of Revelation.* New York: Charles Scribner's Sons, 1940.
SCOTT, J. J. *The Apocalypse.* London: John Murray. 1909.
SCOTT, WALTER. *Exposition of the Revelation of Jesus Christ.* London: Fleming H. Revell Company (fourth edition), n.d.
SCROGGIE, W. GRAHAM. *The Great Unveiling.* Birmingham, England: The Hulbert Publishing Company, Ltd., n.d.
SEISS, J. A. *Lectures on the Apocalypse.* (3 vols.) New York: Charles C. Cook, 1913.
SIMCOX, W. H. "The Revelation of St. John the Divine," *The Cambridge Bible,* ed. J.J.S. Perowne. Cambridge: University Press, 1902.
SMITH, JUSTIN A. *Epistles of John to Revelation* ("An American Commentary on the New Testament," ed. Alan Hovey, vol. VII) Philadelphia: The American Baptist Publication Society, 1886.
STATT, JOHN R. W. *What Christ Thinks of the Church.* Grand Rapids: Wm. B. Eerdmans Publishing Company, 1958.
STAUFFER, ETHELBERT. *Christ and the Caesars.* Translated by K. and R. Gregor Smith. London: S.C.M. Press, 1955.
_____. *New Testament Theology.* Translated by John Marsh. London: S.C.M. Press, 1955.
STAGG, FRANK. *New Testament Theology.* Nashville: Broadman Press, 1962.
_____. *The Book of Acts.* Nashville: Broadman Press, 1955.
STEELE, DANIEL. *Jesus Exultant.* Boston: Christian Witness Company, 1899.
STRACHAN, R. H. *The Fourth Gospel: Its Significance and Environment.* London: S.C.M. Press, Ltd., 1958.
SUMMERS, RAY. *Worthy Is the Lamb.* Nashville: Broadman Press, 1951.
SWEDENBORG, EMANUEL. *The Apocalypse Revealed.* (2 vols.) New York: Swedenborg Foundation, Inc. 1949.
SWETE, HENRY B. *The Apocalypse of St. John.* Grand Rapids: Wm. B. Eerd-

mans, 1951.
TALBOT, LOUIS T. *The Revelation of Jesus Christ.* Grand Rapids: Wm. B. Eerdmans Publishing Company, 1937.
TAYLOR, DANIEL T. *The Reign of Christ on Earth.* Boston: Scriptural Tract Repository, 1882.
TENNEY, M. C. *Interpreting Revelation.* Grand Rapids: Wm. B. Eerdmans Pub. Co., 1957.
THAYER, J. H. *A Greek-English Lexicon of the New Testament.* New York: Harper, 1889.
THIESSEN, H. C. *Introduction to the New Testament.* Grand Rapids: Wm. B. Eerdmans Publishing Co., 1944.
THORNTON, L. S. *Revelation and the Modern World.* London: Docre Press, 1950.
TORRANCE, THOMAS F. *The Apocalypse Today.* Grand Rapids: Eerdmans, 1959.
TORREY, CHAS. C. *The Apocalypse of John.* New Haven: Yale University Press, 1958.
TRENCH, R. C. *The Epistles to the Seven Churches in Asia.* New York: Charles Scribner, 1861.
VINCENT, MARVIN R. *Word Studies in the New Testament.* (4 vols.) Grand Rapids: Eerdmans, reprint.
VINE, W. E. *An Expository Dictionary of New Testament Words.* (4 vols.) Westwood: Fleming H. Revell Company, 1966.
VON ALLMEN, J. J. *A Companion of the Bible.* New York: Oxford, 1958.
WALVOORD, JOHN F. *The Revelation of Jesus Christ.* Chicago: Moody Press, 1966.
WERNECKE, HERBERT H. *The Book of Revelation Speaks to Us.* Philadelphia: The Westminster Press, 1954.
WESLEY, JOHN. *Explanatory Notes Upon the New Testament.* London: The Epworth Press, 1950 edition.
WESTCOTT, B. F. *The Gospel According to St. John.* London: Clarke, 1958.
WHEDON, D. D. *Commentary on the New Testament.* New York: Phillips S Hunt, 1880.
WHISTON, WM. (tr.). *The Works of Flavius Josephus.* "War of the Jews.' Hartford: Scranton, 1905.
WICKS, H. J. *The Doctrine of God in the Jewish Apocryphal and Apocalyptic Literature.* London: Hunter and Longhurst, 1915.
WOLF, WILLIAM J. *No Cross, No Crown.* New York: Doubleday & Company Inc. 1957.

www.ingramcontent.com/pod-product-compliance
Lightning Source LLC
Chambersburg PA
CBHW062012220426
43662CB00010B/1297